Time and Social Theory

Time and Social Theory

Barbara Adam

Temple University Press
Philadelphia

Temple University Press, Philadelphia 19122
Copyright © Barbara Adam 1990
Published 1990
Printed in Great Britain

Library of Congress Cataloging-in-Publication Data

Adam, Barbara, 1945–
   Time and social theory/Barbara Adam.
     p. cm.
   Includes bibliographical references and index.
   ISBN 0-87722-788-8
   1. Time—Sociological Aspects. I. Title.
   HM208.A33 1990   90–40870
   304.2′3—dc20   CIP

Contents

Acknowledgements

I would like to express my gratitude to Martin Albrow and the Department of Sociology, University College Cardiff, for supporting the initial research and to the ESRC for making this research possible by granting me a pool award for the period of 1983–6. I want to thank Paul Atkinson for having been such a wonderful supervisor and Jan Adam and J. T. Fraser for having scrutinised my grasp of theoretical biology and physics respectively. Many people have encouraged me during these years. I thank them all. The following persons, however, need to be acknowledged individually for their significant role in the writing of this book. I am deeply grateful to Ronald Frankenberg and Michael Young for their support of my work and for persuading me to turn the thesis into a book. My very special thanks go to my husband and colleague Jan for his sustained listening, his insightful and perceptive responses and, most importantly, for his critical reading of the manuscript. My children Miriam and Tobias need a special mention since this book would not have been written without their wholehearted support, help and willingness to be self-sufficient. Last, I want to express my gratitude and appreciation to Anthony Giddens for his inspiring work on time and for making time a legitimate topic of investigation for social theory. His thoughts proved relevant for nearly every aspect of time I endeavoured to highlight and discuss and thus provided the provocative backcloth against which my own understanding developed.

Barbara Adam

Introduction: Time is a Fact of Life

'Time is a fact of life,' said a friend to me recently, 'so what is there to write about something as obvious as that? Are you not just complicating something that is fundamentally straightforward and simple?' After many years of research on this topic, responding to that challenge should have posed no problem. However, it did. Instead of getting easier, dealing with this common query had got increasingly more difficult as my study progressed. So I asked my friend to say a bit more about what he meant by his statement. He explained how time was an obvious fact of life because we sleep at night and get up in the morning. Shops are open at certain times of the day, work has starting and finishing times, and our day is structured according to this fact of life. I told him that his examples applied neither to all societies nor did they to our own society in the past. Before Western societies were structured to clock and calendar time, I argued, this 'fact of life' must have been fundamentally different. I also suggested that he had only talked about two out of an immense range of aspects of time. He had mentioned the time of the diurnal cycle and our social structuring of the day with the aid of clock time thus excluding, for example, our getting older or having different concerns at different ages. What is important to a 70-year-old may be quite outside the range of experiences for a young person. I could see some agreement among the other people around the table but my friend remained unimpressed. 'Yes', he said, 'so what? In all of these examples time is still a fact of life.' I had to agree with him and explained that I do not question time as a fact of life but take as problematic how social scientists understand time, and the way they incorporate it into their theories.

Many more aspects of time, I continued, form an integral part of our lives. Some have to do with synchronisation, ordering, sequencing or timing, others with control or measurement, and still others with the time aspects of machines and artefacts. All have a bearing on our lives not as separate abstracted entities but as an interconnected whole. If we accept social science to be about studying, understanding and explaining that reality then we can expect social scientists to take account of time in this multiple and connected way, to know and acknowledge the many aspects of time in their relation and not on an either/or basis. He understood what I was saying but could not see the problem and certainly could not see how one could spend years studying what, to him, still seemed eminently obvious. He was not the only one who felt like this. The sentiments of my sociology colleagues were not far removed from those expressed by my friend. Everyone was still waiting to be convinced.

I went on to tell them that sociologists have studied a wide range of social time issues which include people's budgeting and organisation of time, activities they are engaged in regularly at certain times, the effect of retirement on the structuring of a person's life as well as on their family, the change in time experience after a person has been made redundant, the rhythms of social life, and the control of people's time. Anthropologists, on the other hand, place more emphasis on the different culture-based meanings and forms of time, whilst historians are predominantly concerned with the past. Most disciplines, I stipulated, seem to have their very own subject-specific focus on time. Looking at those studies as a collective whole, however, it becomes obvious that time has played an important part not only in people's lives but also in their thinking. It is integral to human beings contemplating their existence, their own finitude and the inescapability of death. To study time in this way, my friend conceded, sounded really exciting but he could see no reason for going beyond this existing body of work. 'What could there possibly be achieved in a book on time and theory', he asked, 'that cannot be accomplished through those studies, and that every thinking person does not know already anyway?', thus bringing the discussion back to his original statement that time is a fact of life.

Still no one else wanted to participate in this discussion. Everybody was waiting and the onus continued to be on me to make some progress. I had to stop moving on the spot with my explanation. I acknowledged once more the centrality of his insight but pointed to my emphasis on the complexity of time. I stressed how I did not understand time as '*a* fact of life' but as implicated in *every* aspect of our lives and imbued with a multitude of meanings. In our everyday life, I argued, time can mean a variety of things. We can have 'a good time at a party', be 'on time for work', 'lose time' due to illness, choose the 'right time' to plant potatoes and even 'live on borrowed time'. We can make time pass quickly or slowly, which is different from getting impatient because we have to wait or from feeling rushed because time is passing too fast. We need to distinguish between getting old and feeling old and between planning one's day as a pensioner or as a university student. We move freely between those varied sorts of time without giving much thought to the matter, using the idea as if it were a unitary concept. We do not fuss over the differences, and it does not seem to concern us that the time of our imagination knows no boundaries, that the time of our thought is open-ended but has a beginning, and that our sentences our bounded by both a beginning and an end. Neither are we troubled that none of these times are comparable with, for example, the time associated with our finitude and certain but unknown death or our labour time which we exchange for money at the end of the week, the month, or the completion of a job. We seem to weave in and out of a wide variety of times without giving the matter much conscious consideration.

When social scientists investigate human social life, however, we can expect them to rise above the common-sense and the-taken-for-granted. We can presume that they are not only consciously aware of those various aspects of time but know them in relation to each other and account for them in their studies and theories. This very reasonable expectation, however, is not met. Not only does time seem to be a non-reflected aspect of social theory, it also lacks the multifacetedness displayed in thought, language, and the concomitant everyday life. Much like people in their everyday lives, social scientists take time largely for granted. Time is such an obvious factor in social science that it is almost invisible. To 'see' it and to recognise it in not just its dominant but also its many less visible forms has proved to be hard work.

My initial interest, I explained further, was captured by a perceived mismatch between social theory and the social life within my own range of experience. I had noticed that when theorists focus on structure they present a world without change. When they focus on change, this is charted within a static framework which defines the boundaries of before and after. I found social scientists measuring people's experiences in clock time units without taking account of all the other aspects of time and with little discrimination between the measure and the quantity that is being measured. A social event, for example, might be defined in terms of the number of years, months, or days it lasted; yet the process itself may not relate to calendar time but seasons, a person's life cycle or a historical period. Furthermore, what seems timeless or eternal from a personal point of view may be seen as a major change from a historical perspective or as an insignificant shift from an evolutionary position.

There is a tendency in social theory for any one of these aspects to appear as absolute where a focus on time shows them to be relative. Theories and whole perspectives seem further to force choices with respect to time. Thus, the social world is explained in terms of either how it is, how it is changing, or how it ought to be; how it is structured or how it is developing, timeless, or timeful. Functions are explained as frozen realities without time or temporality. Social science, I continued my 'defence', has a long tradition of explaining on an either/or basis and the focus on time forms no exception. Time is understood accordingly as either social or natural, as a measure or an experience, as cyclical or linear. It may be associated with the clock or the rhythms of nature, with ageing and entropy or with the timing, sequencing, and rhythmic organisation of activities. With few exceptions, social theorists conceptualise as single parts in isolation what bears on our lives simultaneously. They exlude in an absolute way what is not focused on, instead of implicating it in their understanding. 'Yes . . .', my friend replied very slowly and thoughtfully, 'I think I know what you are saying. It seems reasonable, but it has lost any feeling of reality for me.' By moving my explanation from examples of what people do to principles and structures of understanding, those thoughts had, despite their apparent sense, no longer any real meaning. Structures of thought carried no reality value for him. For me, on the other hand, they form a central part of the 'empirical' data of my research.

'But it is all so simple', he continued, 'why do you academics keep on complicating what is unproblematic and staightforward?' For the first time in this discussion I found myself no longer in a defensive position but in strong disagreement. Far from accepting that academics in general, and social scientists in particular, complicate the reality they seek to describe, understand, and explain, I have found the reverse to be the case. I have come to recognise that once we begin to observe and contemplate our social reality we find it to be immensely complex and we consequently set out to simplify it until we have reduced it to choices of single or paired aspects. We tend to eradicate complexity to a point where that reality becomes conceptually manageable. Worse still, the simplified aspects are then taken as the basis from which to understand and explain the whole. This is what people do in their daily lives in order to cope with an otherwise unmanageable complexity. It is a strategy for doing and getting on with life. I want to propose, however, that both an assumed and imposed simplicity is no longer a valid approach once we want to understand and conceptualise that reality as social scientists.

'But does it really matter? What difference does it make to our lives how social scientists understand time; whether they conceptualise time in this, that, or any other way?' How could I begin to respond to this innocently posed question? Little did he know that the answer to it has irresolvably separated idealists from empiricists for hundreds of years. Whilst I understand that division to be a mere artefact of the way of thinking that we have inherited from the classical Greek philosophers, my own answer did, nevertheless, locate me quite clearly within the tradition of German idealist thinking. It does matter, I argued, because our concepts and theories, our seeing, and our action are all mutually implicating and fundamentally interconnected. It does make a difference to our lives whether we understand our social organisation by the clock and calendar as an inevitable fact of life, as a fact of history, or as something we have created and imposed on ourselves and maintain by our daily actions. It constitutes the difference between having choices and seeing one's social life as determined. It matters at a global level with respect to nuclear power, for example, whether our understanding is still tied to Newtonian machine technology or to that of the contemporary physics on the basis of which that power has been created. Choice and responsibility can only be taken for that human creation once our understanding is at least adequate, if not ahead of the knowledge that informs that technology. Without such a change in understanding we remain helpless and controlled by our own creation. Our conceptualisations of time and the way we utilise time in our social theories matter with regard to our social construction of the future, our relationship to death, our identity, our daily living, our participation in social life, and our interaction with all that we have created. I therefore do not think that an adequate understanding is an end in itself but have allowed myself to be fundamentally guided by my belief in the constitutive nature of our ways of understanding and our frameworks of meaning. In other words, I see my research of this 'fact of life' as a meaningful contribution to our present lives and to our future.

These comments provided an entry point for the sociology members of this small gathering. My responses, one colleague thought, identified my approach as part of the critical theory tradition in sociology and suggested a tendency toward historical rather than structural analysis. My emphasis on the constitutive nature of knowledge was consistent, she thought, with the critical theorists' concerns and their stress on the future as an explicit component of the analysis. Like them, I seemed to consider understanding as a precondition for action which in turn makes reconceptualisation as important a part of the intellectual enterprise as the accumulation of data. My focus on temporality, on the other hand, demonstrates my leaning toward a historical approach. With one easy sweep my research was classified back into the fold of existing social science traditions. Once I had found my perspective, this fellow sociologist suggested, my research would become manageable within the existing boundaries of the discipline. I agreed that this was possible but voiced my disquiet that such adaptation could only be achieved at the expense of a concern with the anomalies and paradoxes that my explicit focus on time had brought to the surface.

In none of the sciences, and not even the perspectives within them, for

example, were people talking about the same thing when they made use
of the idea of time. They seemed to be talking about phenomena, things,
processes, qualities, or a dimension, a category, and a concept, using the
word unproblematically as if it had only one meaning. Some scientists
talked about motion 'through time', others about change 'in time'. Some
social scientists located time in the capacity for memory and intent along
the axis of past, present, and future, others in the routine and repetitious
nature of everyday life. Some insisted that all time is necessarily social
time and related this to clocks and calendars whilst others asserted that
power and control are the irreducible aspects of social time. To integrate
the study of time within an existing perspective would mean that none of
these transperspectival anomalies could be explored and discussed. Yet, I
consider these inconsistencies and paradoxes as the major challenge and
an opportunity not to be missed.

The general social science practice of separating change from structure,
I suggested further, goes far beyond the dualism of diachronic and
synchronic analyses. Structure and historical change appear as mutually
exclusive theoretical choices but this is not the only problem. Where
change is central to the analysis this process often seems to be based on a
physical theory of billiard balls in motion and on the behaviour of dead
matter. Alternatively, the diachronic analysis might be dealing with
points 'in time' without temporal extension, temporality, or orientation
towards the future. Life, growth, novelty, the possibility of self-
knowledge, the temporal extension across physical boundaries inherent
in consciousness, and the power which I have come to recognise as an
integral part of all relations in which the abstract quantity of time is used
or allocated; all these are mostly excluded. Furthermore, where one or
even more of these aspects are included, they tend to be presented as
serial, linear, progressive, or cumulative when in most situations these
aspects would be present simultaneously.

To gain a clear understanding from those unconnected theoretical,
perspective-based fragments requires that we grasp not merely one or two
approaches to time but all of them. We need to get to know not just the
single meanings of time as clock time, chronology, timing, commodity,
measure, '*t*-coordinate', *Dasein* and *durée*, for example, but the relations
between them. Not merely their identification within single social science
traditions but knowledge of their meanings and differences in relation to
each other has to be the task. To become aware of discipline- and
perspective-specific times is an important but small part of the work that
needs to be done. It requires that we leave the safe comfort of a
perspective and embrace the threatening uncertainty within our own
discipline and beyond. Social science comprises the whole spectrum of
'times' from the most physical, mechanical, and artefactual to the

experiential and cultural. This realisation, in conjunction with my conviction that we interact with and modify not only our social but also the physical, living, and artefactual world on a daily basis, convinced me of the importance of understanding the times of physics and biology in addition to those of the human sciences. We need to study the times inherent in those theories in order to establish the connections between them as well as their relation to the time of the clock. Clock time is, after all, the one aspect of time that all scientists utilise. It is employed as the measure for the events and processes under investigation.

It is one thing to try to understand the underlying and often unexamined assumptions of our own and other disciplines, I explained, it is yet another to forge the links between those assumptions. This, however, is necessary since it is only in their connection and relation to each other that they begin to resemble the seamlessly integrated aspects of our lives: the times of work and social encounters, and the times of our consciousness, our existence, and our tacitly known, lived experiences. To see together what is at present known in isolation requires a constant, conscious effort to keep our theoretical understanding in touch with and checked against the complexity of our ongoing experience in its histori-cal, natural, and artefactual context; in other words, all those aspects that make up the totality of our everyday lives. This entails that we acknowledge the personal not only as valid, but as essential, and our theoretical understanding as inseparable from our biography and biology, our context, beliefs and values, our needs and our motives. We need to recognise our learning, seeing, and experiencing, as well as our thinking, doing, and judging as mutually implicating. To pretend oth-erwise is to falsify our work. In agreement with prominent twentieth-century physicists such as Bohm, Heisenberg and Prigogine, for example, I have therefore replaced the classical science ideal of objectivity with the recognition that the subject–object relationship in scientific activity is one of fundamental implication.

With such an emphasis on the personal plus context, the idea of truth also takes on a different meaning. No longer fixed, permanent and absolute it becomes understood as an ongoing process, socially con-structed as well as constructing, and open to challenge. Doubt of that which we take to be natural and unproblematic, the acclaimed 'tool' of radical humanism in the arts and social sciences, needs to get extended to include ourselves, our own understanding and our base assumptions. This process of doubting and the resulting layers upon layers of reflection force our focus onto that which is normally disattended and help us to break through its taken-for-grantedness. It enables us to see the invisible. Once the process of breaking through the natural attitude has begun, it quickly becomes obvious that the enigma of time reflects our failure to grasp the essential interconnections between its different aspects and we realise that the task is not to know one aspect well but to know all of them in their totality and in their dynamic relation. Understanding time thus does not only allow but forces an approach which transcends perspectives. This necessitates new ways of understanding and a different use of existing concepts. It demands a very specific approach to theory. Transdisciplinary exploration is only possible if we conceive of social theory as something one does and not as a hermeneutic or historical exercise of reinterpretation. In contradistinction to the history-of-ideas approach, for example, where the development of ideas is traced in its socio-economic and intellectual context, I see my approach to theory as entailing an exploration of inherent principles, assumptions, and key questions and their relation to the object of understanding. I isolate basic properties and processes of that which is not generally reflected upon and try to bring my findings in relation to each other in order that I may understand what, up until now, I had only tacitly known. Instead of seeking to render new and better interpretations of existing thoughts about past presents, I want to utilise thoughts for the extension and development of understandings of the present. An understanding through time cannot simply be added on to existing perspectives and theories of social science. It requires a reconceptualisation of not merely social time but the very nature of 'the social'. Despite the inevitable continuity with existing perpectives, it alters the method and the vision, the epistemology, and the ontology. Frequently it invalidates the traditions.

1

Time in Social Theory:
Destiny, Necessity, and Enigma

Time is our destiny because we live our lives unto death and in the knowledge of this inevitability. Time is our necessity because there can be no un-living, re-juvenating, or un-knowing. There can be no un-doing only 'making good', since moments past cannot be lived again. Time is not only a necessary aspect of change but also of stability, since the latter is nothing but an awareness that something has remained stable whilst its surrounding environment, and even the components within, have changed. In addition to change and stability, time is central to order since, as Moore (1963: 8) observed, without a temporal order there is no order at all. Time is both destiny and necessity for all human societies, even if their language does not have a separate concept for it. It is inextricably bound up with human reflexivity and the capacity for self-consciousness (Hegel 1967: 800, 1952: 558). For contemporary indus-trialised societies, however, time is fundamental in a further sense. The members of such societies use the concept of time not merely to synthesise aspects of mind, body, nature, and social life, but they also employ it on a world-wide basis as a standardised principle for measure-ment, co-ordination, regulation, and control. In these multiple forms time is a deeply taken-for-granted aspect of social life. It is everywhere yet it eludes us. It is so deeply implicated in our existence that it is almost invisible. This poses problems for understanding and analysis not only for the ordinary members of society but also for those members who see it as their professional task to provide theories about this reality. Despite this difficulty, however, the centrality of time for the subject matter of the social sciences remains and so does the need for that complexity of times to be reflected in our theories.

The question then arises how such an explicit representation of social time is to be achieved given that the nature of concepts is traditionally regarded as outside the competence of the social sciences' investigations.

'Normally neither historians nor sociologists', Luhmann (1982c: 299) points out, 'ask about the nature of time. If this question is posed directly and framed as one about essences, it cannot be adequately answered. On the other hand, there is a substantial danger that, if we leave this question unaddressed, we shall think about social history in crude and inadequate ways.' For Luhmann this applies not only for social history but for sociology generally, with all the perspectives it encompasses, since its subject matter consists of meaningful human experiences and actions. This includes that human beings are able to reflect on their actions and that they could have acted otherwise. Because of it, Luhmann (1982c: 290) argues, 'temporality too becomes a constitutive dimension of its subject matter. As a result, time can no longer be treated merely as a category underlying our knowledge of social life.' To him, the philosophical theory of time therefore becomes a necessary pre-condition to an adequate theory of social time. Not all theorists who accept the centrality of time for social theory, however, advocate this approach. The writings of Bergmann (1981a, 1983) and Jaques (1982) corroborate Luhmann's position whilst others like Elias (1982a, b, 1984) reject the idea that philosophy holds solutions for social science analyses. Giddens, who legitimated the concern with time in British social theory, holds yet another view on the question of how to deal with the enigma of time. Time is central to his theory of structuration and is implicated in his key concepts of routinisation, 'time-space distanciation', sedimentation, recursiveness of knowledge, commodified time, and the simultaneity of *Dasein*, *durée*, and *longue durée*. Unlike Luhmann, however, he does not pay attention to the nature of time itself. Giddens (1984: 35) makes 'no particular claim to elucidate this matter' before incorporating time into his theory. He is content to utilise and adapt for his own purposes the conceptualisations of time by theorists like Hägerstrand, Heidegger, Lévi-Strauss, Marx, Mead, and Schutz. In his theory of structuration he seeks to show how 'life passes in transformation' and how time is linked to both the contingency of *Dasein* and the possibility of becoming, both being implicated in the recursiveness of social life as constituted in social practices. Giddens (1979: 4–8) endeavours to connect the theory of action with that of institutions and intended actions with their unintended consequences. In his contemporary re-working of the conceptions of human being and doing, social reproduction and transformation, time therefore comes to be of central importance without ever being the explicit focus of his attention. Investigating contemporary approaches to time, we are thus faced with a substantial degree of consensus with respect to a recognition that time is central for social theory but little agreement about the legitimacy of a social science concern with time *per se*.

As destiny and necessity of human social life, time is recognised to be implicated in social theories in a multiple way. Theorists associate it with change, stability, order, control, and measurement or combinations of these. Little thought, however, is given to the relation between those theoretical dimensions of time, and opinions diverge on the question of whether or not an understanding or a theory of time is a necessary pre-condition to social theory. Yet it seems quite clear to me that progress can only be made if we seek to understand not one aspect of time or one perspective's approach to it but aim to grasp time in its multiple expressions. This entails that we allow time to become our explicit focus. Theorists recognise time as a problematic aspect of their work but disagree with respect to their understanding of the nature of the difficulty and how to deal with it. Luhmann (1980: 32–3) proposes that the question of time touches base assumptions in social theory and he sees this as one of the reasons why so little progress has been made. This important assertion seems to be reiterated by the observations of a number of theorists.

Giddens, for example, notes repeatedly (1979, 1981, 1984) that in functionalist theories time is identified with change and sequence whilst stability and order are conceived as timeless. Maintaining this distinction between synchrony and diachrony, statics and dynamics, process and order, leads to a repression of time in social theory. 'To speak of social stability *cannot*', Giddens (1979: 199) insists, 'involve abstracting from time since stability means continuity over time. A stable order is one in which there is a close similarity between how things are now and how they used to be in the past.' The very notion of pattern or structure is in fact nonsensical viewed from the vantage point of functionalist analysis which understands these as timeless snapshots of interaction. 'The flaw in this', Giddens (1979: 202) argues, 'is exactly the same as that involved in the presumption of "static stability": such a snapshot would not in fact reveal a pattern at all, because *any patterns of interaction that exist are situated in time*; only when examined over time do they form "patterns" at all.' He proposes further that social systems are different from material structures, since the former only exist as systems through their continued reproduction over time (1981: 17, 1984: xxi).

Similarly fundamental issues are identified by Schöps (1980), Bergmann (1981) and others. They locate the social scientists' problem with time in the nature of quantitative social research and, more generally, in positivist social science. The search for invariant repetition and pattern in conjunction with a time that is conceptualised as a neutral quantity and used as a universal measure is taken by them as the problematic aspect of sciences dealing with human time.

The explanation offered by contemporary European culture – which, during
the last two centuries, has increasingly marginalised other explanations – is
that which constructs a uniform, abstract, unilinear law of time applying to
all events, and according to which all 'times' can be compared and regulated.
This law maintains that the Great Plough and the famine belong to the same
calculus, a calculus which is indifferent to both. It also maintains that human
consciousness is an event, set in time, like any other. Thus, an explanation
whose task is to 'explain' the time of consciousness, treats that consciousness
as if it were as passive as a geological stratum. If modern man has often
become a victim of his own postivism, the process starts here with the denial
or abolition of the time created by the event of consciousness. (Berger 1984:
9–10)

These writers argue that the problem lies with the kind of time that is
being used exclusively. In contradistinction to the popular view they do
not see time excluded from positivist science. Bergmann (1981a: 12)
explains how the multiplicity of social time cannot be encompassed by
positivist social science since complexity is crowded out by an emphasis
on the measurement of motion, the establishement of causal relationships
and the conceptualisation of an absolute parameter of time within which
events take place. Jaques (1982: 163) presents a corresponding argument
when he points out the discrepancy between the multidimensional
complex time that characterises social life and the one-dimensional time
of social analyses and research. This, he suggests, has little to do with the
popular notion of the previous decade which saw time as needing to be
brought back in to a spatial and physicalist social science.

Time, however, does not merely touch the base assumption of
positivist social scientists. Elias (1984: x–xl) shows that theorists in the
Kantian tradition do not fare any better. They too conceive of time as an
invariable structure. But, unlike the former who see time as an aspect of
external reality the latter view it as an a priori intuition, a pre-condition
to experience. We can therefore agree with Luhmann's (1978: 96)
assertion that sociologists put time theory on too small a basis.

It is considered only with respect to the concept of duration or the mere
sequence of events. No attention is paid to the difference between the past
and the future which is essential for all temporality. Therewith, the specific
internal problematic of time – i.e. the constitution of the present through the
difference between two time horizons, past and future - remains unnoticed.
Whatever time has to offer, in every present, as a space for orientation and
arrangement for the constitution of social relations, thus disappears from
view. (Luhmann 1978: 96)

This implies that studies of how we use time and how we organise social
life by it must be flawed until social scientists have better understood the

nature and function of time. We must therefore make explicit what forms
a largely implicit aspect of our theories. We must be aware, however, that
we can grasp time in its complexity only if we seek the relations between
time, temporality, tempo and timing, between clock time, chronology,
social time and time-consciousness, between motion, process, change,
continuity and the temporal modalitites of past, present and future,
between time as resource, as ordering principle and as becoming of the
possible, or between any combination of these. We need to stand back
and get a wider perspective on the matter. We need to see together what
at present are isolated incommensurable bits. This will lead us to new
insights and take social theory into a new direction. It may help to make
time less of an enigma. Time may even cease to be an irresolvable
problem for social theory.

The diversity of contemporary approaches

Time has occupied sociologists ever since sociology became developed as
a separate discipline. Durkheim, Sorokin, Merton, Mead, Schutz and
many others have set out to delineate the social nature of time. This
social science work on time is characterised by a pattern where a diversity
of pioneering thought is followed by papers and treatises that bring these
disparate thoughts together into a coherent whole and utilise that
understanding for novel time studies. The work of Durkheim (1915),
Spengler (1926), Sorokin (1964), Mead (1959), Schutz (1971), and
Gurvitch (1963) serve as examples for the pioneering thoughts; that of
Sorokin and Merton (1937), Coser and Coser (1963), Moore (1963),
Zerubavel (1979, 1981, 1985), and Bergmann (1981a, 1983) for bringing
those thoughts together. Yet, despite this substantial body of work,
time has also been identified as the missing or neglected dimension in
social theory and research. Tiryakian (1970), Lüscher (1974), Martins
(1974), and Heinemann and Ludes (1978), for example, focus on change,
process, order, and structure when they argue that time is the lacuna,
the forgotten dimension of social theory, and that it is not appropriately
taken account of in social science analyses. Others suggest that the
problem has nothing to do with a lack of studies and writing on time but
with the lack of cohesion. Bergmann (1981a, 1983), Lauer (1981), and
Schöps (1980) demonstrate that much work has been done which remains
isolated from the main body of sociology, lacks coherent theorisation,
and resists integration into existing perspectives. Despite this diversity
of opinions, however, there is agreement among contemporary theorists
who have given attention to time on three interrelated points: that time
has neither been adequately understood nor satisfactorily dealt with

in social theory; that time is a key element of social life and must
therefore be equally central to social theory; and that all time is social
time. On the basis of that agreement we shall begin this exploration by
focusing not on studies of social time but on the way time enters social
theory. In other words, we examine the way social theorists conceptualise
time in both its taken-for-granted and explicated form.

A first look presents us with an array of theories and a multitude of
ideas with little to unite them. None of the writers has the same focus.
Everyone asks different questions. No two theorists have the same view
on what it means to make time central to social theory. To Jaques (1982)
it means studying the form of time. He seeks a theoretical understanding
of time and a clarification of its dimensions. He provides a conceptualisation and social theory of time which is based mainly on philosophical and
psychoanalytical knowledge. He develops an axial scheme which he
applies to the study and measurement of social and psychological
phenomena. For Elias (1982a, b, 1984) it entails an investigation of the
nature and history of time reckoning and reflections on its implications
for social science; for Hopkins (1982) an exploration of the subjective
experience of time in conjunction with the time of institutions, and for
Schöps (1980) a study of the effect of time on social structure. For Hohn
(1984) it involves a historical exploration of time-consciousness, social
time, and processes of change. He establishes an inextricable link
between the time-consciousness, cosmology, and mode of production of
Western societies of different epochs. To Young (1987) it means utilising
biological theories for the analysis of contemporary society, its rhythms
and their changes. A ray of hope appears when we realise that both
Bergmann (1981a) and Lauer (1981) construct typologies as conceptual
tools for social theory. That optimism, however, is premature. Neither
the content of their theories nor its application bear any resemblance to
each other. For Giddens and Luhmann the aim to make time central
forms an integral aspect of their theories. As a key issue that permeates
their work it is a by-product of their writing rather than a centralised
preoccupation resulting in a treatise on social time. For Giddens the issue
of time is so intimately tied to his theory of structuration that one could
almost think that the problem of time for social theory had simply been
the lack of a theory of structuration. Through that theory we can account
for people's location in time-space, for the continued maintenance and
reproduction of institutions, and for the difference between traditional
and modern societies with their respective 'time-distantiations'. Through
the conceptualisations of *durée*, *Dasein*, and *longue durée* we can allow
for a variety of time-scales and modes of being in every human practice
and event. We can accommodate the multiple nature of time-consciousness and understand the commodification of time and its attendant

relations of power. The breadth of Giddens' appproach to time appears all-embracing until we explore Luhmann's writings on the matter, find them equally wide-ranging and notice that he is focusing on entirely different issues. Luhmann establishes distinctions between chronology, time, and temporality and he theorises contemporary world-time. He makes us aware of the historisation of time. He conceptualises time as constituted at every level of existence and provides a time theory that unifies the social theory perspectives of systems and action.

On the basis of this diversity it is hard to believe that these theorists have made the same 'phenomenon' central to their work. Between them they associate time with death, ageing, growth, and history, with order, structure, synchronisation, and control. They view time as a sense, a measure, a category, a parameter, and an idea. They define it as an a priori intuition for the conceptual organisation of experience (Jaques 1982), a social construction with multiple aspects and dimensions (Lauer 1981), an ordering principle and force for selection and prioritising (Schöps 1980), the difference between the past and future and its social interpretation (Luhmann 1982b), a process by which consciousness is formed (Hopkins 1982), and a tool for co-ordination, orientation and control (Elias 1984). Some coherence emerges around the explanations of time by Bergmann (1981a), Elias (1984), and Hohn (1984) who emphasise its symbolic nature. The consistency does not, however, reach to the nature of the symbol which is conceptualised by them respectively as an abstraction, a synthesis, and a construction, from and for experience. Not only are we faced with an incompatible array of definitions but we also have to cope with incommensurable ideas about the source of our experience and concept of time. The rhythms of nature or society, information processing, the capacity for memory and expectation, sociality, language, and social synchronisation are all identified as the bases upon which our knowledge of time is built. There is no warning for the unsuspecting researcher. There are no signposts for orientation in this maze of conceptual chaos. The theories are constructed around a common aim and focus but those who seek enlightenment from this body of thought are left with a sizeable problem: how to make sense of the diversity, and how to relate the isolated bits and conceptualise them into a coherent meaningful whole. On the basis of this heterogeneous body of thought (Adam 1987: 43–111) we need to find a way to do justice to time's coherence in nature and social life.

Closer investigation shows that over and above these irreconcilable differences there are some shared concerns and common assumptions about social theory. Once we shift our attention from the issue of time itself to the theoretical implications arising from the theorists' focus on time, there emerge common threads that criss-cross between these studies to create a web of tenuous connections. These threads relate to a rejection of classical dualisms and disciplinary isolation as well as an acceptance of philosophers' deliberations on the topic of time. They are tied to the recognition that historicity and the symbolisation of time require analysis. They signify a general conviction that all time is social time and agreement that contemporary Western time needs to be understood in its historically developed uniqueness. They show a general commitment to the view that a better understanding of time not only brings to the surface problems and shortcomings in social science analysis but that it will also improve contemporary social theory. This common ground can be utilised as a basic structure for our exploration and for this initial survey of contemporary and classical thoughts on time.

Dualisms and disciplinary isolation rejected

Dualisms are deeply anchored in the structure of our thought and they permeate social theory. As synchrony and diachrony, structure and change, individual and society, nature and nurture, quantity and quality, objectivity and subjectivity, order and control they haunt our theories and our analyses. A focus on time brings those dualisms into high relief and shows them to be untenable. It is not either winter or December, or hibernation time for the tortoise, or one o'clock, or time for Christmas dinner. It is planetary time, biological time, clock and calendar time, natural and social time all at once. Most theorists writing on time therefore find it necessary to confront the tradition of thinking in opposites and to seek ways to transcend it. Duality rather than dualism becomes a favoured option.

Giddens leaves none of the traditional social science dichotomies untouched. His work therefore serves as a prime example for this dualism–duality conversion. Giddens proposes to achieve this mutation with the theory of structuration and his central focus on human practice located in time-space. He makes connections and shows the mutual implication of synchronic and diachronic analyses, change and structure, of human doing, institutional reproduction and social transformation. For others the shift from dualism to duality means that there is no longer a need to choose between the timeless and the temporal, between system and action, form or content. A conceptualisation in terms of duality allows for the timeless form of time to be formed, maintained, and recreated in human practice. This formed and constituted time may then be viewed as both product of and medium for interactions of people in and with their natural and social environments. Alternatively it may be associated with consciousness since time, as Hopkins (1982: 28–9) points out, 'not only forms part of consciousness, it is the process by which consciousness develops and forms'. What appears like a dualism of external and internal experience and consciousness of time is shown by her to be a duality of mutual dependence where the created, external and shared aspects of time re-enter consciousness as constitutive features and vice versa. Jaques (1982) identifies two time dimensions along which the experience of process, change, object constancy, and permanence is organised conceptually: the time axes of succession and intent. He too suggests that the perception of permanence and change is not a matter of choice but they mutually define each other like figure and ground. Our understanding, he argues, oscillates between them. As we focus on one, the other recedes. Thus, his two time dimensions are not two different types of time but relate to the way we order our experience of time passing and of the time of purpose and will. Both in turn depend on experience and knowledge of the past. Jaques proposes that neither the clock time of succession nor *Kairos* the time of intent are sufficient on their own for the understanding and explanation of the human world of hope and intent. His axes of succession and intent therefore stand in a necessary relation to each other, a relation where the latter always incorporates the former but never the other way around.

Whilst the message is the same, Young's (1988) focus is different yet again. He structures his analysis around the concepts of cyclical and linear time which he conceptualises as mutually implicating ways of understanding two sorts of change. No either/or distinction can be made, insists Young (1988: 14). 'The two dimensions are best conceived as two often but not always complementary ways of looking at the same thing, two alternative conceptualizations of the same phenomenon which do not exclude each other.' In a historical analysis of Western time-consciousness Hohn (1984) escapes the dichotomy of traditional and modern society by proposing not a duality but clusters of characteristics. In his analysis, modes of work, cosmology, and conceptualisations of time are established as mutually constituting. Instead of dualisms he focuses on a spectrum of change-continua. He finds either/or choices useless for the description of the slow historical change from natural rhythms to *Takt* (metronomic beat), a development that has also been identified by Young (1988) in his analysis of *The Metronomic Society*. The transcendence of the restrictions of classical dualistic analyses is also of central importance to Elias (1982a, b, 1984). Not duality or clusters, however, but synthesis is the key concept with which he manages to overcome that pervasive tradition of thought. He proposes that clock time is a highly sophisticated social construction for the co-ordination of the body, the person, society, and nature. Not society or nature, not even human beings and nature but humans in nature and as an integral part of

it are to Elias the basis from which to begin the analysis. He shows that
we use time not merely as a measure but as a tool for social interaction.
We utilise it for orientation, regulation, control, co-ordination, syncho-
nisation, and for the comparison of social and natural events. Elias
suggests that this symbol helps us to structure what is in continuous flow.
It allows us to refer to specific points in the continuity of existence in
individual lives, social processes, or natural events. By emphasising the
synthesising power of the symbolic representation of time Elias
transcends the dualisms of nature–culture, individual–society, and
natural–social time without recourse to the conversion of dualisms into
dualities. As a symbol at the highest level of synthesis, he argues, time
brings aspects of the universe, the natural and social environment, and
our personal lives into an ordered relationship. It synthesises what we
tend to separate and dichotomise in our social analyses. Elias's approach
to time therefore underlines my proposition that an explicit focus on time
invalidates the social theory traditions; that it requires us to reassess our
assumptions and to find a way through uncharted ground.

Elias extends his attempt to reunite what scientists have tended to
separate and compartmentalise to the division of knowledge into academic disciplines. Time, dating, and time reckoning, he argues, cannot be
understood on the base assumption of a divided world.

> It is one of the difficulties with which we have to grapple when reflecting on
> time, that time does not fit neatly into one of the conceptual compartments
> which we still use as an unquestioned means for the classification of objects
> of this kind. (Elias 1984: xv; transl. B. Adam and E. King)

This view is echoed by Giddens, Luhmann, Bergmann, Schöps, Jaques
and Lauer who find it necessary to go beyond the boundaries of their
disciplines to philosophy, psychology, geography, history, and even
biology to do justice to their respective analyses. No one, however,
expresses more strongly than Young (1988) the belief that we need to
transgress the boundaries of our discipline because the study of time is a
topic quite unlike any other academic subject.

> Increasingly biologists will need to become sociologists and psychologists, as
> sociologists will need to become biologists and psychologists, and psycho-
> logists the other two, all with as much interchange as possible with historians
> and philosophers; and for any of the students to ignore physics, the queen of
> the sciences, would be to ignore the field in which the largest advance has
> been made so far in the conceptualisation of time. All the disciplines, and
> new hybrids between them, will be required to join in the coming unification
> of the human and natural sciences in the next century. (Young 1988: 246)

Such a requirement, it seems to me, is difficult to meet as long as we do
not first attend to the perspective-based divisions that demarcate our

positions within social science. Even a superficial glance at the different approaches to time allows us to identify these by their key concepts as marxist, functionalist, interactionist, and phenomenological, for example. Thus, in Giddens and Hohn's (1984) analyses we find time associated with reproduction, theorised as abstract exchange value and resource, identified with the concept of commodification and explicated on the basis of control and, in Hohn's case, alienation. Mead's (1959) emphasis on interaction and sociality results in a focus on the directionality and irreversibility of time, its creation in the present through emergence, and the difference between the past and future. His is a constitutive and constituted time where repetition fundamentally involves variation and creation. Luhmann's approach straddles the bias of Mead and the different emphasis of Schutz whose analysis focuses on the consciousness–society conjuncture. Reflection and memory, intent and projects, multiple realities, time horizons, and episodes are therefore the time aspects Schutz (1971) affirms. Hopkins (1982) as well as Giddens and Luhmann centrally utilise these aspects of time for their respective analyses. In contradistinction to Giddens I have not found functionalist approaches to exclude time or to identify it with change only. Order, organisation, synchronisation, change between fixed points, rates of change, repetition, regulation, duration, sequence, timing, parameter, and measure, are all time aspects that are widely utilised in analyses within that perspective. Moore's (1963) excellent *Man, Time and Society* is organised around this cluster of time concepts and so are the studies of Lauer (1980) and Schöps (1980). Whilst the recognition of these perspective biases is interesting, the divisions are of no avail to our task of developing an approach to time that allows for both the multiplicity of aspects and the relations between them, to feature centrally in our work.

We can summarise, therefore, that despite the expressed aim to transcend dualisms and the recognition that the focus on time plays havoc with disciplinary boundaries, these established traditions have a habit of re-emerging, be it in new guises. All theorists concerned with time make distinctions and these can be located in the writings of classical philosophers. Through them the nineteenth century categorisations and dualisms are reintroduced in theories that were created to overcome that limiting framework of analysis. Since, however, these distinctions give us the best initial access to contemporary and classical social science material on time, we need to focus on some of these before exploring the most widely agreed idea that time is always social time. Knowledge of these classical categorisations will help us to grasp better the limitations of the nineteenth-century way of thinking, understanding, and conceptualising.

Making distinctions philosophy's way

Making distinctions is endemic to the theoretical enterprise since understanding means relating: it depends on relating the object of our enquiry
to that which it is not, to its opposite, to that which it resembles and to
that which is different. It allows us to find explanations for observed
social phenomena and it helps us to delineate their particular characteristics. It is therefore not surprising that theories abound in distinctions
and comparisons. To elucidate the nature of social time social theorists
contrast it with natural time. To understand contemporary Western time
they differentiate it from the times of 'traditional' societies of today and
earlier historical periods. In order to explicate the qualitative time of
experience they define it in contradistinction to the quantitative measure
of clocks and calendars. At the root of all these social science distinctions
we find the thoughts and time theories of non-social science thinkers. We
invariably encounter the writings of St. Augustine and the time theories
of the philosophers Bergson, Heidegger, Husserl, Kant, and McTaggart
with their respective concepts of *durée, Dasein,* time horizons, a priori
intuitions and the A- and B-series of time. These conceptualisations are
therefore important for understanding social theories of time.

McTaggart (1927) developed the distinction between the A- and B-
series of time as a logical argument against the reality of time. Whilst
social scientists are not interested in questions of logic they found his
distinction a useful tool for the explanation of social time. McTaggart
identifies two ways of conceiving or talking about time: objectively, by
differentiating between earlier and later states; subjectively, by implicating the observer in the analysis. He suggests that events are conceptualised *in* time where the relation between them is defined in a
permanent and absolute way. In other words, if event X happened before
event Y, then X will always be earlier than Y. Thus, Caesar died before
Queen Victoria, people are young before they grow old, and the shiny
state of the car precedes the rusty one. Such temporal relations, he
argues, may be expressed in terms of timelessly true statements. He calls
these 'tense-less' relations between events the B-series of time. McTaggart
relates the A-series of time to statements about the past, present and
future. Such statements are relative, he reasons, because the definition of
something as past, present, or future depends on both an observer and
surrounding relations. Tensed statements are fundamentally context-
dependent and this makes them inherently relative, impermanent, and
associated with change and temporality.

Social theorists have either adopted McTaggart's terminology or
adapted it for their own purposes. Jaques (1982), for example, extended

McTaggart's criteria and called his A- and B-series equivalents the axes
of intent and succession, respectively; Elias designated them experiential
and structural relations of time. Yet, over and above McTaggart's
question of logic there is a problem for social theory. If objective time
statements can only be made with reference to succession, simultaneity,
and their being earlier or later, and if relative, tensed statements are
proposed to be the only ones capable of expressing change, then does it
follow that social scientists have to choose? Are we forced into a choice
between 'objectively true' statements about permanent relations and
relative ones where change is subjectively located in experience and the
framework of observation? If the human realm fundamentally involves
the past, present, and future, as social theorists consistently argue, then
how does this affect the social sciences' status of objectivity, given that
both the observers and the objects of their observation are essentially
bound up with their own and their society's past, present, and future?
Contemporary social theorists who have recently addressed themselves to
McTaggart's distinction have only implicitly dealt with this question.
They have used the distinctions for two main purposes: the delineation of
the objective time of clocks and calendars from the relative, subjective
time of experience (Bergmann 1981a; Elias 1984; Jaques 1982) and the
differentiation of social from natural time (Bergmann 1981a; Elias 1984;
Jaques 1982; Schöps 1980).

There seems to be unilateral agreement that human time must
fundamentally include the dimension of past, present, and future since
societies comprise conscious beings for whom the past, present, and
future matter. Whilst the B-series is thought to suffice for the description
and explanation of nature, it is argued that both types need to be
encompassed in analyses of the human world since human time-consciousness depends on two factors: the experience of real growth and
decay and the capacity for memory, intent, and expectation. This human
time-consciousness, Bergmann (1981a: 94–5) points out, is a human
universal. All societies differentiate events by criteria related to both the
A- and the B- series of time, even societies who do not have tensed
language or a separate concept for that which we call time. Members of
all societies, he argues, distinguish between events that are happening
now, have taken place in the past, or might possibly occur in the future.
They judge events to be past, present, or future on the basis of how they
are known, how they are determined, and how they can be influenced. We
know past events by records, perceive present ones directly, and know
future ones in our imagination only. Past events are determined, present
ones are becoming determined, and future ones are yet to be determined.
Lastly, we know that the past can no longer be influenced, that the
present is subject to influence, and that the future is only potentially

influenceable. For Bergmann, therefore, the A-series is a fundamental aspect of human social being and consequently has to be expressed in the theories which explain that social life. But, unlike many other theorists who have utilised McTaggart's distinction, he has encompassed cultural diversity. This means he can incoporate in his social theory societies such as the Hopi Indians (Whorf 1956) who do not conceptualise time and he manages to avoid the highly problematic idea that traditional societies live in reversible time.

Elias (1982a: 852–3) moves the argument in a different direction. He uses the same distinction for another purpose. Elias shows that the B-series of time is the time-structure pertaining to an event only. It excludes from the analysis the person as symboliser. A relation thus described is structural. It is the same for all observers. It expresses sequences of energy and matter that stand in a causal relation. With the A-series, on the other hand, the definitions of now, tomorrow, and yesterday change with the observing and experiencing person. They not only alter with observers but must also include their personal intersubjective awarenesses as an integral part of the analysis. Like many of his colleagues, Elias concludes that the experientially based time statements of the A-series are therefore inappropriate for the description and explanation of the causal event chains of nature. His assertion, however, leads him to an argument that differs from that of other theorists. Elias insists that to talk of the future of the sun, for example, is wrong. It is based on the subjective position of a living person and therefore constitutes an inadmissible fusion of distinct levels of analysis. For Elias humans are not part of nature, they *are* nature at a higher level of integration. Nature without the human element is characterised, and thus understandable, by four dimensions: three of space and one of time. With the representation of the universe in terms of symbols, however, an irreducibly new dimension is introduced: the second dimension of time, where self-reflective awareness becomes a necessary, integral part of the analysis. Unlike Jaques's (1982: 92–5) fifth dimension which is located in the capacity of memory and intent Elias's fifth dimension is delineated as awareness of awareness, as observers grasping themselves as integral aspects of their observations.

> Everything that happens in the human sphere is now experienced and represented by humanly created symbols and thus needs definition not only by four but five coordinates. The developing synthesis, from which the present concept of time emerged, is also characteristic of the distinctive nature of this dimension. Scientific consciousness forbids us to obscure either its natural origin or its irreducibly unique quality.' (Elias 1982a: 855; transl. E. King and B. Adam)

If, however, the idea of time is so ineradicably tied to humans in their environment and to their capacity for mental synthesis and symbol formation as Elias seems to be arguing consistently (1982b: 1014–15, 1984: xvi, xlvi, 44–57), and if this human capacity needs to enter all analyses, then surely this implies that the four-dimensional approach (the B-Series) is inadequate, inappropriate even, for understanding the processes and rhythms of nature. I shall show in the next chapter that contemporary physicists have arrived at that very position. Among social scientists Luhmann is a lonely advocate of that approach. He insists that time has to be understood as the difference between the past and the future and that it needs to be distinguished from chronology and the measure of motion. For temporalised systems, Luhmann (1978: 99) writes, 'there cannot exist a single state for which the past and future would be irrelevant.' Past and future, in other words, are fundamental to all of nature.

Luhmann arrives at this definition by taking a different path from his colleagues (Adam 1987: 93–102). He is not concerned exclusively with the human symbol but with temporality as an essential aspect of nature. He seeks the basis upon which our concepts of time and chronology are formed. Past and future are to Luhmann essential for both time as constituted in systems and time as the social interpretation of reality. The former relates to his theory of systems with temporalised complexity (1978, 1979) and the latter to his understanding of culturally constituted time as a generalised dimension of meaningful reality (1982b, c). The relevance of time, as distinct from chronology, Luhmann insists (1982b: 276), 'depends on a capacity to interrelate the past and the future in the present'. Past and future are fundamental to him because they are a quality of nature and not because they are an integral part of human symbolic knowing. As both horizon and the difference between past and future they are integral to the natural world. This view is supported by contemporary natural science. Temporal time, as I shall show, has been established as a law of nature. It follows that an understanding of nature without this temporal extension must be essentially flawed.

By not getting drawn into the dualistic conceptualisation of McTaggart's A- and B-series and the concomitant contrast between social and natural time Luhmann has managed to evade the dualisms others unsuccessfully sought to transcend. I wish to suggest that McTaggart's conceptualisation of time is too deeply steeped in the classical dualistic tradition of philosophy to be useful as a conceptual tool for the explication of the multiplicity and complexity of social life. Even the conversion from dualisms to mutually implicating dualities has not got theorists closer to a conceptualisation of social time that encompasses its multiple expressions. Instead, it introduced new dualisms such as time in nature and cultural life, and the time-consciousness of traditional and industrial societies. However, the distinctiveness of Luhmann's approach is not only to be sought in his different and wider focus but also in an underlying time theory; a theory that, despite some superficial resemblance, differs fundamentally from McTaggart's conceptualisation. Luhmann draws extensively on Mead's (1959) *The Philosophy of the Present* which in turn is informed by Bergson's philosophy. For our purposes it will suffice to outline Bergson's (1910) concepts of *temps* and *durée* in order to show what makes the theories of Mead, Luhmann, and, more recently, Ingold (1986) distinct.

At first sight there seems no problem of compatibility with McTaggart's A- and B-series of time and Bergson's (1910) *durée* and *temps* as lived temporal duration and spatialised, abstracted, mathematical time respectively. Whilst Bergson characterises *temps* with similar features to those of the B-series *durée* is defined in a fundamentally different way to McTaggart's A-series. Bergson's analysis goes beyond the distinctions encountered so far when he insists that temporal time – his true *durée* – is continuous emergence of novelty. To him the future is *becoming* in a way that can never be a mere rearrangement of what has been. Temporal extension in terms of past and future is essential here, too, but it is so in a different way from the above since the present neither just is nor passes. With the notion of lived *durée* Bergson wants to express that *durée* is not *in* time but *constitutes time in ceaseless emergence*; in other words, that the present is not in time but has to be understood as presencing (Capek 1971: 91). Bergson uses the concept of presencing to express the continual creation of the present. In his theory of time, the past and future are not just bound by memory and intent; they are constantly created and recreated in a present. Bergson's time is therefore not a boundary but constituted in emergence.

Unlike Ingold (1986), who seeks a Bergsonian approach to anthropology, neither Mead nor Luhmann make explicit use of Bergson's theory of time but merely include the principle of temporal time in their work. Both are concerned with the constitutive nature of temporal time, with time as ceaselessly creative emergence, which entails that the future is always fundamentally different from the past and the emergent is necessarily more than the processes that have led up to it. 'There must be at least something that happens to and in the thing which affects the nature of the thing', argues Mead (1959: 19–20), 'in order that one moment may be distinguishable from another, in order that there may be time.' Without emergence there is no time, not even a quantity to be measured. Mead theorises this temporality in conjunction with the

universal principles of sociality and communication (Adam 1987: 139–
50). We can thus see that the Bergsonian framework of analysis pervades
the work of Mead and Luhmann even though the concepts of *temps* and
durée are not utilised in their respective theories of time.

Giddens, in contrast, makes central use of the concept of *durée*. As the
concept changes with the development of his thought, however, the
tenuous connections to its originator get ever weaker. Not emergence and
irreducible difference but the moment of repetition and the recursiveness
of social life come to be identified by Giddens's concept of *durée*. His
theoretical concern mutates from an early emphasis on transformation to
a stress on repetition. It changes from a conceptualisation of social
systems as 'a virtual order of differences produced and reproduced in
social action as medium and outcome' (1979: 3), via a focus on the
reflexive monitoring and rationalisation of action as well as the 'the
human agent as a routine feature of *durée*' (1981: 35), to a conceptualisation where *durée* becomes associated with reversibility. 'The durée of
daily life, it is not too fanciful to say', he writes in *The Constitution of
Society* (1984: 35), 'operates in something akin to what Lévi-Strauss calls
"reversible time". Whether or not time "as such" (whatever that would
be) is reversible, the events and routines of daily life do not have a one-
way flow to them.' In Giddens's recent writings (1981, 1984, 1987), *durée*
constitutes one of three time levels of being which he conceptualises as
mutually dependent and intersecting. The other two are *Dasein* and
longue durée. He uses these three to refer to different time-scales of
existence and to distinguish social processes by their time direction. The
two *durées* are used to characterise the repetitive element of both daily
life and generations, whilst *Dasein* is used to express the irreversible
directionality of living unto death. To state the distinctions in this clear-
cut way is, however, misleading since subtle shifts have occured in
Giddens's conceptualisation of these time levels in general and *durée* in
particular, as I have already indicated.

In *Central Problems in Social Theory*, Giddens (1979: 200) argues that
the idea of reversible time is a misnomer, that 'it is not really time as such
that Lévi-Strauss is referring to, but social change'. Whilst he emphasises
the importance of tradition and routine, he also insists on the need for a
simultaneous conceptualisation of the historical and sequential nature of
social life, and thus its direction and one-way flow. Similarly, he stresses
the directional process of long-term sedimentation for the *longue durée*
(1979: 7, 1981: 20). This vision of direction-in-recurrence and fruition-
through-repetition, which seems to me to be fundamental to his theory of
structuration, is replaced in *The Constitution of Society* with an imagery
of recurring aspects of social life operating in 'reversible time'. By 1984
the complexity of his thoughts on the subject is compressed into a sterile

model where the *durée* of day-to-day experience is characterised as operating in reversible time, *Dasein* in irreversible, directional time, and the *longue durée* of generations, institutions and history in reversible time again. I take this to be a highly problematic conceptualisation and shall therefore return to discuss it further on several occasions. At this point only a few preliminary comments on *durée* and the idea of reversible time will suffice.

In *A Contemporary Critique of Historical Materialism* (1981) Giddens links the *durée* of daily life to both the capacity of human beings to transcend the immediacy of the senses by memory – conceptualised as individual, symbolical, and social storage – and the flow of daily experience and practice. In accordance with Schutz (1971), he sees purposes and reasons as retrospective, routine aspects of action. He also writes about the *durée* of interaction being reflexively categorised into episodes with beginnings and ends. This *durée*, as both the temporality of a present experience transcended by memory and purpose and the directional flow of day-to-day routinised life, is a conceptualisation that Giddens has adopted from Schutz who, in turn, has adapted Bergson's meaning for his own social theory. In this *durée* the element of routine enters as a chronic temporal feature of action in terms of reflexive monitoring and rationalisation whilst the routine aspect of Giddens' later (1984) version of *durée* is associated with the tasks, chores and endlessly recurring phenomena of social life. It appears that it is due to their routine and recurrent nature that Giddens comes to think of the habitual and repetitive phenomena as timeless, as not dependent on either time or space. He gives priority to cycles of return where, he argues, neither past and future nor temporal direction matter since what has been will come again, and what is past will also be the future. The routine aspects of daily life such as working, driving the car, or cooking food are always past and future simultaneously. Without the relevance of the past and future dimension, Giddens seems to be arguing, the essence of unidirectionality and irreversibility of social reproduction are lost (1984: 35). In *The Constitution of Society* the complexity of Giddens's thinking on the matter is thus reduced to a duality of reversible and irreversible time, a mere variant on the more common division into cyclical and linear time. Where Giddens writes of reversible time, Rammstedt (1975: 51–2), for example, refers to cyclical time-consciousness when he suggests that in cyclical processes what has been recurs and what is expected to come has already been before. Put alongside of each other the two conceptualisations can be recognised as expressing the same idea.

Giddens acknowledges that daily life has a flow and duration but he does not see it leading anywhere; hence his imagery of reversible time. Yet, whilst events may recur chronically and in a seemingly unchanged way, they nevertheless have time within them. Sequencing, duration, irreversible direction, passage, and the rate at which events occur, I want to suggest, are integral time aspects of even the most repetitive social phenomena. Their direction and irreversibility only become irrelevant when the recurring events are abstracted from their context. As practice, events are fundamentally contextual, directional, and irreversible. Furthermore, it is not time but events and tasks that are endlessly recurring whilst the flow of experience continues in an irreversible and directional way. Neither irreversibility and directionality nor recurrence and reversibility should therefore be assumed to be interchangeable. Going to work every morning, reading the paper, and doing the washing-up could classify as recurring, repetitive, habit-infused activities but this makes neither them nor the time in which they occur reversible. There can be no un-going to work, no un-reading the paper or un-washing-up since time neither stands still nor goes backwards during those activities.

Not only the specific conceptualisation of *durée* and reversibility distinguish Giddens's theory of time from that of his colleagues but also his understanding of the constitution of time. To Giddens time is constituted in the repetition of day-to-day living. His focus is on social reproduction rather than the social production of action. Social reproduction, however, deals with the replication of practices over time and it is this repetitive aspect that Giddens conceptualises as temporality where others emphasise emergence, life, growth, change, or decay. It is reproduction in the form of routinisation which, to him, is constitutive not only of social order but of time itself. Bergson's emergence, transformation, and becoming seem to get crowded out of the analysis when the focus is predominantly on repetition, routine, and reproduction. Time is no longer used for the conceptualisation of the new, the unpredictable, or the recognition that life passes in transformation; namely that which Giddens (1979) seeks to encapsulate with his theory of structuration.

Giddens's notion of reversible time is informed by Lévi-Strauss's work on the distinction between traditional and modern societies and their respective modes of communication through myths and stories. Lévi-Strauss (1978) in turn has adopted the concept from Newtonian mechanics. He uses it to express the idea that myths and orchestral scores, for example, are machines for the suppression of time. Not only can myths be repeated an infinite number of times, Lévi-Strauss suggests, but their form differs from that of modern, sequenced stories. Unlike their modern counterparts myths resemble loops rather than a sequential forward movement. They can be accessed at any point without the need to proceed from a beginning to an end. As such they are conceived by Lévi-Strauss as time transcending and defined as reversible and non-cumulative (Giddens 1979: 21-2). I want to suggest, however, that myths and musical scores can be time-reversible only in isolation and abstraction; only un-told and un-performed. Without their being told, played, performed, read, or thought about, however, they have no meaning or reality. Their existence, I propose, is to be found in the conjuncture between having been created and being told, performed, or read. This makes them not machines for the suppression of time but for its constitution. It makes them fundamentally irreversible. Lévi-Strauss does concede that they cannot be studied in isolation as a bounded order of signification, but only as sign. Yet, despite this recognition, he pursues the timeless structure. What would follow from the concessions, however, is that meaning is context bound and thus not timeless. Neither myths nor musical scores are reversible since we can never step in the same river twice, to use the Heraclitean metaphor, perform them backwards, or un-tell them.

In addition to the theorists already mentioned, Giddens draws extensively on the writings of Heidegger. Yet, unlike Giddens, Heidegger does not offer repetition and irreversibility as separate or separable concepts but theorises them in their mutual relation. Heidegger shows how repetition is linked to the becoming of the possible and to the one-way direction of time. Stegmüller (1969) explains how Heidegger relates the historical awareness of human beings to their existential reality of repetition and recurrence.

> The more future orientated the *Dasein* the more open it is towards the past potentialities of Being. Thus, human beings, and especially those that exist explicitly (knowingly), are repeating beings. (Their) Repetition (however) is no empty bringing back of the past; not a mere binding of the present to that which is irrevocably gone, but a deep existential response to that which has been whilst simultaneously being a decisive revocation of the effects of the past in the present. (Stegmüller, 1969: 175; transl. B. Adam)

It seems that Heidegger's conceptualisation of repetition has not been taken into consideration by Giddens when he argues that each tradition or daily routine may be experienced as a kind of 'time-threat remover' by providing security through continuity and structured sameness. By emphasising the repetitive aspects of the two *durées*, and theorising these in reversible time, Giddens has allowed both presencing and the difference between the past and future to fade out of his analysis. By conflating repetition, cycles, and sameness with reversibility, the opportunity to theorise presencing and the relation between cycles of return and directional continuity and change, has been missed. Giddens is correct in his observation that time is inextricably linked to repetition. But, as Elias (1982a: 849) points out, it is the symbol that represents as repeatable what is irreversible and unrepeatable. The repetition itself, I would argue, cannot be theorised in terms of sameness if it is to form a coherent part of the theory of structuration. It needs to be understood temporally and, following Heidegger, as a response to, and negation of, the previous recurrence. To conflate repetition and reversibility is like saying that because droughts are a regular occurrence in Africa, or the meeting of political leaders is a frequent event with a long tradition established over centuries, the drought in Ethiopia and the meetings between Bush and Gorbachev are reversible or experienced as such. I want to propose therefore that such terminology is misplaced and should be avoided. In addition to Heidegger's conceptualisation of the human relationship to repetition, I want to suggest that no routine, tradition, or regular recurrence is ever the same in any of its repeats. Between the last winter and this one, last month's pay and the present one, yesterday's washing-up and today's, the world has changed. We have grown older and the other participants and objects have changed. The context is a different one. All one can state is that the more similar and unchanging the events, the more they allow for a speculation on a similar future. None of it, however, is meaningful or observable, apart from their practice in a present, and as such they have irreversible effects that contribute to both change and stability. We have to recognise that repetition can be the 'same' only in abstraction, by artificially excluding contexts and effects as I have argued above and shall discuss further later.

Furthermore, what is generally conceptualised as timeless, refers mostly to rates of change that are very much slower than those of the observer's frame of reference. Traditional societies, for example, are extremely slowly changing when measured and defined against present Western standards. It is the particular frame of reference that makes Lévi-Strauss and Giddens conceptualise such societies as 'cold' and operating in reversible time. From an evolutionary perspective, for example, the changing of such societies would be considered as being extremely fast. The wider the gap between the rate of change and the framework of perception of those who observe the change, the more likely is a conceptualisation in terms of the duality of form and content. Yet once we take account of the relativity of the frame of reference, we recognise that form is forming: that it is being formed at every moment of interaction. Giddens refers to this process as structuration. But as long as he retains Lévi-Strauss's concept of reversible time to describe continuity and transformation – his structuration – he creates misunderstanding and confusion. Not every reader of *The Constitution of Society* will have Giddens's earlier book at their side to remind themselves of both his critique of Lévi-Strauss's structuralism (1979: 24–8, 200), and his theor-isations of the relation of repetition to transformation (1979: 62–5).

In these last pages our focus has shifted from exploring the philosophical bases of our time theories to Giddens' adaptation of them. Becoming aware of the subtle shifts and mutations that occur in the work of just one author allows us to see not only the multiple influences that bear on our theories of time but also lays bare the enormous complexity of the assumptions that underpin our explicit and implicit theories of time. Furthermore, it shows how much is taken-for-granted even when time is the explicit focus of our attention, when the stated aim is to make time central to social theory.

In our everyday lives as in our theories the one aspect of time we take most for granted is that of a frame within which we organise, regulate, and structure our daily lives. We associate the fact that we live 'in time' with clocks, calendars, with the rhythm of day and night, and with the seasons. The sun rises every morning, Christmas returns every year, schools break up in the summer. All these recurring events constitute the basis upon which we live an 'in time' existence. They allows us to plan our lives within the structure that is created by their regular and thus predictable recurrence. Many theorists not only identify the distinctiveness of this time but they also differentiate between this boundary aspect and time passing. Once more, however, it matters how the distinctions are conceived. We have seen that Bergson differentiates between *temps* and *durée* as the structural and time creating dimensions of time respectively. Both McTaggart's B-series and Bergson's *temps* are clock- and calendar-based concepts for the expression and explanation of existence *in* time. Bergson and Mead differentiate their theories of time in which time is a constitutive dimension of life, from theories where time is primarily the parameter within which life takes place. This distinction is one that appears in many guises as we shall see later. I shall identify it as the difference between 'time in events' and 'events in time'.

Heidegger's approach cuts across these distinctions and brings aspects of them together to form a coherent whole. He emphasises the finitude of *Dasein*, our *Sein zum Tode* (being unto death), as the source for our existence in time. He argues that out of our awareness of the finitude of existence arises not only the meaning, the importance, and the urgency of being but also time as the boundary to life. This boundary of birth and death, he insists, must not be thought of like a perimeter fence or a fixed structure but as permeating our being. To Heidegger *Dasein* (Being in the world and the now) is always inclusive of the birth-death penetration and as such allows for objectivity and for human beings to exist in time. It seems worthwhile to quote Heidegger at length on the existential relation of birth and death to *Dasein*.

The 'between' which relates to birth and death already lies *in the Being* of

Dasein. On the other hand, it is by no means the case that *Dasein* 'is' actual in a point of time, and that, apart from this, it is 'surrounded' by the non-actuality of its birth and death. Understood existentially, birth is not and never is something past in the sense of something no longer present-at-hand; and death is just as far from having the kind of Being of something still outstanding, not yet present-at-hand but coming along. Factical *Dasein* exists as born; and, as born, it is already dying, in the sense of Being-towards-death. As long as *Dasein* factically exists, both the 'ends' and their 'between' *are* in the only way possible on the basis of *Dasein's* Being as *care*. Thrownness and that Being towards death in which one either flees it or anticipates it, form a unity; and in this unity birth and death are 'connected' in a manner characteristic of *Dasein*. As care, *Dasein is* the 'between'. (Heidegger, 1980: 426–7)

Heidegger suggests further that this awareness of existence as bounded entails the fear of non-existence. Death, concern, and conscience are therefore fundamental aspects of *Dasein* which force action in the present. He emphasises the *Zwischen* (the between) as not only defined by its boundary permeation but as also defining it. The temporality of *Dasein* gives meaning to birth and death while being given meaning by them. Beginning and end and that which binds them, he argues, are always mutually defining and implicated in the analysis. Heidegger is not alone in emphasising the centrality of the *Zwischen*. In both information theory and cybernetics the interval between signals has been identified to be as important as the signals themselves. Without the interval, it is argued there, processes, entities, or constructs, for example, could not have any meaning. To Heidegger humans are *zukünftig* (future-orientated/dependent) at every moment and *gewesen* (having been/ become from nothingness). Birth and death enter creatively into every moment. Their *Dasein* is therefore both horizon and presencing. Horizon and presencing are not only key concepts in Heidegger's work and the treatises of Bergson and Mead but also form a central component of Husserl's phenomenological writings on time which became an important source of inspiration for classical and contemporary philosophers, psychologists, and social scientists alike.

Husserl (1964) conceptualises the present as horizontality of the flowing present in which impressions and perceptions are extended by protensions and retentions. In contradistinction to psychologists of his time, Husserl insists that even a concern with short term-memory has to fundamentally include the future dimension. Without an extension into both directions, he argues, one could not understand speech, appreciate music, or read a text. Without retention we would not know what we had been saying so far; we would lose the thread of our thought. Without protension we would be incapable of finishing a sentence since the

meaning must precede its being expressed in speech. Husserl's conceptualisation of the past and future as horizon, constituted by and
integrated in a present as well as constituting it, has proved a powerful
idea for social theory.

For our present focus on the different ways to conceptualise existence
in time, however, we need merely to establish the distinction between
time-frames and phenomenological horizons. Not only are the two
conceptualised on the basis of different sources of time but they also
entail very different theoretical characteristics which differentiate
Heidegger and Husserl's analyses of 'in time existence' from that of clock
and calendar time. Husserl's horizon is constituted by the penetration of
the present by protentions and retentions; Heidegger's horizon relates to
Dasein's permeation by birth and death whilst the time-frame of dates
and clock time units is formed by the rhythms of nature and society: by
seasons, diurnal cycles, religious festivals, market days, and faster natural
oscillations of varying speeds ranging from the heartbeat to the caesium.
Unlike boundaries, horizons are relative to their owners and to contexts
and they cannot be reached. The birth–death horizon, for example, can
only be reached in death at which point it ceases to be a horizon.
Horizons constitute a boundary but this border is unlike a fence or a
fixed structure. Horizons are an extension of the present, of our existence
and of consciousness. They radiate outwards from our being like a halo
and resonate towards the centre of our being from its amorph periphery.
Boundaries are very different from this. They are, explains Bergmann
(1981: 108), subject-independent. We can get close to them, even
transcend them, and they always include the reality of the other side. The
'working day' from 9.00 am to 5.00 pm, for example, would be
meaningless without the hours preceding and succeeding it; night time is
permanently bounded and defined by day time. Not permeation but
regular rhythmic recurrence constitutes time-frames and allows for
planning in the interval periods.

The conjuncture of horizons and perimeters is achieved by contemporary phenomenologists through the concept of the life-plan. Through this
idea they are able to bring horizons and perimeters into a meaningful
relation. 'Knowledge of finitude', suggest Schutz and Luckmann (1974:
47), 'stands out against the experience of the world's continuance. This
knowledge is the fundamental moment of all projects within the framework of a life-plan, and is itself determined by the time of the life-world.'
They further argue that the stream of consciousness intersects with the
rhythms of the body, the seasons, and society which constitute the
multiple times of the life-world. Furthermore, they see the life-plan as
determined by finitude yet simultaneously dependent on the principle of
'first things first'. This means that perimeters as fixed, external temporal

structures intersect with the knowledge and permeation of the birth – death horizon. Action, I want to propose further, fuses rhythms and finitude into a coherent whole. Our idea of time must consequently always entail both rhythmic recurrence and beginnings and ends, perimeters and horizons. It is therefore important that we never lose sight of one whilst our focus is on the other. Rhythms and irreversible processes must be understood *together* since, on their own, neither could account for that which is expressed by the idea of time.

A closely related group of distinctions that appear in a multitude of guises in classical and contemporary treatises on social time relate to questions about the nature of the past, present, and future and their respective reality statuses. Whilst interpretations vary on the former, conceptualising the past and future as a boundary, an ever-changing horizon, a focus for orientation, or simply an extension, there is agreement on the latter. Most theorists question the reality status of the past and future and they accord a special position to the present. The origin of these thoughts can be traced back to St. Augustine and his quest for the nature of time. Not every treatise of time refers to Heraclitus, Kant, Hegel, Husserl, Bergson, Heidegger, Schutz, or Whitehead but I have not come accross a single study that does not mention St. Augustine's *Confessions*. Most go further than mere lip-service and utilise his thoughts for their own understanding; and no doubt classical time theorists were also aware of St. Augustine's conversations with God. 'My soul is on fire' he pleaded with his creator, 'to know this most intricate enigma. Shut it not up, O Lord my God, good Father . . .'. (1978: 45).

In Book XI of the *Confessions* (AD 397–401), St. Augustine addresses himself to the enigma of time as measure and to the nature of past, present, and future. He feels he knows time but, whenever he wants to raise it to the conceptual level of consciousness, he ends up with irresolvable puzzles: the nature of time eludes his rational grasp (Bourke 1983: 228–9; Gale 1970: 40). He does, however, come to recognise time past, time present, and future time as the essence of the human mind. For to live life as a human being, he thinks, involves the interaction of memory, perception, anticipation, and desire. Without these aspects of mind humans would be incapable of living their daily lives, since knowledge, experiences, goals, fears, desires, and anticipations are ineradicable aspects of human perception and action. From this he concludes that past and future do not exist outside mind. 'It can only be', he argues, 'that the mind, which regulates this process, performs three functions; those of expectation, attention and memory. The future which it expects, passes through the present, to which it attends, into the past which it remembers' (St. Augustine Book XI, Section 28; p. 277; quoted in Jaques 1982: 5). This understanding of past, present, and future as present past, present present, and present future, coexisting in the mind, has proved a fruitful source of inspiration through the ages and has lost nothing of its potency even today. Both Mead and Schutz, for example, have taken on board this understanding, first formulated at the end of the fourth century AD and so did the contemporary theorists already mentioned. On the basis of those thoughts theorists have developed different approaches. For many, St. Augustine's thoughts have led to the conclusion that time is to be exclusively located in the human mind, for others they have resulted in theories that differentiate between the reality status of the present, on the one hand, and the past and future on the other. For Mead and Luhmann they have culminated in analyses that show memory and anticipation as a fundamental aspect of all living forms.

For Luhmann (1978: 99) human mind and social organisation are part of nature. They are nature extended by meaning and the human dimension. Memory and intent are, to Luhmann, not exclusively human capacities but an essential part of plant and animal life as well since binding the past and future in a present is fundamental to all self-organising systems. It is not an exclusive capacity of human beings. Communication by symbolic language merely shifts this capacity to a different scale. It vastly increases the time-transcending potential. Elias (1982a) conceptualises the difference as one of dimension while Luhmann seems to see it as one of degree. Luhmann suggests further a temporal integration of past and future in the present through the activities of the mind. But, in contradistinction to Jaques (1982), Luhmann proposes that mind is fundamentally interactively constituted. To him, time-consciousness, mind, and language are mutually implicated and it is this, he argues, which makes them both social and objective. For Jaques the objective status of his psychologically based past and future dimension is achieved through the communication of intent.

In Schutz's (1971) work the past, present, and future play a central role. They feature prominently in Schutz's explications of communciation, meaning, action, relations of a personal and impersonal kind, the taken-for-granted realm of practical activity, and the effortless negotiation of multiple life worlds (Adam 1987: 150–8). Schutz's thoughts on the past and future direction of our socially constituted consciousness have had a deep impact on social theories within and beyond the phenomenological tradition. They therefore merit attention and I propose that we look at Schutz's conceptualisation of the different temporalities entailed in the act and in action respectively since the principle of this particular distinction echoes through many other aspects of his work in areas where he focuses on the nature and intersection of individual and collective aspects of social life.

In his distinction between the act and action Schutz points out that an act can only be known once it has been performed, once it is in the past. It can also be projected into the future as a potential act. To be known as an act, however, is crucially dependent on reflection. This applies to past known acts as well as those imagined in a future present. Whilst the latter are in principle uncertain, they may be known in the future-perfect tense. They can be reflected upon as possible acts. Schutz points out that a person may reflect in the past tense, the present-perfect tense, or the future-perfect tense. Whilst he thinks the act to be dependent on reflection, Schutz ties action intimately to the present. Action, he argues, is a process with a forward direction, always orientated towards projects. Action is therefore always projected action which is lived in a continuing process. It is teleological in its nature. Its motive is purposive and described by Schutz as an 'in-order-to' motive. Action motives, he insists, have to be distinguished from act motives which are always presented in the reflective mode as rationalisations. Schutz calls the latter 'because motives'. As rationalised acts, he argues, they are explained with reference to the past. In this distinction between action and acts and the concomitant 'in-order-to' and 'because motives' Schutz is pointing to a difference in the direction of time. Action is always present action in the direction of the future. This is so even when it is taken with reference to something that has occurred in the past. It is impossible for action to go backwards in the direction of the past. Reversibility is an impossibility in Schutz's analysis. In contradistinction to action, the act is always rationalised from the present in the direction of the past. Meaning, argues Schutz, is always attributed reflectively. This entails both a kind of 'stepping outside' the stream of consciousness and future-orientated action, and a looking back at previously performed or imagined acts.

Extending Mead's (1959) argument, Schutz suggests that we can only be aware of our ego or our stream of consciousness in the reflective mode.

> We cannot approach the realm of the Self without an act of reflective turning. But what we grasp by the *reflective* act is never the present of our stream of thought and also not its specious present; it is always its past. Just now the grasped experience pertained to my present, but in grasping it I know it is not present any more. And, even if it continues, I am aware only by an afterthought that my reflective turning towards its starting phases has been simultaneous with its continuation. The whole present, therefore, and also the vivid present of our Self, is inaccessible for the reflective attitude. We can only turn to the stream of our thought as if it had stopped with the

last grasped experience. In other words, self-consciousness can only be experienced *modo praeterito*, in the past tense. (Schutz 1971: 172–3)

This process is further complicated by the fact that we remain in the stream of consciousness even during reflection. The stream of consciousness, Schutz seems to be arguing, is always in the action mode even while it is engaged in reflecting on the past or imagined acts. Actions may be grasped intuitively as a totality in the 'vivid flowing present' but acts, which have their meaning attributed reflectively, have a different temporal structure within the stream of consciousness (1971: 53). He suggests that reflection and representation break the flowing unity and present it as partial elements. This means that the quality of the whole cannot be retained once it has been subject to rationalisation. This is because reflectively attributed meaning is by necessity selective. In other words, aspects of past acts need to be selected from the vastness of the totality within which past and potential acts are embedded. We select from within a horizon of social relatedness and establish causal relationships and 'because' rationalisations. In addition to selection we both order according to priorities and sequence with reference to a hierarchy of values and necessities. Selecting, prioritising, and sequencing, Schutz proposes, form part of the taken-for-granted strategies that people employ in their routine interplay of act and action.

This last point also forms a key argument in Luhmann's (1971b) essay *Die Knappheit der Zeit und die Vordringlichkeit des Befristeten* (the shortage of time and the priority of that which has a fixed time limit) where he suggests that sequencing in order of priorities with reference to values and necessity plays a central role in the allocation, utilisation, and organisation of people's time. Whilst Schutz conceptualises purposive action as future orientated, he does nevertheless argue that it also entails a strong element of influence from of the past. To him the past is fundamentally embodied in projects since these are always utilised in form of mediated, indirect knowledge. In other words, Schutz is arguing here that any present, direct, purposive action is simultaneously bounded by the socially constituted common stock of knowledge, by language, and by the imposed relevances of the group. These common aspects, he thinks, are of historical nature, sedimented over long periods of community life. For Schutz the arena of action is the common-sense world. He conceives of this world as the paramount reality in which people operate as physical beings, and in which they expect their domain of work, play, and communication to be governed by the law of cause and effect.

Let me make these thoughts more real by relating them to my presentation of Schutz's ideas. Giving an account of Schutz's work here entails tailoring the portrayal to suit my overall argument, my style of presentation, and the length of other sections within the chapter. I prioritise, sequence, reject, emphasise, and evaluate with reference to the past and the future; namely, my reflected understanding of Schutz's work and my project. As a biographically unique person, engaged for many years in the study of time with reference to social theory, I communicate this unique understanding through a shared language and on the basis of a common, historically sedimented stock of knowledge. My choices are always guided by a concern with what I think is considered relevant by social theorists and social scientists more generally. My understanding of my colleagues' criteria of relevance imposes restrictions on content. No matter how novel my developing thoughts might be, they can only be expressed in a meaningful way through the shared, mediated knowledge already present in our society in general and the social science community in praticular. Only with a shared medium of communication can I expect the reader to follow my thoughts and partake in my conceptual exploration.

From this very brief excursus on Schutz's time-related writings we can see that the past, present, and future issue primarily in terms of how we act, interact, and know. His focus is on the time differences between doing and rationalising what we have done, and between knowing our actions and attributing meaning to them retrospectively. Those differences are in turn closely tied to language as fundamentally tensed, and to the ability to conceive of pasts and futures in a multiple way. We can think of future futures, future presents, present futures, future pasts or any number of other combinations. The present as the locus of action and communication is accorded special status. Yet, as Schutz shows, it cannot be understood without its penetration by aspects of the past and future. Historically sedimented knowledge, goals, or concerns cannot be separated from understanding the acting, communicating, interacting persons in their everyday life-world.

Schutz's thoughts have become an integral part not only of phenomenological writings on time but of treatises covering the entire range of social science perspectives (Bergmann 1981a; Elias 1982a, b, 1984; Giddens; Jaques 1982; Luhmann; Young 1988). They have become absorbed to such an extent that their origins are no longer referenced; they are presented as 'social fact'. The situation is almost the reverse with Mead's *The Philosophy of the Present*. This work is cited by social theorists almost as frequently as St. Augustine's *Confessions*. Yet, the body of that thought has not been taken on board, let alone absorbed as 'social fact', by contemporary social theorists. There seem to me to be at least two reasons for this. First, *The Philosophy of the Present* is a collection of posthumously published lectures and lecture notes. As a first attempt at major reconceptualisation they are extremely sketchy and difficult to understand. Secondly, the implications of those thoughts are uncomfortable and uncompromising: they require us to reassess our base assumptions. Mead's temporal theory of time, as I shall show throughout this treatise, affects the very foundations of social theory. It goes far beyond mere scientific trimming. Taken on board, it radically alters the way social reality may be understood and theorised.

Showing how mind, consciousness, sociality, and the self have evolved, Mead is able to locate them in and as an integral part of nature. For him, form is forming and mind, for example, is formed and still forming in interaction with the environment. Mead focuses on the problem of the emergence of the 'now' in relation to that which has been in the past, and he investigates the relation of consciousness to the common, shared aspects of both the human social world and the universe. In his analysis of sociality and emergence he establishes the nature of interaction at the levels of the physical world, life, and consciousness. To explain change, continuity, the self, and identity he takes a consistently temporal standpoint, focusing exclusively on the 'time in' things, events, perspectives, or roles rather than the time of an abstract framework within which experience is conceptualised. Despite this strong emphasis on time, his thoughts are not intended as a contribution to the philosophy of time. Whilst time is both central to and implicit in this work it is never the direct focus of his attention. This, of course, is consistent with his rejection of abstract time. He denies reality status to the abstract time of clocks and calendars and regards it as nothing more than a 'manner of speaking'.

In the essay, 'The present as locus of reality', Mead (1959: 1–31) deals with the ontological status of the present, past, and future. As the title suggests, reality to Mead exists in the present. The present implies a past and a future, but they are denied existence. Any reality that transcends the present, he argues, must exhibit itself in the present. He allows that the present may vary in its temporal spread, but insists that it must include becoming otherwise we would not be able to distinuish one event from another. An example might help to clarify the meaning of this abstract proposition. My present, for example, could be defined by my activity of writing, but for this present to be recognisable as a past present, something new will have had to have happened. My going to have a cup of coffee may be such an event which will delineate the old from the new present which is, in turn, defined by the event of having a cup of coffee. The present could, however, also be conceived as a thousand other event-filled episodes, such as my working on this book, the 1980s, or the post-war era. These will in turn become the past either due to their completion or due to emergent events. The present post-war period, for example, would cease to be the present only after some major social upheaval, affecting all other relations in such a fundamental way that the present could no longer be defined by the social turning point of World War II but by that new decisive focus. This is what Mead seems to mean when he argues that for us to be able to conceive of events, change, continued existence, the present or even time, there has to be becoming and disappearing. An eternal present, he explains, cannot be a present at all. To him, the present is the only locus of reality because he understands all past as reconstructed in a present, each moment recreated afresh in the light of a new present. Mead (1959: 11) explains how it is customary to think of the past as 'there' and as not being subject to change. Like others, he admits the past to be irrevocable but, he suggests, it is so only in so far as we cannot change or undo events as they have happened. In its meaning and the way it is preserved, evoked, and selected, however, the past is revocable and as hypothetical as the future. The past is continuously recreated and reformulated into a different past from the standpoint of the emergent present. It has no status apart from its relation to the present. Emergence, he insists further, inevitably reflects into the past and changes its meaning. By focusing on that process Mead can explain how the past is both irrevocable and revocable, and how the present is dependent on both the past and the future. My writing, for example, is a process with a temporal direction. There can be no un-writing and no un-thinking. I may rub out what I have written. In terms of directional processes, however, it will remain something that was written and has been rubbed out later: there is no scope for reversibility here. It is in the interaction of organism and environment, argues Mead, in both the mutual forming and the content of that process that we must locate the source of time. Even in something as insignificant as writing a sentence, for example, I act on my environment while it acts on me and it is in the ensuing process of mutual adjustment and reorganisation that all the past gets readjusted from the standpoint of the present. The world, Mead (1959: 47) argues, is irrevocably different because of it.

If, to Mead, the locus of reality is the present, then how does he theorise the status of the past and the future? They are, to him, the field of ideation and their locus is the mind. Like St. Augustine, Mead argues that they refer to that which is not in but beyond the present, something representational. Unlike St. Augustine, however, he emphasises the need for adjustment and selectivity. Through mind we transcend the present and extend our environment. The real past, just like the real future, is unobtainable for us, but through mind it is open to us in the present. The past 'in itself' is not a past at all; only its relation to the present is the ground for its pastness. What was novel in the old present has become part of the world of the new and different past. It is in this process of emergence and mutual adjustment at the levels of physical, living, and conscious reality, that Mead locates sociality. 'The social character of the universe', he writes (1959: 49), 'we find in the situation in which the novel event is in both the old order and the new which its advent heralds. Sociality is the capacity of being several things at once.' The sociality he has in mind has two essential aspects: *passage* and *emergence* (1959: 77). It is only in passage that an organism can be a member of two divergent systems at the same time. Only in passage do the old and the potential enter into a relationship with the new. In his introduction to *The Philosophy of the Present*, Murphy describes Mead's principle of sociality.

> The abruptness of emergent process is reflected in a plurality of relational systems irreducibly distinct yet so mutually implicated in "passage" that an object, belonging to two such "systems" at once will import into each a character with which its presence in the other has endowed it. The process of readjustment in which the object maintains itself in each system, through being also in the other, is sociality. (Mead 1959: xxxii)

Sociality then is located in that process of adjustment and not in its result, in the being part of the old and the new at the same time. Sociality could therefore be described as the dynamic meeting, the interpenetration of continuity and change, of conservation and revolution. Mead extends his analysis of sociality to include all of nature. He theorises it as a quality of the living world, of conscious beings and of human symbolic interaction. Taking this naturalist approach he avoids the traditional social science position that locates sociality in human intersubjectivity only. To Mead (1959: 49) 'mind is only the culmination of that sociality which is found throughout the universe'.

Several implications arise from these thoughts for a social theory approach to time. First, there is an unalterable temporal direction in things, organisms, events, and human knowledge. There can be no un-being or un-becoming. Secondly, what has taken place issues in what is taking place and, in the world of conscious beings, the future potential forms an integral part of that which is happening in the present. Thirdly, time is not to be located in passage but in the becoming event. No numbering or counting of units could possibly account for time since the chief reference is to the emergent event which is always more than the processes that have led up to it. If we think we are measuring empty intervals we suffer a 'psychological illusion' since without emergence there is no time, not even a quantity to be measured. 'We reach what may be called a functional equality of represented intervals within processes involving balance and rhythm,' writes Mead (1959: 22), 'but on this basis to set up time as a quantity having an essential nature that allows of its being divided into equal portions of itself is an unwarranted use of abstraction.' Fourthly, and in concordance with Einstein's theory of relativity, Mead allows for no overarching universal time standard since all that we know must be done from the perspective of the organism that does the knowing, measuring, or dating. Our own Western time frame-work within which we conceptualise our existence and through which we impose order can therefore be only a 'manner of speaking'.

Whilst I am in full agreement with Mead's view that our time of clocks and calendars is not absolute but dependent on the framework of observation, I would argue that as long as we relate to that time as an absolute, objective reality it is real in its consequences. It must therefore be taken account of in any analysis that seeks to understand and explicate this reality. Mead's exclusive focus on the source of the time of experience without a theorisation of the abstract concept forces him to choose between the static and the dynamic, the time of clocks and calendars and Bergson's constituted time of the lived *durée*. By excluding non-temporal time from his analysis he has chosen to theorise one aspect at the expense of another and, by implication, he has contributed to the dualism that has haunted Western thought on time since Greek antiquity and the teachings of Heraclitus and Parmenides. However, once time is socially constructed and regarded as real we need to take account of it in our social analyses and theorise that constructed time in relation to the constitutive, temporal time that Mead identified and conceptualised. Most social theorists have no difficulty with taking account of clock time, as later chapters will show, they are in fact biased towards the other extreme. In contradistinction to Bergson and Mead's emphasis, the clock time parameter is the only kind of time that enters their analyses. Even theorists who have explicitly noted the importance of Mead's (1959) work have neither incorporated his insights nor adjusted their assumptions in the light of his work. In the following chapters I not only want to show the implications of Mead's thought on social theory but also aim to extend his thought to include the quantitative resource and its attendant relations of power in my analysis.

This overview of the philosophical bases to our social science distinctions has shown that classical philosophy is fundamentally dependent on thinking in opposites. Where old dualisms have been exorcised, new ones swiftly moved into their place. With the exception of Heidegger's work, it seems therefore not to be particularly well suited to the transcendence of this tradition of thought. I therefore propose that we explore a different path for our study of time and social theory, a path where we pursue connections where convention dictates separation, a path where we allow ourselves to be guided by our tacit knowledge of the complexity and multiplicity of contemporary time where tradition offers rationalised simplicity and analytical dissection into component parts. Before we embark on this less conventional investigation, however, we need to return to the juncture where the social theory approach seems to part company with philosophy and the tradition of thinking in opposites. We need to look at the idea that all time is social time; that time is fundamentally embedded in the social forms of life which constitute it and which are simultaneously constituted by it.

All time is social time

Most social science treatises on time establish time as a social fact. As ordering principle, social tool for co-ordination, orientation, and regulation, as a symbol for the conceptual organisation of natural and social events, social scientists view time as constituted by social activity. In other words, irrespective of the differences, disagreements, and incompatibilities of their theories, they share the conviction that time is fundamentally a social construction. If it is that simple, however, why has time proved such an enigma for thinkers of all ages? Is it, as Elias suggests, that philosophers have led us astray by asking the wrong questions or are there paradoxes that stubbornly remain, despite the fact that social scientists have established time as social time?

To theorists with a functionalist bias time is always social time because it reflects, regulates, and orders social life. It is a 'social fact'. For Marxists time is essentially social because it cannot be separated from praxis: the union of theory and practice. In doing, time is thought to find its expression. In practice, it is maintained, transformed, or drawn upon irrespective of the particular nature of the action. In neither of these perspectives, however, is the analysis extended beyond human social life. Where theorists incorporated the insights of Husserl's phenomenology, the different time-dimensions of the physical environment and the body are acknowledged as an integral part of the 'life-world' (Bergmann 1981a; Hopkins 1982; Schutz and Luckmann 1973). For phenomenologists time is social time because it can only be constituted intersubjectively. Only humans, however, are accorded the status of 'subject'. Unlike Mead's principle of sociality, which is a fact of all nature, the conventional social science conceptualisation of 'the social' refers to human activity exclusively. In fact, both implicitly and explicitly, it is developed in contradistinction to nature, as that which nature and natural time are not.

Elias (1982a, b, 1984) and Bergmann (1981a) qualify this position by insisting that it is not enough to define time as social without reference to that which time expresses. Whilst both acknowledge time as irreducibly social, they argue that time may express and symbolically represent a range of aspects from human social life to growth and decay in the environment. Bergmann agrees with Gunnell (1968: 20) that time always presupposes a view of time. But he suggests that we need to recognise that its meaning is not separable from questions of its nature. It cannot be understood without an exploration of its source. As Bergmann (1981a: 19) points out, the question about its nature turns into a question about its source. Its source, one could continue his thought, cannot be understood without an exploration of its function, usage, genesis and expressions (Adam 1987: 178–93). From here we can complete the circle back to the necessity of meaning. To declare time as inevitably and fundamentally 'social' is thus not enough. Neither is it sufficient to convert questions of being into issues of meaning only. Yet these are the traditional ways the human sciences have dealt with time. Bergmann argues that sociology ought to take a different approach from the one established by psychology and other human sciences.

> Sociology could also ignore questions about the origin and reality of time by first conceptualising time as a social construction for its object area from the outset and by secondly converting the question of being into a question of meaning. In fact most sociological treatises on the problem of time proceed in such a way that the relationship of processes of transformation, of time and time consciousness does not even get considered as a subject . . . Sociology can neither simply start out with time as an object of sociological knowledge nor leave the basis of the intersubjective constitution of time unquestioned. (Bergmann 1981a: 17; transl. E. King and B. Adam)

This question of the source of time must not be ignored since it is central to an adequate interpretation of time in social theory. In other words, if time is conceptualised as a socially constituted symbol then it is pertinent to inquire what is symbolically represented. Where this question is addressed, time is found to represent a multitude of phenomena. These include physical entropic processes; life processes of growth, decay, and information processing; mechanical, biological, and human social interactions; natural and societal rhythms; novelty and becoming; selves with identities, memories, social histories; and a capacity to communicate and synthesise. They encompass calendars, mechanical and atomic clocks; the motion of particles and light; and speed, velocity, and acceleration. We can see from this small sample that in those instances where theorists have sought the source of time they have once more arrived at a multitude of seemingly incompatible answers, few of which are easily reconcilable with the idea that all time is social time.

This poses a number of questions. First, how are we to conceptualise the symbol and its multiple sources if we insist on staying within our disciplinary tradition? Secondly, do we need to choose any one or a combination of these sources as more appropriate or correct than others? In other words, what are we to make of this multiplicity of sources? Is there a 'right one'? Thirdly, on what basis could we adjudicate between Heidegger's finitude of existence, Bergson's becoming and Mead's sociality? The dilemma remains even with conceptualisations of the ultimate source of time within the discipline. How could we possibly choose between Giddens's repetition, reflection, and memory; Luhmann's differentiation of systems from their environment, seriality, selection, and meaning; and Jaques's movement, change, and continuity of existence? All seem equally relevant with respect to the source of time.

The material presented so far cannot supply us with answers. It neither provides us with the means to make an informed choice nor is it helpful for understanding connections. Yet, when we look at the theories collectively, the multiple sources, dimensions, aspects and levels of time all appear equally important and it becomes obvious that it would make little sense to choose one in preference to the rest. Every one of the conceptualisations seems to constitute an essential part of the whole. *Dasein*, becoming, and sociality, rhythms and choice, meaning and memory, all form irreducible aspects of the reality upon which our consciousness, knowledge, and conceptualistions of time are based. To understand them collectively, however, entails that we also encompass the relation between these aspects. Not surprisingly, no such attempt at a comprehensive conceptualisation has yet been made in social theory since this would necessitate the transgression of social science perspectives and, worse still, a disregard for disciplinary boundaries. Without such deviation from the tradition, however, time can neither be grasped in its full complexity nor appropriately incorporated into social theory. It is quite apparent that very few identified sources of time are social constructions in the conventional social science sense. It is only their symbolic meaning which is always socially constructed. Our small sample of the diversity of symbolic representations shows that time is implicated in the physical universe, in living nature and in the self-reflective, meaning impregnated, human social world. One solution is to argue for 'level-appropriate' meanings. The need to take account of these levels is thus recognised by many. 'The structure of lifeworldly time', write Schutz and Luckmann (1973: 47), 'is built up where the subjective time of the stream of consciousness (of inner duration) intersects with the rhythm of the body as "biological time" in general, and with the seasons as world time in general, or as calendar or "social time". We live in all these dimensions simultaneously.' Bergmann (1981a) and Schöps (1981) accord the levels similar, if more detailed descriptive attention. With the exception of

Mead, however, social theorists do not theorise that which they identify as represented by the symbol; namely, the times of the material and living world. At best the 'social construction' is delineated *against* the time of the physical world or the living body. It is defined in contradistinction to physical and body time (Bergmann 1981a; Jaques 1982; Lauer 1981; Schöps 1980) and neither the times of these other 'levels of beings' nor the relation between them are being sought. The disciplinary division of labour is upheld. Yet, as Elias (1982b: 1000) rightly points out, these 'levels' do not stand in isolation. They do not exist in parallel but in relation to each other; and it is in their relation that they have to be understood. This is not an easy task in our divisive approach to knowledge. It is in fact extremely difficult to think and speak in a manner which does not tacitly imply that physical time, biological time, social, and experience-related time exist in parallel and without connection to each other. What started out as a non-dualistic statement results in new dichotomies: social time and that which it is not. Yet, without understanding the relations and connections, I propose, social theory has no base from which to conceptualise and explain the source of the difference between time and temporality, between time as structured or structuring, as measure of motion or as duration, as rhythm or as process of becoming of the novel, as resource or horizon.Without it there is ultimately no escape from dualism. In agrement with Elias and Luhmann I therefore propose that the task for the future is to relate the various scientific domains with a theoretical relational framework and to use time as the central common denominator. In order to grasp social time in its complexity, we shall therefore transgress our disciplinary boundaries and endeavour to understand together what theories of social time have separated. We shall explore the unity of that which emerged as a new dualism: social and natural time.

Reflections

Destiny and necessity are affirmed. The enigma is brought closer to the surface but in no way dissolved. We have surveyed some contemporary work on time and explored some of the philosophical writings which inform it. This helped us to appreciate the complexity, range, and boundaries of the debate to-date. It established that the problem of time is not the exclusion of time from social theory and that the solution is not merely one of fusing synchronic with diachronic analyses. It demonstrated that meanings have stayed persistently different and that paradoxes remained despite the various categorisations of approaches. No coherent social science approach was discernible. It showed that social theorists had integrated time into existing perspectives and that these in turn coloured their foci, emphases, and assumptions about social time. The prevalent practice of conceptualising the social world into opposites had not been overcome either. On the contrary, the tradition has been affirmed and new dualisms added: the A- and B-series of time; horizons and perimeters; experiential and structural time; reversibility and unidirectionality; rhythm and metronomic beat; social and natural time; 'time in events' and 'events in time'; time as constituting and constituted.

On the basis of existing approaches it seems therefore neither possible to conceptualise the connections between the multiplicity of these aspects of social time, nor feasible to establish relations between the times of the different spheres of being. The favoured dualism–duality conversion merely results in new dichotomies. Furthermore, understanding reality through mutually defining pairs is not suitable for the understanding of multiple realities, 'embeddedness', and simultaneity. As antinomies and pairs they tend to dominate and thus make it difficult to sustain an awareness of the complexity that lies outside their narrow focus. Mead's analysis provides a possible basis for theorising relatedness, interaction webs, and multiple times. Yet it too is not sufficient if we do not simultaneously take account of Elias's fifth dimension, Giddens's knowledgeable agents as users of time, and the power dimension of contemporary Western time. Grouping existing contemporary perspectives on time into their different foci, emphases, and philosophical traditions has neither enabled us to develop a framework with which we could establish the connections and meaningful relations between the diversity of those ideas nor made it possible to explain the differences and incompatibilities. The perspective clusters merely demonstrate the limitations that are highlighted by this focus on time. Looked at collectively, they demonstrate that all aspects are important, that none should be prioritised or excluded. A conceptualisation in terms of levels, it seems, is more useful than that of polarisation or perspective clusters since it necessitates an understanding of relations, interconnections, and mutual implications. As an approach, it provides a superior analytical tool to the philosophical distinctions since a focus on relations aids the transcendence of what Elias calls the old code of nineteenth-century thinking which is steeped in Newtonian physics and Cartesian dualism.

Since the physical universe, living nature, human social groupings, written language and symbolic knowledge, social records, technology, artefacts, clocks and calendars, all form an integral part of our social life today, and since they are all implicated in a full understanding of time, it seems essential that they are explored in their own right. Elias's challenge to utilise the focus on time for relating some of the scientific domains, will therefore be taken up. This necessitates the pursuit of unfamiliar principles, novel connections, and insights which are alien to most social theory perspectives. Only then will it be possible to show a meaningful relation between existing perspectives, between the times of nature and society and between time, timing, temporality, and tempo. Only then may the enigma become less daunting.

2

From the Measure of Motion to Entropy

Throughout the history of natural philosophy and science each major shift in the understanding of the natural world has brought with it a reconceptualisation of the nature of time and space. This applied to the philosophies of the ancient world and the natural sciences since the Enlightenment. Physicists of the twentieth century, for example, had to turn philosophers in order to understand the strange reality which was forced upon them through their discoveries; a reality which they could no longer explain with Newtonian physics. Unlike their colleagues from the social sciences, physicists have not considered their inquiries into the nature of time and space metaphysical and therefore 'unscientific'. Whenever physicists have been confronted with the limits and boundaries of their knowledge, they have produced studies which are quite explicitly concerned with the nature of time, space, light, or matter (Ball 1892; Feather 1959; Larson 1965; Ridley 1976; Prigogine 1980; Denbigh 1981; Landsberg 1982; Powers 1982; Jones 1983; Prigogine and Stengers 1984; Hawking 1988). Most social scientists would argue that these reconceptualisations in physics and the physicists' focus on the nature of time have no bearing on the social sciences. I want to present a case to the contrary: that far from being irrelevant, natural time and the contemporary natural scientists' reappraisal of their base assumptions are of central significance to social science theory and practice. They matter because scientific conceptualisations of reality have deeply influenced not merely our common-sense understanding of the world but also our assumptions as social scientists. They are of interest because the practice of social science is affected by the 'scientific method'. They should be of concern because the subject matter of the social sciences fundamentally implicates physical and biological dimensions. Finally, and as I shall show in later chapters, the social scientists' understanding of natural time is critical because it is intimately tied to the conceptualisation of social time.

Theories of natural time should therefore be recognised as an important focus for social science inquiry.

As we have already seen, there is considerable agreement among social theorists that the natural and social sciences have their own level-specific time concept: that biological time is insufficient for the description of the human social world in the same way as physical time is inappropriate for the analysis of living nature. This generally accepted idea is, however, jettisoned in practice whenever the 'scientific method' is applied in social science studies. With respect to time this means social scientists assume the general distinctions when they delineate social time in contradistinction to natural time but ignore it when they use time as a neutral quantity and an abstract, standardised measure. It is therefore pertinent for us to get to know the multiple expressions of time. The other equally important reason for social scientists to concern themselves with natural time relates to the nature of human being. Humans are simultaneously cultural, living, and physical beings that interact with and relate to their environment and are constituted by it. Humans beings create artefacts and technologies that constitute physical environments for themselves and others. Time is implicated in all these dimensions of our being but is expressed differently in each of them. Since the entire range of natural times is central to our existence it seems appropriate for us to explore and explicate what would normally be considered outside the sphere of social science competence.

As social theorists we may not be capable to do physics or biology, in the same way as we might well not be able to write a symphony. We can, however, appreciate and understand the theories, the music, and their respective inherent principles since, as Infeld (1953: 3) assures his readers, 'the underlying ideas are both simple and essential'. Understanding can proceed at many levels and thankfully contemporary physicists have communicated their ideas and base assumptions in a way that is understandable to lay persons. My reading of these studies consequently revealed three clusters of approaches with a direct relevance for social science theory and practice. The first includes time as both a measure and a quantity to be measured. As such, it is used in mechanics, Newton's laws, Einstein's theories of relativity, and in the empirical studies and synchronic analyses of social scientists. The second is concerned with directional processes and events as expressed in the laws of thermodynamics, the theory of dissipative structures, some historical analyses in social science, and the work of Mead and Luhmann. The third approach is that of quantum theory which conceptualises the ultimate reality as fundamentally temporal and which has so far not had an impact on the social sciences. The Newtonian measure, thermodynamic change, and quantum temporality will therefore be the focus of my attention. Not the theories or their historical development, however, but the nature of time inherent in those theories has to be the goal of the exploration. This means that our involvement with the theories can be kept to an absolute minimum. Screening the theories in this way allows natural time to be raised from a tacit to an explicit level of understanding.

The Newtonian measure

In classical physics motion cannot be described without time. Time and motion are inseparably linked. If something moves, then it changes its position in space in a certain time interval. In Newtonian science time is not studied in its own right but used purely operationally as the measure of things and events. It is understood as a unit, equal to the other fundamental quantities of space (length) and matter (mass). These three constitute the basic trinity of the exact sciences. All other physical quantities can be defined by them. In the case of a car in motion, for example, the three are employed whether one is calculating the speed with which it travels (speed = distance ÷ time), its acceleration, or the force with which it hits an object. They are used to calculate the car's efficiency, the power generated by its combustion engine, or the work done.

The time of Newtonian physics is fundamentally conceived as a quantity: invariant, infinitely divisible into space-like units, measurable in length and expressible as number. It is time taken; the duration between events, which is unaffected by the transformation it describes. Newton conceived this physical measure to be located in an absolute time. He believed all things and events to have a distinct position in space and to occur at unique moments in time. Newton wrote: 'Absolute, true and mathematical time, of itself, and from its own nature, flows equably without relation to anything eternal, and by another name is called duration. . . . All motions may be accelerated or retarded, but the flowing of absolute time is not liable to change' (quoted in Shallis 1983: 17). This means that Newtonian physics deals with measurements and laws which pertain to the motion of things *in* time only, on the one hand, and absolute time within which motion and change are thought to take place on the other. We further need to appreciate the very specific change that is expressed by the laws of motion. Newton's innovative mathematical technique is applied to calculate not change but rates of change. It does not deal with change explicitly as an external quantity, but incorporates time only implicitly in the description of events. Absolute time, which he conceived of as flowing continually without relation to anything, has in fact been removed from the description. Motion has been stabilised. In Newtonian physics, we can summarise, time is defined operationally. It is linked to number and the measure of motion, duration, and rate. As such it depends on the postulation of absolute time within which the laws of motion find their expression. The assumption of absolute time, however, remains untheorised and exluded from the laws.

Let me compress what I see as key features of Newtonian time so that we may become more clearly aware of what is entailed when social scientists conceptualise time as reversible, as measure of motion and spatial units, as duration, and as rates of change. The Newtonian mathematical description of changing events, as we have seen, is dealing with a non-temporal quantity which is generally applicable without the need for a temporal context or reference to the past, present, and future. There is change, but this is external and related to position, rather than changing that which does the moving. Change in position is motion and motion, in theoretical physics, can proceed forwards or backwards. It is understood as invariant with respect to time. It is postulated as reversible, as symmetrical with respect to the past and the future. In Newtonian equations, it can therefore be argued, motion proceeds in non-temporal time.

In order to appreciate what is meant by this idea and what is entailed when social scientists employ the concept of reversible time for social science analyses, we need to probe a bit further. Physicists use this term because it excludes all those aspects which form an integral part of human time: the effect of the past, present, and future; rhythmic repetition with variation; processes of interaction and their irreversibly changed outcomes. It excludes decay and ageing, the unidirectionality of energy exchange, and the asymmetry of interactions, the irreversibility of living processes and the cumulation of knowledge. The Newtonian concept of reversibility is based on the assumption that everything is given and that, irrespective of the number of changes a system undergoes, it will return to its original state. What one change has achieved another can undo and thus restore the initial state. The physicists' equations are fundamentally indifferent to context and any distinction between the past and the future; and location in a unique present is immaterial. 'The structure of these equations', explain Prigogine and Stengers (1984: 61), 'implies that if the velocities of all the points of a system are reversed, the system will go "backward in time". The system would retrace all the states it went through during the previous change.' This means that raindrops flying back up to the clouds they came from, old people getting younger, and a cooked pie being separated back into flour, water, salt, eggs, apples, and sugar have to be considered possible in principle. Not only that, but it also implies that such reversals have to be judged *as likely* as raindrops falling down to the ground, people getting older, and the baking of a pie.

Even today the sought after ideal of Newtonian physics is the absolute and the timeless and we need to appreciate that this is only achievable on the basis of total abstraction. In other words, the process by which this is accomplished is one of extracting single units from interactive wholes and seeking that unit-part in the ultimate simplicity. Only at this level of simplicity is the motion of atoms thought to be time-reversible. We need to recognise that this reversibility is postulated on the basis of idealisations. In other words, if one excludes friction, if one excludes gravity, if one excludes radiation, and if one excludes interaction, then one is left with a universe of perfect symmetry, single parts in motion, and non-temporal, directionless time. Time-reversibility is only possible, therefore, on the basis of absolute abstraction and the fundamental exclusion of all boundary conditions (Prigogine and Stengers 1984: 106).

Today natural scientists recognise that Newtonian physics describes only part of our physical reality, that it does so in a highly abstract manner, and that its validity is limited. Time, I want to suggest, is at the very centre of the changes which have taken place since and which have thus far failed to penetrate social theory. Social science is still imbued with the general classical conceptualisation of the time of Newtonian physics and more specifically the time of the clock. We therefore need to look at the machine time of clocks as an expression of Newtonian understanding of reality before focusing on the conceptualisations of time in contemporary physics.

All machines can be understood as the realisation of Newtonian laws and theories. Interacting with machines we are not merely relating to moving parts but we are, as Pirsig (1979: 92) shows so persuasively, dealing and working with Newtonian concepts. Whenever we interact with a machine we are living Newtonian physics in that very practice. Driving a car would be impossible without a full, if tacit, working knowledge of the physical principles involved. Through the pervasive experience of machine technology in almost every aspect of our reality, Newtonian physics has become an integral part of contemporary existence in industrialised societies. As such a fundamental aspect of our lives, I suggest, it needs to feature in the science that seeks to understand and explain that reality. For our purpose here time will serve as the exemplar for the more general point.

In any system of organisation where parts and subsystems are designed to interact in a repetitive, non-variant way and intended to bring about transformations, time as duration and rate needs to be extended to cover these aspects of organisation. In mechanically organised systems we therefore find time implicated not only as duration and rate of change, speed, or acceleration, but also as sequence, timing, and periodicity (conclusion of a full cycle of motion and transformations). Car drivers and motor cyclists, for example, have to interact with their machines according to the above principles. Every engaging of the clutch involves them in timing, duration, rate, and periodicity as well as the necessity to execute the actions in the right sequence. Even if they do not know the laws of physics drivers interact with their machines on the basis of a tacit knowledge of Newtonian mechanics.

Clocks play a dominant role in our lives and as machines they too constitute an integral and coherent expression of the mechanistic and causally orientated Newtonian science. They can be seen as mechanical models of the universe that represent time as distance travelled in space. Like all other machines they function according to the above-mentioned time principles: duration, rate, tempo, timing, sequence, and periodicity. In addition, clocks not only include time as a measure, they also measure time. It is this dual function of clock time that requires some attention since the two are qualitatively different. The invariant measure is a human abstraction whilst that which is being measured is a physical, natural phenomenon whose very essence is repetition with variation. The difference is analogous to Bergmann's and Elias's distinction between the symbolic expression of time and its source. In other words, the neutral and invariant measure of time by clocks is based on natural events that recur without ever being the same in their recurrence. The planets are not in step with each other which means that their overall configuration never repeats itself with the same constellations. The earth's rotation too is slightly irregular with reference to other timekeepers, and the hours of daylight change minimally with each diurnal cycle. All natural *Zeitgeber* (time givers/sources of time) are characterised by repetition with variation. Clocks and calendars, the devices we use to keep a record of the natural passage of time, have to be calibrated with these natural sources of time and this involves adjustment on the side of the human device. Despite this realisation, however, it is increasing abstraction and standardisation coupled with a decreasing reliance on the sun and stars which characterises the historical development of the clock. Two of the latest identical atomic clocks, beating to their own frequency of atomic resonances, are calculated to get out of step by one second over three million years (Fraser 1987: 72). Yet, we need to appreciate that the measures are based on convention only since we have no way of comparing past or distant intervals with those of here and now. We can only ever measure time with reference to whatever countable units have been chosen as a yardstick.

The clock, as a mechanical device symbolising time, translates a recurring regularity – pendulum, crystal, or caesium oscillation – into a directional flow. This direction, however, is irrelevant for the measurement of the units since these need only to be counted. Newtonian time, we need to remember, is conceptualised as consistent in either direction: forward or backward in time. I want to propose that the direction of clock time is an artefact of the number system; that it is given by the mathematical convention of the number two following the number one and not vice versa. The position of the moving hands on the clock-face indicates a now-point spatially in relation to past and future within a frame of mathematically represented invariable units. The meaning of time, however, is not encapsulated in either the counting of units or the number system. The meaning of time is dependent on its relation to real environmental changes since the clock does not tell us whether it is 12 o'clock noon or midnight, summer or winter, in the northern or southern hemisphere.

The clock incorporates recurring cycles as well as the linear, unidirectional flow of time; duration as well as instants; and lastly, a spatiovisual representation of time. It is a purely spatial measure of the length of time. More generally, spatial time is evoked whenever time is linked to measurement.

> When we speak, for example, of time intervals and durations or of time order and sequence, we have in mind an imaginary long straight axis of time with points on it locating events and distances along it measuring the elapsed time between events. The very words *interval, duration, sequence* evoke spatial images that help us to think about time and its measurement. In other words, for quantitative and related conceptual purposes, we picture time as a kind of one-dimensional continuous space. And one finds this spatial view of time throughout scientific literature. (Jones 1983: 79)

This, of course, includes the social sciences. It applies to the social science focus on the measured quantity, organisational interaction, linear sequence and cyclical pattern, timing and order, as well as the concern to measure rates of change, duration, and periodicity.

To gain a basic understanding of clock time and the paradox of time measurement can be extremely useful to social scientists. The recognition of the purely conventional nature of this 'scientific measure' can serve as a basis for liberating social science research from the compulsion of the scientific method. For this purpose time as measure and as mechanical organisation need to be appreciated not as facts but as ideas; as abstracted human constructs that are given material expression. It is this abstractness and conceptual nature of time in classical physics which we have to bear in mind when time is used as measure of motion. This time is non-temporal. It is bi-directional, reversible, symmetrical, and invariant, and its definition is inextricably tied up with space. Our world of experience, on the other hand, is asymmetrical. It is filled with unidirectional events and repetitive cycles with variation. The study and explanation of that reality has therefore to be based on different principles and a temporal conception of time. Before we move to this more familiar terrain, however, we need to look briefly at the changes in understanding that have arisen from the work of Einstein and the quantum theorists.

Relative time and quantum temporality

Einstein's theories of relativity and the work of the quantum theorists revolutionised the physical concepts of time and space. From a social science point of view, however, these shifts in understanding are less significant than those associated with the theories of thermodynamics and dissipative structures since time in the former is still defined operationally. In other words, the symbol of time t, which is conceptualised as a unit length without a time direction, still plays a central role in relativity and quantum theories. Physics, Denbigh (1981) explains, treats all aspects of time equally.

> It knows of no means of picking out a unique moment, the now or the present. The t-coordinate is an undifferentiated continuum, and, if this coordinate is 'taken for real' as has been the tendency among many scientists and philosophers, the familiar distinction between past, present and future, so important in human affairs, comes to be regarded as a mere peculiarity of consciousness. It is as if every event along the coordinate is, in some sense, 'equally real' even those events which (to us) 'have not yet happened'. On this view of matter it is a function of consciousness that we 'come across' those events, experiencing the formality, as it has been said, of the events 'taking place'. (Denbigh 1981: 4)

However, these contemporary physicists have brought about changes that are of interest to social scientists and it is these I want to bring to attention here. Focusing on Einstein's work first, I have identified three aspects of his work: *Eigenzeit*, curved space-time, and the finite speed of light. Collectively they affect not only our understanding of time but of reality, causality, and the relation of observer and observed.

Einstein demonstrated that simultaneity and instantaneousness can only be defined in relation to a particular frame of reference; that two events which may be simultaneous in one frame may occur at different times in another. 'For Relativity tells us', writes Barnett (1957: 41), 'there is no such thing as a fixed interval of time independent of the system to which it is referred. There is no such thing as simultaneity, there is no such thing as "now", independent of a system of reference'. Einstein, like the physicists before him, utilised time operationally as a measure, but he no longer understood it as absolute. He established time as relative to observers and their frames of reference and he used the concept of *Eigenzeit* (local, proper, or system-specific time) to elaborate that distinction. *Time has become a local, internal feature of the system of observation, dependent on observers and their measurements.* Despite the fact that his work deals with acceleration speeds at or near the speed of light, the principle of his theory affects the status of the B-series of time as objective and absolute. On the basis of the principle of the theories of relativity not only social but natural time needs to be understood as relative and pertaining to the system of observation.

Whilst Einstein's work has no direct practical application for social science, we need to take note of it at the level of theory since most social scientists understand natural time exclusively through the conceptual framework of Newtonian physics as absolute, objective, spatial, and clock-like. I am moving to this unfamiliar area of study to demonstrate the multiple sources and conceptualisation of natural time. This is not the place for detail and depth, but I am sure that even a brief look at the physicists' understanding of natural time will prevent a social science definition of natural time in a pure and simplified contradistinction to social time. Einstein's work leaves no doubt that relative, contextual time is not, as social scientists and philosophers insist, the preserve of a social world where the past, present, and future matter. It is integral to all of nature which includes the human social world. It is therefore up to social scientists to establish in what way the relativity and contextuality of social and natural time confer or differ, and to incorporate their conclusions into the knowledge of their subject matter. Acquaintance with the physicists' comprehension of natural time, as I have argued above, forces us toward a new understanding of social time and the nature of the social.

Einstein's formulation of a fundamentally fused space-time is one of the few post-Newtonian ideas that have been adapted by social scientists for their own purposes. Giddens (1979, 1981, 1984), for example, works extensively with the concept of time-space and geographers use space-time diagrams and draw space-time trajectories to account for the movement of human beings in their daily lives (Carlstein 1982; Carlstein et. al. 1978; Hägerstrand 1975). Unlike the space-time and time-space of social science, however, Einstein's time-space is curved. It is bent under the influence of mass. Einstein thus created an image of a circular, curved space-time where notions of before and after lose their meaning. Despite the fact that the theories of relativity apply only to the cosmic scale of travel at the speed of light, they have inspired calculations and speculations about the extent of this curvature and the possibility of time folding back upon itself; the past intersecting with its own future (Hawking 1988).

In addition to the contextual nature of time and the fusion of time and space Einstein defined the limits of the physically possible. His work, as Shallis (1983: 33–62) and Jones (1983: 102–113) show, was influential in making the close connection between time, light, and causality more explicit. Light is therefore the third aspect of Einstein's work I have selected as important for the changing understanding of physical time. Physicists of an earlier period, who had none of the tools necessary to measure signals at the speed of light, thought that light travelled at infinite speeds. Today the speed of light has been experimentally established as finite and absolute. Its finite speed represents the upper limit to all physical signals and it is the same for everything and everybody regardless of how fast they move. Light, which includes the entire spectrum of electromagnetic radiation from low frequency radio waves to X-rays and gamma-rays, is a prerequisite for the communication and transmission of signals. This knowledge has become an integral aspect of our lives. The phonecall from my mother, for example, is not synchronous with my receiving it because it takes about one-hundredth of a second for her voice to reach me, and we can experience the finite speed of light and sound waves when we watch a satellite interview on television.

Time and the speed of light, argues Jones (1983: 112), are the key to understanding causality because a causal relationship can only hold between events if they are separated temporally so that a light signal, or anything slower, can pass between them. He suggests that it is only because it takes time to cross distance, that causality can be envisaged at all. At the macro level of the physical world every effect is assumed to have a cause and this causality is intimately tied to the sense of order with which we experience our reality. The laws of classical physics provide a rational connection between causes and their effects and the theory of relativity places an upper limit on phenomena that can possibly be causally connected. Anything travelling below the speed of light is feasible. Anything faster is no longer physically possible and thus outside the realm of what physics and allied sciences can meaningfully deal with. The finite speed of light is therefore one of the causes for the sciences' incapacity to deal with non-causal connections, coincidences, and such phenomena as *Zeitgeist*, telepathy, and precognition.

Yet these are the very kind of phenomena that quantum physicists encountered in the world beyond atoms. They found that the causality which forms an integral part of the world of experience ceases to be meaningful at the subatomic level. They experienced a reality of non-local connections and acausal events; an indivisible, dynamic, patterned whole that resisted abstraction and sequencing. Shallis (1983) explains the implications of these findings on the principle of causality. 'In turning to smaller and smaller time intervals,' Shallis (1983: 117) explains, 'a level is reached where causality is no longer distinguishable in nature. This temporal view of the quantum world leads to the insight that causality is itself a temporal phenomenon which only appears at longer time intervals. Causality is a principle that nature displays at the macroscopic levels of time.' Quantum physicists had to abandon the Newtonian conceptualisation of particles in motion, caused by push or pull, and sequentially ordered. At the subatomic level physicists found no ordered sequences and serial changes, the characteristic of causal chains of machine action, but fundamental oneness. Here nature emerged as a complicated web of relations of a unified whole. The connections are no longer serial and local but instantaneous. This, Capra (1982: 75) proposes, makes them fundamentally different even from Einsteinian signals and information transfer.

Before physicists could encompass non-causal, non-local connections and fundamental oneness, however, a whole host of other basic assumptions had to give way to a fundamental shift in understanding. Reality, according to classical physics, is constituted by atoms which exist in time and space. In quantum physics this understanding has radically changed (Capra 1982: 63–85). *The word 'quantum' stands for unit of action which contains energy and time.* This conceptualisation, it will be remembered, forms a pivotal part in the social systems analysis of Luhmann (1978, 1979). These quanta, explains Capra, are not hard, indestructible bodies, but have to be conceived as four-dimensional space-time entities, as dynamic patterns of activities. This description is based on the realisation that matter cannot be separated from its activities and that it exists only in the form of energy patterns. It is important to note that both action and the very notion of pattern are fundamentally temporal; a view echoed by Giddens in his condemnation of functionalist approaches to pattern and order as timeless. The quantum world, however, displays a temporality which is different from that of our experience. 'At the subatomic level,' explains Capra (1982: 83), 'the interrelations and interactions between the parts of the whole are more fundamental than the parts themselves. There is motion but there are, ultimately, no moving objects; there is activity but there are no actors; there are no dancers, there is only the dance.'

Where Newtonian physicists conceptualised the ultimate reality as hard, material, and permanent, quantum physicists find particles to exist for a while and then to disappear again into a background of energy. They see them as temporally emerging; transient rather than permanent, displaying simultaneously the characteristics of both particle and wave.

Zohar (1983: 122–36) explains how their movement, instead of being smooth and continuous, as thought previously, jumps unpredictably from one energy state to another like a 'jerky' film which keeps skipping frames. At that level reality is no longer knowable but merely describable in terms of probability waves. The Newtonian idea of inert matter has ceased to be appropriate for the description and explanation of the behaviour of particle-waves that try out all possibilities simultaneously before settling down. The future dimension, another area which social scientists had regarded as the sole preserve of human time, is identified by quantum physicists as an integral part of physical reality. This extension of matter into the future is conceptualised as a virtual transition.

> If, for example, an electron is struck by a photon, it will have picked up energy from the photon and thus can no longer carry on happily circling round the nucleus in the orbit it had been occupying so stably. It must instead go off in search of some new orbit more suited to its newly excited state. But given that nothing is determined in quantum physics, there are *many* new orbits where it might possibly settle down. While only a proportion of these would offer the electron a stable, permanent home, how is it to know which one unless it tries them all? And this is exactly what it does.
>
> An excited electron, in the guise of a probability wave, puts out 'feelers', during the course of which it simultaneously situates itself, temporarily, in *all* of its possible new homes. And until such time as it registers itself as living at some permanent address, it *really is* living at all of its temporary ones. (Zohar 1983: 128)

Action and wave-particles coming into being are thought to happen without any direct cause or signal. Time and space lose their conventional meaning where action seems to happen instantaneously across distance. Neither time nor space seem to exist as distance between places and moments. Time as distance has become replaced by relationships, fundamental action, and the 'trying out' of all possibilities before actualisation. Action at a distance, defined as physically impossible in relativity theory, has become an accepted, experimentally validated fact in quantum physics.

Capra (1976, 1982) shows further how, in addition to understanding the fundamental reality as active, interconnected wholeness, physicists had to take account of their own consciousness whenever they observed or measured that reality. This consciousness works on the basis of irreversibility, and it distinguishes between that which has happened and what might happen in the future. Physicists today allow for their own macro-world time-consciousness to become intimately connected to the objects of their observation. Whilst these objects are thought to have none of the time characteristics of consciousness, they are accepted as being influenced by them. Social scientists have known for a long time that their research affects that which they are studying; that it changes the nature of the phenomenon under investigation. This is believed to pose an irresolvable dilemma for the scientific status of their research since objectivity is one of the most fundamental requirements. Quantum physicist have established this Newtonian imperative as an impossibility. It is therefore in the interest of social scientists to take note of the changes that have taken place in physics during this century.

Our focus on time has shown that the quantum physicists' view of reality appears almost like a reversal of mechanics and Newtonian physics. Non-temporal time, motion of inert matter, causality, truth, and objectivity have had to give way to temporality, fundamental uncertainty, the relevance of the future dimension, becoming and extinction, the fusion of action, energy and time, and the mutual implication of observer and observed. Parmenides, Pythagoras and Archimedes have to step down as the founding fathers of science and make room for Heraclitus. Whilst the quantum world is far removed from the macro-world of everyday life, some of the quantum theorists' basic insights have had a deep influence on the understanding of consciousness and on global, ecological interconnectedness. The social sciences who could gain so much from those developments in physics have been virtually untouched by the fundamental shifts in understanding that have taken place during this century. The writings of Giddens, Mead, and Luhmann, as I have shown above, form partial exceptions. Giddens acknowledges the importance of Einstein's theories of relativity and the concomitant fusion of time and space into curved space-time, whilst differentiating his own conceptualisation of time-space from that of Einstein and the contemporary physicists. Mead discusses the physical theories of his time in their own right and theorises their implications for social theory. Lastly, Luhmann incorporates the physicists' fundamental shift in understanding into his own social theory. His stress on communication and change, and on action as the fundamental unit, in fact all of his writing, becomes more meaningful when it is contextualised in this way. Once we appreciate that his scientific base assumptions belong to the contemporary paradigm of theoretical physics and thermodynamics, Luhmann becomes understandable. From being seen as an old-fashioned systems theorist, and an incomprehensible one at that, he becomes a social theorist working at the forefront of social science on the difficult task of trying to integrate social theory into an emerging reconceptualisation of science. Our exploration of these developments is, however, not complete until we have looked at change in the physical world through the theories of thermodynamics and dissipative structures.

Thermodynamic change

During the late eighteenth and nineteenth centuries a shift of focus from quantity and timeless laws to change, growth, and evolution occurred almost simultaneously in physics, biology, astronomy, philosophy, and the arts. In the social sciences this change of emphasis is exemplified by Marx's theories and the evolutionism of Spencer, and in the physical sciences by thermodynamics. Physicists learned about the relationship between heat and work and found the two to be interchangeable. They also realised that all forms of energy, from mechanical to thermal, are convertible to each other. These realisations led to an understanding which was fundamentally different from the idealised world of a clockwork universe and mechanically organised systems of transformations without friction where moving objects would continue their motion indefinitely unless they were stopped by an object in their path. It involved both a shift from time-symmetry to a distinction between past and future, and a move from idealisations to descriptions of nature.

> When we compare mechanical devices to thermal engines, for example, to the red-hot boilers of locomotives, we can see at a glance the gap between the classical age and ninteenth century technology. Still, physicists first thought that this gap could be ignored, that thermal engines could be described like mechanical ones, neglecting the crucial fact that fuel used by the steam engine disappears forever. But such complacency soon became impossible. For classical mechanics the symbol of nature was the clock; for the Industrial Age, it became a reservoir of energy that is always threatened with exhaustion. The world is burning like a furnace; energy, although being conserved, also is being dissipated. (Prigogine and Stengers 1984: 111)

The study of processes and change found its most prominent contemporary physical expression in the laws of thermodynamics and the theory of entropy. Both relate to the experience and working knowledge of our daily lives and should therefore form a component of social science knowledge. All dynamic theories conceptualise energy as being conserved. In thermodynamics, unlike Newtonian dynamics, however, energy is conserved but cannot be reversed. This knowledge allows an observer to distinguish processes on a before and after basis.

The first law of thermodynamics deals with the conservation of energy. It states that the total amount of energy in a process is conserved despite complex forms and changes. In other words, energy can never be created or destroyed, it can only be transformed from one form into another. The second law places an important restriction on this idea of endless transformations (Briggs and Peat 1985: 166–87; Capra 1982: 59–65;

Rifkin and Howard 1985). We know from our daily experiences that there is a certain irreversibility about those transformations. Wood which has been burnt, heat which has been applied to cook the food, petrol which has been used up for driving a car cannot be used again for the same work. This knowledge is contained in the meaning of the second law of thermodynamics which states that, while the total energy is constant, *useful* energy is diminishing due to dissipation into heat and is thus rendered unavailable for work.

The second law of thermodynamics thus provides an explanation for the physical world of our experience. Every time we have boiled a kettle, for example, we know that the water gets cold, and the room imperceptibly warmer if we leave it standing for a while. We also appreciate that in order to get the water boiling again, we need to provide an external source of heat energy. The reverse process would seem quite impossible. We know further that an ordered deck of cards loses its ordered sequence when it gets shuffled, and that it is highly improbable that we would ever shuffle a random deck of cards back into its ordered sequence. Reversibility, as proposed by Giddens and Lévi-Strauss, is unachievable for even the most repetitive social actions. Every person who cares for a family and a household knows that clothes get dirty not clean, objects wear out rather than getting newer, and the house has a tendency to get untidy and never spotless. It takes constant effort (i.e. energy input) to maintain a certain level of order, tidiness, and cleanliness. This means that physical systems tend toward disorder and a decrease in information unless they receive input from outside to maintain or increase their order. The second law therefore expresses explicitly what is known tacitly in everyday life: that all systems tend towards disorder; that things, just like people, are impermanent; and that every time something occurs, some amount of energy will be unavailable for future work. Rifkin and Howard make the connection between this unavailable energy and pollution.

> Many people think that pollution is a by-product of production. In fact, pollution is the sum total of all available energy in the world that has been transformed into unavailable energy. Waste, then, is dissipated energy. Since, according to the First Law energy can neither be created nor destroyed but only transformed, and since according to the Second Law it can only be transformed in one way – toward a dissipated state – pollution is just another name for entropy; that is, it represents a measure of the unavailable energy present in a system. (Rifkin and Howard 1985: 45)

Entropy is an alternative expression for the knowledge contained in the laws of thermodynamics. It represents the amount of energy no longer capable of being converted into work. It is conventionally interpreted as both a measure of disorder in a system and the degree of physical evolution. The concept of order refers to structure and pattern. Disorder relates to the lack of structure, distinction, extension, or identity of any kind. Examples for the distinction would be an ordered deck of cards that has been shuffled, a hot and a cold liquid that have been mixed, and two colours that have been thoroughly stirred together. In all these cases order, structure, and distinction are lost to random uniformity. Gardner (1982: 247–57) shows how entropy has a precise definition not only in thermodynamic theory but also in information theory. He explains how the two measures – entropy and information – vary inversely; how the information content goes down when entropy in a system increases and vice versa. He first demonstrates the connection with a deck of cards and he then extends his explanation to the city of London. 'A city such as London', Gardner (1982: 255) argues, 'represents an enormous growth of order and information. London could not have evolved except as the result of vast movements towards disorder in the world outside it. The city's millions of branch systems, living and non-living, operate on entropy disequilibrium produced by chains of systems that ultimately link to the sun.' All social systems involve unidirectional exchanges of energy and information. The nature of that exchange, however, is unlikely to be analogous to that of steam engines and other machines which, after all, depend for their perfect and predetermined functioning on human designers and maintenance engineers. Yet, inadvertently, social theorists employ the theories of machines for the elucidation of social processes. It is therefore important for us to begin to get to know these theories as a basis for more adequate conceptualisations and explanations of social life. Whatever the differences between machine and social exchanges, it is clear that all theories of interactive processes have to utilise time as an integral property of the system. Not the abstract non-temporal time of the measure but the temporal time in processes has to become central to the analysis. It is this temporal time of interactive systems that Mead and Luhmann sought to elaborate and theorise. To appreciate the changes that have taken place in the understanding of processes and time in the physical world during the last two decades, we have to turn to the work of the Nobel laureate Prigogine (1980; Prigogine and Stengers 1984). His theory of dissipative structures provides us with a new conceptualisation of physical time and helps us better to see the distinctions between Newtonian science and what he calls the 'science of becoming'.

Prigogine developed his theory to explain natural phenomena and flow-structures that operate on principles that are fundamentally different from those of machines. The former function far from equilibrium whilst the efficiency of the latter is judged by how close to equilibrium they manage to operate. For machines, in other words, there has to be just enough heat-energy difference to make them work, but the aim is to achieve a differential that is as close as possible to non-dissipation. Far-from-equilibrium processes which cover both living and non-living flowing structures suddenly organise into new orders: stable flow systems emerge from fluctuating energy flows. Prigogine found these systems to be dramatic and unpredictable. One critical fluctuation can 'flip' the whole system into a newly ordered flow. The behaviour of electrons, sand dunes, tapwater and traffic are all examples of dissipative flow-structures. Contrary to machines they generate high levels of entropy and are open to a continuous flow of matter and energy. Whereas a machine's efficiency stands in an inverse relation to its openness and fluctuation, far-from-equilibrium systems increase their stability with the degree of openness. Newton's linear, time-reversible world is a world without surprises; a machine reality which could be taken to bits and then rebuilt again. The world of dissipative structures is unpredictable, non-linear, flowing, irreversible connectedness; a world of broken symmetry and 'time-fullness'. The heat transfer in dissipative structures, unlike that of Newtonian systems of exchange, is not to be conceptualised merely as waste but as a source of order and creativity.

Prigogine's evidence further suggests that irreversibility is an aspect of the physical world; that it is fundamental to all of nature. His work invalidates theories that locate the source of irreversibility exclusively in the human realm of mind and the foreknowledge of death. To Prigogine and Stengers (1984: 298) it is important that the internal feeling of irreversibility is no longer conceived as a subjective sensation that separates us from the outside world. It needs to be understood as human nature, as marking our participation in an evolving world. Time reversibility, equilibrium, and perfect symmetry only apply to idealisations and closed, isolated systems. This finding, however, was totally unexpected; the outcome of an exploration rather than the confirmation of a hypothesis.

> We were seeking general, all-embracing schemes that could be expressed in terms of eternal laws, but we have found time, events, evolving particles. We were also searching for symmetry, and here also we were surprised, since we discovered symmetry-breaking processes on all levels, from elementary particles up to biology and ecology. . . . A new unity is emerging: irreversibility is a source of order at all levels. Irreversibility is the mechanism that brings order out of chaos. (Prigogine and Stengers 1984: 292)

Like the quantum theorists before them, Prigogine and Stengers think that such a shift in understanding shows the important role of the theoretical framework on the perception of reality and, because of it, they too argue for the necessary inclusion of observers in their analyses. No scientific activity is without communication, time orientation, distinction between earlier and later states, past and future extension, historical embeddedness, or presencing. The reality scientists seek to understand must therefore include themselves in the object of their study. Scientists must embrace their own symbol-constructing nature, their theoretical framework and their symbolisms and implicate them in the analysis. Quantum theorists and Prigogine would therefore argue that Elias's fifth dimension is not exclusive to the human sciences. It is essential for understanding and explaining anything, anybody, and any process in the universe.

Prigogine further proposed a new conceptualisation of physical time. In distinction to the Newtonian *t*-coordinate he introduced a time operator *T*. He demonstrated that the broken symmetries of real events can only be described with time *T* rather than the *t*-coordinate of Newtonian and quantum physics. This *T* time is to be understood as analogous to historical time; as the internal age of a system which expresses irreversibility, directionality and an essential difference between past and future. Prigogine's historical time must, however, not be confused with the time used by historians. Whenever they describe social processes 'in time' and locate events within an external, absolute time-frame, they utilise the *t* time of Newtonian mechanics. Only with *T* time, rather than the *t*-coordinate of Newtonian and quantum phsysics, however, can scientists explain the broken symmetries of real events. *Prigogine has established T time as a law of nature and with it he has changed the nature of a scientific law.*

This shift in scientific understanding, as I shall show later, is of deep significance to social science. As long as laws are conceptualised as outside time and space, dissipative processes cannot be thought about in a meaningful way. As soon as scientists focus on far-from-equilibrium processes and think of nature as timeful, the classical conceptualisation must become redundant. Today the laws of nature are no longer separated in principle from the evolving nature they are to explain. Laws themselves may be understood as devoloping and evolving. This means that reversibility, far from being the primary and most fundamental aspect of nature, is agreed to be a product of the consciousness of human observers. Once again we find Luhmann in tune with twentieth-century scientific thinking whilst his colleagues who preserve temporal time for the human social realm exlusively remain locked into the dualisms of classical nineteenth-century thought.

Reflections

Let me summarise the natural times and their social science applications before reflecting more generally on the implications for social theory. In

Newtonian physics time is defined operationally and enters as measure of motion, duration, and rates. It is conceptualised as reversible which entails that past and future are identical and that due to the symmetry of idealised motion one has no means by which to tell the difference between earlier and later states. This reversible time is thought to operate in an absolute, unidirectional, and irreversibly flowing time, and to exist independent of any event, process, or change. This time is evoked when social scientists utilise time as measure and rates of change, when Giddens and Lévi-Strauss employ the concept of reversible time and when historical change and uniqueness are plotted within a parameter of calendar and clock time. All these are 'in time' analyses and conceptualisations of Newtonian time.

In mechanical technology time is extended to include the time aspects of mechanical organisation: timing, duration, sequence, and periodicity. Time here is still in the reversible form, but the number system, function, meaning, and environments of the mechanical devices are no longer so. They are irreversible, directional, and dependent on the possibility of defining a now in relation to a past and future. In other words, anything beyond the design which is based on Newtonian principles entails irreversibility and asymmetry, thus an 'arrow of time'. Lauer (1981) and Moore's (1963) work on social time are prime examples for social theories informed by the machine time of Newtonian mechanics.

Einstein retained the Newtonian operational definition of time but relativised the measure by locating it the framework of observation. The speed of light is established as the basis to communication and causality and is postulated as the boundary for both time and all that is physically possible. Causal analyses therefore operate with a tacit acceptance of a physics perspective that operates within the limit of the speed of light. Einstein's fusion of space and time has affected social theories and inspired a new perspective in geography associated with Hägerstrand and the Lund School.

Neither the Newtonian reversible measure nor the Einsteinian causality have been abandoned but they lack application and meaning at the quantum level. Quantum physicists have come to accept that the connections need to be conceptualised as non-causal and non- local; as simultaneity and instantaneous oneness, stretching into possible futures. With regard to time a fundamental shift in understanding occurred once the ultimate unit was no longer conceptualised in terms of particles but action. When matter is thought to be no longer separable from its actions, time and energy become an integral part of the fundamental reality. As far as I am aware, Luhmann is the only social theorist who has sought to take on board some of the important insights of quantum physics and thermodynamic theory. But, as I shall show in the following chapters, there are many areas in social theory where the insights of the quantum physicists could lead to significant advances.

With the shift from action to interaction asymmetry abounds. Time becomes internal to the event, a system-specific process that leaves a record. In physical theories of change time is therefore irreversible and unidirectional. The direction itself, however, differs in thermodynamics and the theory of dissipative structures. Thermodynamic processes change in the direction of increased entropy and disorder whilst the transformations of dissipative structures change toward negative entropy, increased order, and creativity. Mead is the social theorist most explicitly concerned with the theorisation of temporality and sociality as principles of nature. Like the contemporary physicists Bohm (1983), Capra (1982), and Fraser (1975, 1987), Mead (1959) sought to conceptualise a single, integrated living universe. Working on principles of the boundary phenomena betweeen the inorganic and organic realm, Prigogine (1980: xii) has made the traditional divisions inapplicable and highlighted the importance of a new approach. 'How can we relate these various meanings of time', he asks, 'time as motion, as in dynamics; time related to irreversiblity, as in thermodynamics; time as history as in biology and psychology? It is evident that this is not an easy matter. Yet, we are living in a single universe. To reach a coherent view of the world of which we are part, we must find some way to pass from one description to another.' The passage from one description to another is being sought in this treatise. It is attempted in a way that recognises with Prigogine (1980) and Elias (1982: xxiv) that we are not dealing with clear-cut divisions and isolatable principles that exist parallel to each other, but with aspects that interpenetrate and implicate each other. Furthermore, it is the understanding of the relation between them that I take to be one of my central tasks in this book.

In a way, this chapter could be said to have started at the wrong end since the abstract measurement is a development from organic, qualitative experiences of cycles, periods of change and variation, growth and decay, development and purpose. 'It is the quality of experience', Jones (1983: 86) suggests, 'that precedes the continuum in which we imagine it to exist.' In other words, the objectified measure is a simplified metaphor for that experience. However, it made sense to begin our exploration with the Newtonian measure of motion since the abstract, spatial time of the clock has come to dominate the Western world to such an extent that it is related to as being time and as if there were no other times. Social scientists chart a historical development of the awareness and understanding of time from 'time in events' to 'events in time'; the former being associated with traditional societies and the latter with Western industrial ones. In the physical sciences the developments seem to have been the reverse: *events occur in time* in classical physics whilst *time is in action and events* in thermodynamics and the work of Prigogine. Those two developments are both related and distinct. The point at which the social time-consciousness changed from an event-based time to clock time roughly coincides with the historical development of science and what we today regard as classical physics. Any contemporary social science conceptualisation of time in events thus needs to be differentiated from its earlier form since it includes Newtonian time and as such forms part of the tacit knowledge of the members of Western, industrialised, scientific, technological societies today. By working towards an elucidation of the multiple principles and sources of time, it is hoped that time will lose some of its taken-for-granted status in social theory.

A number of further insights with implications for social theory have emerged from this brief exploration of the changing conceptualisations of natural time in physics. It is noticeable how none of the historically developed understandings gets lost or replaced, but becomes incorporated: the same concepts take on a different meaning in the new theories. Similarly, in the broad area between the inorganic and the living world, meanings differ even though principles and aspects of time are shared. Dissipative structures, for example, are no longer reducible to the understanding of classical thermodynamics but they share the concept of entropy with the latter perspective. With the introduction of the theory of dissipative structures, the meaning of entropy has changed and so have the characteristics of time related to that understanding. We need to take note of this general principle when we explore aspect of biological and social time.

An understanding based on the metaphor of levels emerged as more suitable for the multiple times of the physical world than that of dualities favoured by most social theorists. The usefulness of such a 'level' approach relates to the recognition that it would be inappropriate to choose between single and paired aspects of time. The perception of levels has the further advantage that it takes us away from the tradition of presupposing one primary mode of description and explanation since, as Prigogine and Stengers (1984: 300) point out, 'each level of description is implied by another and implies the other. We need a multiplicity of levels that are all connected, none of which may have a claim of preeminence.'

I proposed that the importance of understanding physical time is not confined to physics or even to an understanding of the global issues of pollution and resources. Physical time forms a deeply sedimented aspect of our everyday working knowledge. Newtonian physics pervades our daily lives through both our technologies and the way physics is taught at school: not as a way of understanding but as *being* the fundamental reality. We live and practice thermodynamics each time we put the kettle on, tidy the house, take shoes to be mended, polish the car, wind the clock, or buy a new battery for it. As dissipative beings we function far-from- equilibrium and with massive energy conversions. Having a meal and taking exercise, for example, we are tied into the energy exchange of the entire universe. Making a telephone call across vast distances or receiving television pictures via a satellite, we partake in a process that demonstrates the upper limit of the speed of light and with it any physical signal and causally connected events. At the quantum level we are flowing oneness where everything affects everything else. As a fundamental part of our everyday life physical time thus needs to become recognised as integral to the domain of social science inquiry. Furthermore, as integral aspects of our socially constituted life they should also feature in the theories about that life.

With respect to the substance of social theory an acquaintance with the natural scientists' understanding of natural time affects the social theorists' conceptualisation of social time. In contradistinction to most social theorists who have been concerned with the study and theory of social time, contemporary physicists recognised that McTaggart's B-series of time does not suffice for the description of the physical world. It is a fundamental insight of contemporary natural scientists that nature entails the past and future dimension; that it has a history. Far from being appropriate for the description of the physical world, the B-series of time has been clearly shown to be an aspect of abstraction and idealisation. As such, it can be understood as a mode of organising experience. Furthermore, we need to appreciate that earlier and later states are impossible to recognise without entropy production, past and future extension, presencing, and T-time; in other words, without a grasp of 'time in' events, interactions, and systems. Time statements about 'objective' temporal relations *necessarily* implicate the past, present, and future of both the observer and the phenomena under investigation.

At this point it needs to be stressed once more that this discussion of the physical aspects of time was highly selective and required extensive simplification in order that the physical principles of time could become clearly visible. The focus was on time. This meant that many of the interesting ideas and insights of theoretical physics, which have important general implications for social theory, had to be excluded. For the same reasons a similarly focused selectiveness will be applied to the following exploration of biological times.

3

Rhythmicity:
Source of Life and Form

When social scientists contrast social with biological time they emphasise the qualitative experience of time, the reckoning of time, and they stress memory, foresight, identity, and symbolic representation as the distinguishing features of human social time. They identify the past, present, and future dimension as fundamental to the human realm and argue that social processes are characterised by context-dependence, relativity, and repetition with variation. The biological dimension of human time is largely associated with the ageing process of the body, with the fact that our lives are lived from birth to death (Giddens 1984; Schöps 1980). At the level of theory, it is suggested that the B-series of time is the appropriate conceptual tool for the description and explanation of natural time. In other words, the evidence presented in the first chapter has shown that the structural time relations of succession are thought to suffice for the causal event chains of nature. This view is refuted by biologists whose work shows this to be a misguided perspective on the temporality of nature.

Biologists provide evidence that requires social scientists to reconsider their understanding of natural time. They show that the past, present, and future, the qualitative experience of time, temporally based uniqueness, and even the aspiration to beauty, are characteristics of all living nature and not the sole preserve of human social life. Their writings and their findings establish that the biological dimension of human time is not exhausted by the ageing of the body, and leave us in no doubt that the B-series of time is an inappropriate conceptual tool for the description of the rhythmic temporality of nature. Portmann (1952: 456–8) conceptualises the rhythmic sequences and timing of living nature as a time *Gestalt*, permeated by qualitative expressive power rather than mere survival value. Portmann, the natural scientist, resorts to language that resembles poetry when he tries to express the nature of living forms. He wants us to appreciate that living beings are, from the depth of their temporal being, practising centres of action rather than perpetrators of fixed behaviour. Portmann expresses wonder and simultaneously acknowledges the limitation of scientific knowledge when he writes about life.

> The richness of life is given to us as an immense and impenetrable whole. It is mysterious in all its forms, its perfection, and the meaningfulness of its adaptation to the different conditions of the environment. It is still more mysterious in those forms in which each comprehensible purpose of life appears transgressed; in those forms which we can only manage to describe in the language of our own pure [non-utilitarian] creation, in the language of art. It is difficult to grasp these living forms in which the long past of millions of years of transformations still forms part of the present today and in which future formations already live in our midst and prepare the next transformations through an incomprehensible treasure-store of formative potential. (quoted in Gebser 1986: 173–4; transl. E. King and B. Adam)

To Portmann, past and future exist in the present and his biological time is non-spatial, qualitative *Innerlichkeit* (internality), the very nature of which is inaccessible to quantitative scientific methods. Science, he argues, can be no more than an aid to expressing with language and number something for which we have not yet developed an adequately expressive mode. To him the search in contemporary biology is, and will have to be, one for a science of life that can encompass non-material, temporal quality.

Quantum theorists suggest that the reality they are seeking appears like a dance without dancers. The biologists' subject matter, I propose, entails both dancers and the dance. At the biological level of explanation all physical aspects of time are relevant but no longer sufficient to explain phenomena of the living world. Understanding organisms, their growth and their evolution, involves not only similar but also irreducibly different aspects of time from those of machines, their entropic processes and our measurements. The continuity as well as the discontinuity with the physical times will therefore have to feature in our understanding. All processes, for example, have 'time in them' but only living beings have a time-sense. The idea of a life-span may be applied to inorganic and organic phenomena. We talk of the expected life-span of a washing machine but the machine's 'life' would not involve growth, healing, and reproduction. All interactive systems age but machines decay according to the principles of the second law of thermodynamics. They are neither able to age biologically, which would involve a decay that is balanced by repair, nor experience a moment of death which would enable them to re-enter the ecological cycle of life. Some of the key concepts of biology

such as rhythmicity, reproduction, regeneration, metabolism, and morphogenesis have no equivalent in the physical sciences. Different principles apply and the machine metaphor is no longer appropriate. To show
continuities, establish distinctions, and to render the inherent time
principles visible is the task of this exploration in order that we may
compare it to the social science view of natural time. Organisms, their
rhythms and biological clocks, their evolutions and their morphogeneses
will therefore be at the centre of our attention. Where appropriate, we
shall establish their distinctness in contrast to machines and the behaviour of dead matter, since the machine metaphor not only dominates the
social but also the life sciences.

Like the enquiry into physical times this investigation has to be highly
selective in order to maintain a relevant focus and avoid losing the thread
in the detail of studies and debates. I must also alert the reader that many
of the theorists chosen for this chapter are not representative of the
dominant perspectives in biology which are deeply embedded in classcial
physics and Newtonian mechanics. To make visible those aspects that
distinguish biological from physical times, and living creatures from the
behaviour of inorganic matter, requires an explorations at the fringe
rather than the centre of the discipline.

Biorhythms: the clocks that time us and know time

Biologists show us a world of orchestrated rhythms of varying speed and
intensity, of temporally constituted uniqueness, a realm of organisms
with the capacity for memory and foresight and of beings that time their
actions and reckon time. Rhythmicity is the key to this time-world of
nature. It is also the concept that links biological analyses to those of
human organisation and culture. To understand the rhythmicity of
nature is therefore important for social scientists at both the substantive
and the theoretical level. The work of chronobiologists, for example, has
a direct bearing on the lives and social organisation of members of
contemporary industrial and industrialising societies as the social science
treatises of Luce (1977), Rifkin (1987), Stüttgen (1988), Wendorff (1980,
1984), and Young (1988) show. It demonstrates the link between
rhythmicity and health, sanity, performance, and accidents at work. It
provides a new perspective on contemporary existence. Rifkin (1987)
suggests that the work of chronobiologists shifts the emphasis away from
philosophical speculation and grounds our understanding of time in the
empirical evidence of their studies. 'With each new discovery in the field
of chronobiology,' writes Rifkin (1987: 30), 'we come closer to redefining
ourselves in temporal as well as material terms. The social implications of

this metamorphosis in thinking are likely to be enormous and far-reaching.' Understanding the nature of rhythmicity therefore fuses the empirical and theoretical domains. This makes its pursuit a rewarding enterprise. In this treatise I shall select from the vast body of research only those aspects that illuminate and further our understanding of natural and social time.

Sunlight as radiant energy is the source of life; and the movement of our earth and its moon in relation to the sun constitutes the basis for nature's rhythmic character. In this dual capacity as the provider of energy and rhythmicity the sun influences the cyclical nature of life. All living beings regulate their cycles of activity and sleep with reference to it. Our physiology as well as our social processes are governed by it. Birds migrate and mate in relation to it, and nearly all of what we understand as plant behaviour is linked to it. For living beings the sun has therefore a multitude of functions. It is a source of energy, a carrier of physiologically relevant information, and the root of rhythmic organisation. Contemporary natural scientists agree with Cloudsley-Thompson's statement that 'rhythmicity is a characteristic of nature' (1961: 1). We need to find out how biologists understand that rhythmicity so that we may check it against the social science conceptualisation of natural rhythms. We have already seen that the idea of invariant repetition is inappropriate for planetary motion. We now need to explore to what extent this idea of 'sameness' applies to living nature. For social scientists natural rhythms mean seeds growing into plants that make more seeds and grow new plants; they imply winters preceding and succeeding summers, and days following nights, following days *ad infinitum*. A far more complex picture, however, emerges from research conducted in the life sciences.

All organisms, from single cells to human beings and even ecosystems, display rhythmic behaviour. Rhythmicity is a universal phenomenon. Scientists conceptualise atoms as probability waves, molecules as vibrating structures, and organisms as symphonies. Living beings, they suggest, are permeated by rhythmic cycles which range from the very fast chemical and neuron oscillations, via the slower ones of heartbeat, respiration, menstruation, and reproduction to the very long range ones of climatic changes. Their activity and rest alternations, their cyclical exchanges and transformations, and their seasonal and diurnal sensitivity form nature's silent pulse. Some of this rhythmicity constitutes the organism's unique identity; some relates to its life cycle; some binds the organism to the rhythms of the universe; and some functions as a physiological clock by which living beings 'tell' cosmic time.

If we focus on the rhythms of our bodies we find that we eat, sleep, breathe, use energy, digest, perceive, think, concentrate, communicate, and interact in a rhythmic way. Not just everything we do, but all of our body's physiological processes are temporally organised and orchestrated. Our activities and our sleep are linked to the light and darkness cycle of the earth and our lives follow the natural cycle of growth and decay. 'Though we can neither see nor feel them,' writes Luce (1977: 16), 'we are nevertheless surrounded by rhythms of gravity, electromagnetic fields, light waves, air pressure, and sound. Each day, as the earth turns on its axis, we experience the alternation of light and darkness. The moon's revolution also pulls our atmosphere into a cycle of change. Night follows day. Seasons change. The tides ebb and flow. And these are echoed both in animals and in man.'

Research on circadian rhythms shows that daylight and darkness act as cues to keep us synchronised with our environment (Aschoff 1965, 1981, 1983; Brown et al. 1970; Cloudsley-Thompson 1961, 1980, 1981; Wever 1979). All the varied cycles of physiological activity – temperature, blood pressure, respiration, pulse, haemoglobin and amino acid levels, hormone production, organ function, and cell division – rise and fall within it and are synchronised into a cohesive temporal whole. The image of a symphony is frequently used to stress the complexity, the interdependence, and the fine-tuning involved. This body symphony, however, is not played in isolation. It is performed in synchrony with all the earth's other symphonies. In other words, our body rhythms are not merely orchestrated into a coherent whole but they are also synchronised with the rhythms of the environment. In this rhythmic co-ordination of cyclic physiological processes, Fraser (1982: 153) discerns the birth of presentness. In the calibration of these multiple rhythms, he argues, a communal present is created. This physiologically constituted present, however, needs to be distinguished from the indication of a now-point on a clock. Like a symphony, the physiological orchestration of a present is irreversible and implies its past and future. Furthermore, the entire range of rhythms exists simultaneously and continuously, beating in finely tuned synchrony. 'We do not consult our internal clocks intermittently,' writes Young (1988: 30), 'as if we were wearing daily, monthly, and annual watches on our wrists which we glance at now and then. We consult them continuously and together. They are part of us.' Neither an either/or, nor a sequential analysis would therefore be a very useful tool for the explanation of this important organising principle of nature. The concept circadian means *circa* one day. It indicates an openness to variation rather than sameness, invariant repetition, and fixed accuracy. Fine-tuning, adaptation, and context–based, projective and retrospective changes are only possible on the basis of such fundamental openness. The circadian cycles are in turn embedded in equally open and variant lunar and seasonal rhythms. Aschoff's work further demonstrates that the existence of such 'circa-rhythms' facilitates the prediction of the future.

Aschoff (1983: 139) writes, 'Whoever is in possession of such a programme can predict what will happen – they can take precautions.' What social scientists associate with human life – the creation of a present, memory, foresight, and anticipatory behaviour – must be accepted as an integral aspect of all living nature. Qualitative variance, the other preserve of human organisation cannot be upheld either. Not just planetary motion but all of plant and animal life, including our own physiology, are witness to that principle. Pregnancies, the woman's time of the month, spring time when plants grow almost visibly after their dormant time during the winter, these times are not merely regularly recurring cycles but are characterised by an intensity and a quality that differentiates them from other times. No two pregnancies nor any of a woman's periods are the same and those hours of extraordinary spring growth are, as Berger (1984: 35) points out, 'incommensurate with the winter hours when the seed lies inert in the earth'. In the rhythms of nature we thus find variant repetition, past and future penetration, and context-dependence: time characteristics that are traditionally preserved for the socially constituted rhythmicity of human social life. With the conventional distinctions dissolving, we are not merely affected in our understanding of natural time but that of social time. What has thus far been considered distinct has to be recognised as an integral part of all nature and what has been designated adequate for the explanation of nature turns out to be a principle that is *only* found in the realm of human culture.

Sociologists make much of the modern dominance of clock time and its effects on our social lives and institutions, neglecting that we also *are* clocks. They ignore that we are timepieces that beat the multiple pulses of our earth and oscillate in synchrony with nature's rhythms. Once we take that knowledge on board, however, we recognise that our modern machine-based rhythms beat to a different frequency from those of the ancient beats within which they are embedded. Our own multiple physiological clocks vary in intensity and rate. Their speed varies with both internal and external conditions, whilst invariance and uniformity are the characteristics of the created clock time that underpins our contemporary social organisation. The body clock, unlike its abstract standardised counterpart, tells 'real time': it knows whether it is 3 o'clock in the morning or the afternoon, summer or winter, in Iceland, Namibia, or Antarctica; and it could tell the difference between the Ice Age and the twentieth century. The difference is one between *being* time and symbolising it. In other words, rhythmicity and body clocks are part of that which the mechanical clock symbolises. But compare the body clock with Jones's (1983: 79) description of clock time: intervals, durations, sequence, order, and periodicity, imagined as a straight axes along which elapsed time is measured and events are plotted. Whilst order and mutually related sequence, duration, and intervals are also principles of body clocks, the nature of these temporal principles is fundamentally different in living systems. Once more the same concepts take on a different meaning. The imagery of clock time is spatial whilst that of body rhythms is fundamentally temporal. I am not suggesting that space is not important, merely that temporal aspects predominate. I am proposing that not only time but also space has to be conceptualised temporally when the subject matter is life.

Once we become aware of our natural rhythmicity, we recognise the the dissonance between the metronomic beat and the multiple rhythms of nature. We realise that biological time, both in its nature and its 'knowing', is quality whilst the social construction is a quantity without contextual knowledge, a resource that can be used as a measure or a medium for exchange. Context independence has made the synthesising symbol fundamentally different from that which it synthesises and symbolises. We therefore need to reverse the social science approach and accept that the quantitative time measure and the B-series of time are not appropriate tools for the explication of the natural world. They are only suited for the realm within which they were created: the human world of objectified abstractions and symbols. Even there, however, those conceptual tools are not universally applicable but have to be used in conjunction with such conceptualisations as the A-series of time, Bergson's *durée* and Heidegger's *Dasein*. Furthermore, clock time needs to be located in a particular cultural tradition, albeit one that is dominating and rapidly spreading. Even in societies that organise their social lives to the clock, its hold is not universal. The metronomic beat is superimposed on a massive base of variable, qualitative rhythms that precede the cultural 'newcomer' by millenia. This superimposition, however, takes place not merely at the substantive level but also in the theories we have to explain that reality. In other words, the machine metaphor is used for the understanding and explication of natural rhythmic organisation. Sociologists like Spencer and Parsons who have used the organism analogy for their explanation of society, have in fact utilised a conceptualisation that is based on an understanding of machine organisation. A brief explanation of the difference thus merits our attention.

Organisms and the machine metaphor

The view that our technological and chemical inventions are copied from nature is held by many. 'We have reproduced,' suggests Vester (1979: 62), 'more and more intrinsic features of our biological nature: mechanisms and technical principles like levers, filters, pumps and motors, energy transfer and chemical factories, all of them being structures and technologies long present in a perfect form in nature.' Once recreated to human design, however, we tend to use the copies for understanding the original: we end up understanding bones, muscles, and the heart, for example, through the postulates of mechanical organisation. Problems arise when the principles of mechanics and life no longer coincide; when the mechanical replicas – the source for understanding the 'original' – exclude cybernetic and metabolic principles and the symbiotic relationship of beings with their environments.

All complex systems – mechanical, biological, social, ecological, and even planetary – have interconnected parts; and their identity as wholes is constituted on the basis of their relationship with the environment and the internal relationships between their parts. Similarly, all system processes involve sequencing, timing, duration, and rate, the time aspects of machines we have encountered in the previous chapter. This means that precise timing and sequencing are not only vital to the smooth functioning of machines but also to the existence and development of living organisms. All organic processes are accurately timed, explains Denbigh (1981: 141), 'so that the various organs and tissues are created at mutually related rates, resulting for instance in the limbs growing at a suitable speed in relation to the rest of the body.' The breakdown of any one of them would result in illness or death just as a machine would cease to function if the timing or sequencing of any one cycle were to be changed or stopped. At first sight, therefore, the time principles of machines and organisms seem to coincide. Closer investigation, however, reveals subtle and irreducible differences.

Focusing on machines first we find that they are created to a design of Newtonian mechanics which is based on idealised invariance, motion without change, and spatialised, measurable time. They are constituted by unit parts and subsystems that interact in terms of non-temporal sequence, timing, and periodicity. The activities of machines are determined by their design and their functions can be explained in terms of causal event chains within the system. They use up energy according to the laws of thermodynamics which means that the total energy is not lost but exists no longer in usable form. Their efficiency is defined in relation to entropy: minimum entropy means maximum efficiency. In other words, there has to be enough energy difference to make the machine work but the aim is to achieve a differential that is as close as possible to non-dissipation. Machines can be taken apart, fitted with new parts, and reassembled. Organisms are different on most of these counts and where principles are shared, their meaning has to change once they are applied to living beings.

If we want to get to an understanding of organisms without the mediation of the machine metaphor we have to turn to the work of biologists such as Bateson (1979, 1980), Portmann (1952), Sheldrake (1983), Vester (1979), and Weiss (1939, 1973), who have recognised that the assumptions of mechanical biology are inadequate for the elucidation of the living world. From this body of thought organisms emerge as growing, self-replicating, temporally, and metabolically organised inter-action networks that stand in an existential relation to their multiple environments.

In contradistinction to machines, organisms have the capacity to repair damage from within. They do not need an engineer or maintenance crew to keep them in working order. They can heal a wound, grow a new part, even renew themselves by cell division or sexual reproduction. Biological 'parts' are therefore more appropriately conceptualised as incessant self-renewal processes. Like machines, organisms retain their identity in spite of replacement and renewal of all their 'parts'. Nothing within our body, for example, is preserved. Yet, we are recognisably the same person despite the fact that every cell in our body and nearly all the protein in our brain is replaced in less than a month. Even after years of absence, people can recognize each other. Characteristics of shape, movement, and expression have remained sufficiently constant for this recognition to be possible. In contrast to machines, however, the replacement of the 'parts' is achieved by the organism in an incessant process of balancing decay with renewal. The resultant stability is fundamentally dynamic. Organic processes can neither be explained in terms of linear causal chains nor defined within a system only. In contrast to machines, the functioning of organisms is guided by cyclical patterns of information flow: the information is 'fed back' in the form of feedback loops. To understand living systems requires therefore a wider angle of vision. As Capra (1982: 289) explains, 'component A may affect component B; B may affect C; and C may "feed back" the influence to A and thus close the loop. When such a system breaks down, the breakdown is usually caused by multiple factors that may amplify each other through interde-pendent feedback loops. Which of these factors was the initial cause of the breakdown is often irrelevant.' This emphasis on multiple cycles and feedback loops does not imply that single cause and effect links have become redundant. It simply means that for an understanding of systems the time-span has to be expanded from single steps to a whole network; and that there has to be an appreciation that outcomes cannot be traced back to single causes. Furthermore, it is the interplay of processes – the multiple interconnections within the organism and between the organism and the environment – that hold the key to understanding. 'The living cell presents an incessant metabolic activity,' explain Prigogine and Stengers

(1984: 131). 'There thousands of chemical reactions take place simultaneously to transform the matter the cell feeds on, to synthesise the fundamental biomolecules, and to eliminate waste products. As regards both the different reaction rates and the reaction sites within the cell, this chemical activity is highly coordinated. The biological structure thus combines order and activity.' To understand biological 'wholes' and their 'structure' is therefore synonymous with the idea of being temporally organised in such a way that all aspects are existentially dependent upon one another. Dissection into parts, be it physical or theoretical, destroys the organism and so does its abstraction from the environment, since the boundaries of living forms extend beyond the organism to its environments. Each system is interdependently nested in a multitude of environments while simultaneously being environments for a multitude of others. We need to be careful here with generalisations and bear in mind that Western medicine has built its successes on the foundation of a Newtonian machine understanding of the human body. For all those not trained in Western medicine, however, the dissection of a rat will result not in a 'rat in bits' but in an irretrievably dead rat. Anatomical dissection is a process by which we enquire into the nature of dead parts of something that was once alive. Dissection of any kind eliminates the principles of life because living beings are fundamentally tied to an energy exchange that transcends the laws of thermodynamics. Organisms exchange their energy according to the ecological principle: all dissipated energy is reabsorbed into the whole where it constitutes a source of life for other living creatures. Life is constituted in this interdependent, living network where any one exchange affects the whole in an irreversible, yet never-ending and never-beginning way.

Biologists have established links between metabolic rate, life-span and time. They attribute a time-sense to all metabolically organised systems (Fischer 1981; Hoagland 1981; Luce 1977: 23–9). In cold-blooded and hibernating animals, for example, the sense of time as duration and passage varies with the seasons. With the drastic slowing down of the metabolic rate, a hibernating animal could be postulated to experience the period of hibernation as just 'one night's sleep'. With respect to humans we know that the metabolic rate of young children is higher than that of old people and that the experience of the speed with which time passes is consistently different between the young and the old. The last birthday seems like a very long time in the past to a five-year-old child but feels like yesterday to an eighty-year-old person. Years fly past for old persons but for children they can seem like an eternity. I do not want to suggest that the metabolic rate is the only factor influencing the sense of the passage of time, only that the experience of time differs with metabolic rate and, more importantly, that a sense of time seems to be integral to all expressions of life.

The change of focus from mechanical organisation to living organisms involves therefore the use of some new concepts, and it changes the meaning of existing ones that biology shares with the machine technology of classical physics. Systemic processes, interrelated and mutually dependent transactions, symbiotic relations, self-organisation, self-renewal, and a sense of time emerge as irreducible time characteristics of organisms, whilst the time concepts of mechanical organisation reapppear. Timing, sequence, duration, periodicity, and rate are temporal aspects of all organisation, but they take on a different meaning in the context of rhythmically organised living beings. Furthermore, we need to bear in mind that the machine metaphor, so readily used for the explanation of living processes, is a simplified abstraction from organisation in nature and therefore a problematic conceptual tool for anything other than machines and the behaviour of dead matter. When the living characteristics are allowed to come to the fore, the conceptualisation of 'parts' and 'wholes' loses its meaning. Organisms emerge not as entities but as processes; and 'wholes' appear as fundamentally embedded in an infinity of connections where everything affects everything else. Similarly, the structure–change dichotomy is one of many dualisms that ceases to make sense at the level of life where structures are not static but forming.

The implications for social theory are manyfold. They relate to our use of biological analogies, to the conceptualisation of social science 'parts' and 'wholes', namely individuals and society, to our understanding of causes and consequences, and they have a bearing on our practice of imposing a standardised time-frame on the phenomena under investigation. As we have seen from this brief exploration, the difference between understanding natural organisation through the machine metaphor and through the principles of life is a deep and far-reaching one. I see the implications for social theory not so much with respect to a need to use the living organism analogy but in relation to the ecological principles of life. Organism analogies will be problematic whatever kind we chose. But to recognise the difference between the principles of machines and life respectively gives us choice for understanding human organisation: whether we liken it to dead matter and the human creation of the machine, or whether we think of it as a living, self-replicating entity; whether we view its stability through the principles of thermodynamics or through the extreme fluctuations that characterise process-stability. If we favour an understanding through the principles of life, then we are still left with the difficult task of establishing the distinctiveness of the social process. Appreciating that organisms cannot be defined as entities has implications for our conceptualisation of individuals and society. It opens up new prospects for a debate that has run aground (Lukes 1978; Mandelbaum 1978; Popper 1979). We shall pursue such a different understanding of individuals in chapters six and seven.

The analysis of living processes through the principles of feedback loops has its equivalent in social theory approaches where it is recognised that we are not dealing with stimulus–response situations and that we cannot stipulate backwards from consequences to causes, and less still to intentions (Giddens 1976; Popper 1979). The biological theories, however, go further than that and recognise that single steps can never give us access to the 'whole' no matter how wide a time-span of observation we choose. Lastly, the biological evidence corroborates Einstein's theories of relativity. It demonstrates that time is local, that it is organism, species, and context specific. It leaves little doubt that the overarching time-framework is our creation and has little to do with the objects of our observation. Berger puts the point beautifully.

'The life span of the hare on the one hand and the tortoise on the other are prescribed in their cells. The likely duration of a life is a dimension of its organic structure. There is no way of comparing the time of the hare with that of the tortoise except by using an abstraction which has nothing to do with either. Man has introduced this abstraction and organised a race to discover which of the two would reach the finishing post first.' (Berger 1984: 9)

An acceptance of the findings of physics and biology would allow us to move away from the present situation where we feel compelled, in the name of science, to standardise and impose a unified time framework. It would enable us to stop imposing the clock-time measure irrespective of context and suitability.

Living change

An understanding of change in living nature has to encompass becoming, rhythmicity, and form, and it has to broaden the time-scale of analysis. This poses a difficulty for the conventional tools we employ for the conceptualisation of change. The mere plotting of events on a before and after basis cannot accomplish this task; neither can the Newtonian theory of reversible motion nor the abstract measure expressed by the clock. The similar rather than the same recurs with rhythms and, since only the recurrence of something similar in relation to what has passed signifies its renewal, we can state with Klages (1934: 32) that '*Takt* (metronomic beat) repeats and rhythm renews'. Such renewal is not change *in* time but it constitutes time. To encompass such change requires non-Newtonian theories of change such as those of Bergson, Mead, and Whitehead. It necessitates theories of forming and structuration rather than form and structure; and it requires an extension of vision from causal event chains to cycles within cycles within cycles.

Cycles of change that are of relevance at the biological level extend over far greater time-spans than those conventionally used by the social sciences. The time-scales of human biology, for example, range from the atomic and microscopic to the evolutionary and even cosmic. Biologists traditionally identify three time scales which are of importance to human beings: metabolic, epigenetic, and evolutionary rates of change. However, only the middle range which covers changes of growth, development, and ageing, and which includes life-spans ranging from seconds to decades is accessible to our conscious experience. Vester (1979) argues that, in order to survive, humans have to extend their thought levels, their concerns, and their planning: the time-scale has to be expanded so that we may see linear cause-and-effect processes connect with others and then form feedback loops which elicit responses, until we recognise whole webs of interconnections. By extending our vision to follow the curved path of a multitude of intersecting and interconnecting arrows, we can appreciate cause and effect relations as integral parts of biological systems which link events to multiple system processes. In other words, cause-and-effect may then be conceptualised as component aspects of biological processes which encompass direction, forming and form, uniqueness, and novelty.

Change in nature involves the exchange of energy and information. Convertible but not reusable, energy is exchanged in all action. In thermodynamic systems the resultant change is towards an increase in entropy, in dissipative structures towards an increase in order. Living organisms dissipate energy too, but in the living world this energy is being transformed, recycled, and used for self-repair and self-renewal. As dissipative structures, organisms are always existentially linked to their environments and energy is transformed, shared, and exchanged, which results in an increase of order. Like inorganic systems, organisms cannot reuse their dissipated energy, But, unlike their machine counterparts, they can use the dissipated energy of others in the ecological chain. The waste of one becomes a source of energy for another who is able to take it in and transform it. This process continues until the cycle is closed and the numerously transformed energy reaches the original organism in the recycled form. The ecological principle is like a never-ending, never-beginning story where, concomitant with everything affecting everything else, there is evolution.

Both evolution and entropy are concepts pertaining to irreversible processes. Species may become extinct but their evolution cannot be reversed. Entropy is expressive of spontaneous process towards disorder and a decrease in information. The process of evolution, in contrast, is characterised by an increase in both information and order. Both entail change, which in turn implies something that is sufficiently unchanging to ensure an identity that can be said to be changing. Evolution is not conceivable without past and future extension and the change for both entropic and evolutionary processes is considered to be unidirectional. Only evolutionary processes, however, are accorded creativeness and inventiveness (Denbigh 1981). Thus, both processes share the temporal principles of irreversibility, unidirectionality, change, and a past and future extension but their content differs and this fundamentally changes the meaning of the temporal principles according to their application. The situation is, however, further complicated by the biologists' absorption of the Newtonian framework of meaning. As Ingold's (1986) work demonstrates, this separates theorists into temporal and static evolutionists.

Biological processes of change fundamentally entail cyclicalities, such as the life-cycle, metabolic cyles, and metamorphic processes, to name just a few. Metamorphosis, the change of form, is of interest here since it involves a multiplicity of temporal principles. For example, the development of a butterfly involves a series of stages and transformations – egg, larvae, pupae, butterfly – where each expressive form is fundamentally different from all the others. Metamorphosis entails single steps while simultaneously being a cycle which is in turn integrated with the cycles of the environment. Each stage of the cycle is accurately timed, both internally and to the relevant times of the environment. Within each full cycle and its stages there are sub-cycles of activity and rest. Specific forms precede and follow each other in an invariant sequence and each single form implicates all the others: it entails all the past forms and those that are to follow.

The biologist Sheldrake (1983) offers some fascinating insights and ideas with respect to form and its relation to time. Whilst I am in no position to judge the much debated validity of his theory, I am interested in his thoughts for their theoretical implications. Morphogenesis, the coming into being of form, cannot be grasped through causal theories, he points out, because form, unlike energy, is not conserved. It can be destroyed and has therefore to be created, recreated, and maintained. Neither effective nor formative, teleological causation can explain the creation of something new as long as form is understood as merely pre-given with no questions being asked about where form might come from or how it might be created. These are the issues to which Sheldrake addresses himself. In a published lecture he describes the problem.

What is it that gives organisms their form? When we walk in the countryside
we see dozens of different kinds of plant. All of them are living in the same
earth, getting the same sunlight, with the same carbon dioxide in the air and
using the same water from the soil. Yet their forms are different, and each
species has its own kind of form and organisation . . . Just think of our own
bodies. Consider the arms and legs. The chemicals inside them are identical;
the muscles, the bones, the proteins are chemically the same in both, and so
is the DNA – indeed the genetic material is identical in all the cells in our
bodies. Yet in spite of their chemical identity the arms and legs have a
different shape. Their shape is not explained by the chemicals they contain.
(Sheldrake 1986: 203)

Sheldrake's concept of form includes shape, gesture, expression, and
movement. His conceptualisation of the process of morphogenesis covers
three central interdependent aspects: regeneration, reproduction, and
regulation towards a morphological goal. Not one, he argues, is grasp-
able with the tools of classical science. His theory of life and the relation
between form, single units, and wholes deeply affects the understanding
of the temporal processes at the sphere of life and, as we shall see, it bears
a strong resemblance to Giddens's theory of structuration.

Sheldrake postulates morphogenetic fields which he understands to be
similar to the conjectured magnetic fields in physics. The idea of
morphogenetic fields is not a new one. It has been suggested by biologists
since the turn of this century (Gurwitsch 1922; Weiss 1939, 1973;
Waddington 1957, and many more). Sheldrake, however, proposes a
process of formation that differs from those earlier teleological conceptualisations (Sheldrake 1983: 33–52). He suggests that *morphogenetic
fields both originate and become strengthened from real phenomena and
their repetition*. This involves an influence of repetition and like upon
like. Once something has been designed or accomplished, he postulates, it
should become easier on subsequent occasions. This should be the case
regardless of where in the world the subsequent occurrences take place
since he conceives of those fields as 'outside the laws of time and space'.
Whilst he is not spelling this out explicitly, the laws he is referring to
appear to be those of Newtonian physics. Each repeated action should
get easier, he proposes, until a critical number of repetitions has been
reached and the field stabilises. Sheldrake's theory can therefore explain
what Portmann (1952) considered inexplicable: how ancient forms,
which developed millions of years ago, are still present and how they are
related to potential future forms.

Like Giddens's theory of structuration, Sheldrake's theory of morphogenesis stresses the important role of repetition. Its influence, however, is not conceptualised on the basis of cause-and-effect links between

individuals but 'through the whole'. This means that Sheldrake sees each present moment of action, interaction, or communication as being related to the previous one through the morphogenetic field. This differentiates his understanding from that of his predecessors, contemporaries, and colleagues in the other sciences. They see the relation between past and present action in terms of actions in the present drawing on a store of genetic and culturally learned knowledge. To Sheldrake each present is a reflection of all the past while simultaneously affecting all the future. In contradistinction to Plato's eternal forms, Sheldrake's forms are both forming and formed in a present. Platonic forms are pre-given and are thus consistent with the Newtonian, causally determined framework of understanding where nothing new enters the cycles of endless transformations; Sheldrake's forms, in contrast, are constituted in the present and based on non-Newtonian assumptions. He describes morphogenetic fields as resonating cosmic memory, incessantly and creatively formed in the present. Because everything – signals, actions, thoughts, designs, inventions – passes through and gets constituted and strengthened through the morphogenetic field, it is not only actions but also thoughts that make an irreversible difference.

Sheldrake's focus on repetition and his idea of something being formed by that which it is forming and vice versa bears thus a strong resemblance to Giddens's theory of structuration and the concomitant conceptualisation of the duality of structure as both medium and outcome of action. Both theorists seem to be chasing the same relational idea. Yet, as Archer (1982: 457) points out in a critique of Giddens's theory, something seems to be missing in the theory of structuration when 'structuration is ever a process and never a product.' By implication it excludes form. Archer suggests that Giddens evokes two images: that of recurring, routine action, and that of fundamental change. She identifies the latter with metamorphosis. 'There is also metamorphosis,' writes Archer (1982: 459), 'the generation of radically new practices when agency rides on the coat-tails of structural facilitation to produce social change of real magnitude. Although the "duality of structure" spans both images, it provides no analytical grip on *which* is likely to prevail under what conditions or circumstances.' Archer favours the 'morphogenetic approach' of general systems theory and she associates this with metamorphic changes. My reading of biological theory and Giddens's theory of structuration, however, suggests different conclusions. Metamorphosis, as I have explained above, produces a series of radically different forms *without* generating something radically new. Its determinism matches that of effective causality. Each form, it will be remembered, is enfolded and internally present in all the others. In metamorphosis nothing new is being created within its cycle of changing forms. Archer's image of

metamorphosis is thus unwittingly appropriate for my reading of the
theory of structuration, since I have argued that Giddens provides no
basis from which to explain true creativity and emergence of new social
practices and institutions. Metamorphosis, I propose, is a very fitting
image for a theory that stresses transformation by focusing on the
chronic recursiveness of habit and repetititon. Structuration as a creative
coming into being of form, rather than formed by pre-given causes, on
the other hand, requires a non-Newtonian conceptualisation of time,
space, matter, and cause. It belongs to a different scientific framework of
understanding.

Archer's proposed alternative provides no solution to Giddens's
theoretical problem since it contains the very shortcoming that Giddens
identifies and seeks to overcome with his theory of structuration, namely
the dualism of repetition and transformation. Archer (1982: 461)
criticises Giddens for '*not answering "when" questions* – when actors be
transformative (which involves specifications of degrees of freedom) and
when are they trapped into replication (which involves specification of
the stringency of constraints).' However, the systems theory she advo-
cates as an alternative is firmly and explicitly based in Newtonian causal
science and Cartesian dualism. It is an affirmation of dualistic thinking
resolved by dialectics, the very conceptual framework that Giddens's
theory is directed against. What Archer shows as a virtue is identified by
Giddens as a problem: transformation and repetition are not separable,
they implicate each other. They must therefore be theorised accordingly.
What Giddens fails to achieve, however, is to make the relationship
between repetition and transformation convincingly explicit. Like Sheldrake, Giddens conceptualises structure 'outside time and space', as
having a virtual existence through rules and resources as both medium
and outcome of social action. What Giddens does not make explicit is
how (rather than when) society is transformed in repetition. I therefore
agree with Archer that neither form nor radically new practices are
theorised by Giddens, but disagree with her alternatives since they retain
the very features Giddens seeks to transcend.

While Giddens's and Sheldrake's approaches look alike, they diverge
with respect to these base assumptions and thus belong to different
traditions of thought. Mead's (1959) theory of sociality and Sheldrake's
theory of morphogenetic fields, on the other hand, do not appear similar
but are in fact consistent with respect to their assumptions about time
and natural processes. In both theories reality is created in the present. In
both pasts are thought to be recreated and possible futures changed. To
Sheldrake *form is not caused by either preceding or future forms and
conditions. It is being formed in the present by thoughts and actions.*
'Like forms' are both medium and outcome of that process. Where their

theories differ is that Mead understands forming as being achieved by a multiplicity of interactions, whilst Sheldrake sees each action and thought as contributing to the whole and vice versa. To Sheldrake every thought, action, interaction, and transaction resonates in the field and thus not only changes the pasts and futures for individuals but for all. Every action affects everything else. The universe is a different place because of it. With Sheldrake's theory this idea no longer remains just a statement but is given substance. By proposing mechanisms and suggesting ways of testing his theories, he brings this important ecological principle within the fold of contemporary science. We are witnessing the emergence of a framework of meaning that leaves room for making connections and seeing relationships where classical science erected disciplinary boundaries and emphasised discontinuities. 'Causal time', a pillar of classical theories of change, seems to lose its explanatory power once scientists begin to step out of the dominant scientific framework for understanding reality.

Reflections

If in physics the shift of understanding was from particles to action, in biology it is from structure to rhythm. What is considered to be separate in the inorganic realm is united in living phenomena. The non-causal time of dynamic, fundamental oneness of the quantum sphere combines with the causal, sequential order of the world of experience. All forms of physical time are relevant but not exhaustive for the living world. Time is internal to living processes not just as temporality but as bioclocks beating time. In addition to beating their own time living beings have a time sense and respond to cosmic time. They are rhythmically organised which endows them with memory, foresight, and a capacity for synthesis. With respect to its form, the most appropriate image of biological time might be of many intersecting spirals where linear, irreversible processes fold back upon themselves in multiple feedback cycles. This cyclicality must not, however, be conceptualised as reversible recurrence but as change. Whilst the degree of change is context dependent, it is in the very nature of those rhythmic processes to differ in their recurrence. In all of nature there is emergence and disappearance but this is expressed differently at the various levels of existence. Particles come into being and disappear again; humans and animals are born and die. Growing, ageing, healing, regeneration, and reproduction are all aspects of the dynamics of organisms with form.

We know of the typical life-span of living organisms and this includes ourselves. We know the typical age of a cat, a fly, an oak tree, and fellow humans, for example. What is not generally known, but forms part of the biologists' specialist knowledge, is that in living beings this typical length of life within species is related to their metabolic rate; the faster their metabolic living, the shorter their lives (Phipps 1980). Both physicists and biologists work with the concept of rate but for metabolic rates the mathematical expression is not enough: they fundamentally imply the organism's time sense. With respect to time this has turned out to be a generally applicable principle. In other words, the same time aspects of organisation and process apply almost universally but take on different meanings at the various realms of nature.

With reference to the time-scale of processes it is important to take account of the entire range and to recognise its relativity. Typical time-scales of an infinite range are an aspect of nature and not, as social theorists suggest, of the social scientists' analysis only. It is due to their existence that social scientists ought to seriously and urgently consider to expand the time-scale of relevance for their discipline. Our subject matter is about beings whose understanding is affected by phenomena with process speeds that range from close to the speed of light to that of light years, beings who have also created technologies with time-spans ranging from nanoseconds to millenia. Can we afford to exclude those time-scales from our analyses? Such an expansion of the time-scale of our analyses is possible without recourse to the language of adaptation and determinism. Contrary to Giddens's (1981: 20–4, 1984: 228–43) warning, an evolutionary perspective is not fundamentally tied to determinism since the principle of causality is not necessarily an inherent characteristic of nature but of Newtonian science. 'The relativity of our reference point,' explains Fischer (1981: 372), 'can be demonstrated by taking a moving picture of a plant at one frame a minute and then speeding it up to thirty frames a second. The plant will appear to behave like an animal, clearly perceiving stimuli and reacting to them. Why, then, do we call it unconscious? To organisms which react 1800 times as quickly as we react, we might appear to be unconscious. They would in fact be justified in calling us unconscious, since we would not normally be conscious of their behaviour.'

Rhythmicity too is fundamental to nature and not an arbitrary retrospective grouping into episodes with beginnings and ends, which depended on the human capacity of reflection. For some periods and episodes such human structuring may well apply, but this very activity of the mind has a natural source in the rhythmicity of all phenomena that are regarded as living. Mind does not retrospectively impose the cycles of light and dark, the seasons, the tides, menstruation, the digestive system, or attentiveness. These rhythmic cycles constitute living nature which includes humans and their capacity to experience rhythms and to order impressions, actions, and thoughts in a rhythmical fashion. Rhythmicity, which entails cycles, structure, and processes with variation, would therefore be a more useful key concept for social theory than reversible time.

We live Newtonian and thermodynamic theory but we are biological clocks and organic beings. We breathe, eat, digest, and use energy in a rhythmic way. Our activities and our sleep are linked to the light – dark cycle of the earth and our lives follow the natural cycle of growth and decay. This, I want to suggest, has an effect that cannot be limited to our physiology but permeates our social lives. I therefore propose that the biological aspects of time are of interest to social science not as a backcloth against which to define social time but as an integral part of it. Biological time, however, is neither just about the ageing of the body, as Giddens and Schöps seem to argue, nor merely central to the genesis and evolution of life and organisms. It is our human nature. What we conventionally conceptualise as anatomical structure is, in the light of the latest biological knowledge, of temporal nature. We can therefore agree with Bergmann (1981a) that biological time is based on real growth and decay but must recognise that this does not exhaust its characteristics. It is qualitative time linked to the natural rhythms of our earth, constituted by life, and experienced by all living beings. As such it is far removed from the classical physicists' t-coordinate, and the measure of motion. Hohn (1984: 6) suggests that time is neither a quality of nature nor of consciousness but exists purely as a social concept which is constituted in conjunction with the cosmology and the relations of work of specific societies. As a concept, one has to agree, time is irreducibly social since human culture is a pre-requisite to the development of concepts. The source of these concepts, however, is to be found in the multiple temporalities of nature and in ourselves as living organisms. Whilst the language-based concept belongs exlusively to the human social realm, the same cannot be said about the sense, experience, and knowledge of temporality which are existential to being. It is these existential aspects of being, I want to propose, that need to become legitimate concerns of social theory.

Twentieth-century physics has changed our understanding and the meaning of physical reality. Similar shifts of understanding have occurred in chemistry and biology, with the result that *all of nature is emerging as fundamentally dynamic*. The contemporary natural scientists whose work was explored in the last two chapters all found it necessary to come to terms with the fundamental qualities of the phenomena of their respective fields. This involved them in a conceptual struggle for post-Newtonian perspectives on their various subject matters. This leaves social scientists in a predicament. Not only do they portray an outmoded picture of the nature of the natural sciences but, in their quest for scientific respectability, they are also seeking the very approach that leading contemporary scientists have found to be inadequate for the description and understanding of the natural world: the classical goal of abstract idealisations and context-free, timelessly true statements.

A different view of nature directly affects our understanding of that which we regard specifically human. If the experience of time, choice, purposive action, sociality, communication, and even the beginnings of consciousness are recognised as fundamental aspects of biological nature, then our traditional distinctions between biological and human nature and natural and social time must yield. They need to give way to an understanding that takes account of the conceptual shifts that have taken place in the natural sciences during this century (Adam 1988). This means that, in order to understand the times of human social life, we need to explore 'human time' in both its continuity with, and distinctiveness from, the times of nature. As seen earlier, however, existing social science approaches are not helpful to this task. First, as I have shown already, physical and biological nature are delineated as 'the other': that which human society is not. Not only is this approach based on a faulty understanding of nature, natural science, and natural time, but it is antithetical to recognising continuities and relations. Secondly, existing models for the structuring of our understanding of social life are based on unacceptable dualisms and take as separate what is fundamentally indivisible. Thirdly, social theories are constructed within clearly defined disciplinary boundaries. They are not concerned with an understanding that connects and relates those separate realms. New ground has therefore to be broken, which means that the structure and content of the remaining chapters might well strike social scientists as unusual.

The following chapters are organised to develop from the traditional to the unconventional. They begin with an overview of empirical studies of 'human time' before focusing more explicitly on studies concerning the use of time as a resource in contemporary industrial societies. However, since not all human societies relate to time as an abstract quantity that can be used, allocated, or sold, it will be necessary to explore aspects of time that are shared by all human societies past and present. Power and transcendence are chosen as key concepts for the demarcation of the times of industrial societies and humanity respectively. In the last chapter I shall return to the issues raised in the beginning of the book and show how an explicit understanding of time offers not merely a basis for a more adequate social theory but a chance to be participating agents in a world where our creations have become the controlling factor of our lives.

4

Human Time Studied

In this brief look at studies of human time I am not concerned with the conceptualisations of time in social theory but with the more explicitly investigated time aspects of human existence in both their individual and social expressions. Not the detail but an overall picture of time studies needs to be the aim so that we may relate our findings to the previous chapters. What emerges as important can then be examined further.

Aspects of mind

Psychology has a long history of studying time. In 1891 Nichols reviewed the multitude of approaches to time by psychologists.

> Casting an eye backward we can but be struck by the wide variety of explanations offered for the time-mystery. Time has been called an act of mind, or reason, of perception, of intuition, of sense, or memory, of will, of all possible compounds and compositions to be made up of them. It has been deemed a General Sense accompanying all mental content in a manner similar to that conceived of pain and pleasure. It has been assigned a separate, special, disparate sense, to nigh a dozen kinds of 'feeling', some familiar, some strangely invented for the difficulty. It has been explained by 'relations', by 'earmarks', by 'signs', by 'remnants', by 'struggles', and by 'strifes', by 'luminous trains', by 'blocks of specious-present', by 'apperception'. It has been declared *a priori*, innate, intuitive, empirical, mechanical. It has been deduced from within and without, from heaven and from earth, and from several things difficult to imagine as either. (quoted in Ornstein 1972: 80, 1975: 16)

Nichols's thoughts could have been written today. We still designate time a priori, a general sense, subjective and objective, and a multitude of other things. In psychology, however, the focus narrowed. Since the end of the last century the emphases of the psychological investigations of time have shifted from issues of ontology and consciousness to those of perception and behaviour. The studies conducted during the first half of this century have been concerned with the time aspects of experience, behaviour, and cognition. The most well known of these have focused on time perception and people's capacity to estimate time against the standard of clock time. They were concerned with the 'psychological present' and the estimation of duration and intervals. Psychologists have further explored the timing, planning, coordination, and anticipation of behaviour, and they have researched time with respect to memory. In all these studies the clock was utilised as the base against which the perceptions, memories, and behaviours were measured. Contemporary psychologists no longer tie their understanding to the empty unit of time through which classical studies estimated perceptions of duration and intervals. Ornstein (1975), in his seminal study '*On the Experience of Time*' related the human time sense to the content of experience. He found that our experience of time differs according to how much happens in the intervening period. Michon (1985) has developed that thinking further and theorises human time in terms of information. The change to this conceptualisation, he suggests, is based on the 'realisation that time is the manifestation of the need to exchange information with the environment' (1985: 47). We need to remember, however, that this is an aspect of time that is shared by all living beings. It is not a prerogative of the human psyche.

We saw in the previous chapter that information exchange is an important source of sentience and of the most basic form of consciousness, the two characteristics of all living organisms. As such it allows for prediction, anticipation, self-observation, and modificatory behaviour. Information exchange is therefore a reality of the biological order generally. Even at the level of inorganic nature, time is associated with information through the transmission of light and other signals. The exchange of information with the environment needs therefore to be linked to the irreversibility in all of nature and human 'information time' must be regarded as differing merely in its expression. The human processing of information, as Michon (1985: 8) rightly points out, 'appears to be a highly complex symbolic construction, not in any way something that might affect a time sense, and probably not even analogous to the way we perceive space, but rather more comparable to the way in which the semantic comprehension of a verbal sentence is constructed.'

The importance of language in relation to the human awareness of time is pointed out by many. Only humans, argues Fraisse (1979), communicate information that not only refers to the present but to things that existed in the past and are planned, anticipated, and conceived for the future. He sees this conceptual aspect inextricably bound up in that which psychologists study: the 'psychological present', the evaluation of duration, or orientation within temporal horizons. A distinction thus needs to be made between the information processing of signals and that of symbols. Wessman and Gorman (1977: 5) seek to achieve just that. Yet they seem to go too far when they argue temporal awareness to be a human development, and the idea of time to have its 'origin in the mind of man'. Their proposal, that time may best be viewed as a 'complex of developed abstract-conceptual frameworks gradually constructed and acquired', severs the idea of time from its sources. This in turn poses a problem when they use the idea of 'representational schemata' – a key concept of contemporary cognitive psychology (Neisser 1976) – to describe the distinctiveness of human symbolic internal representation and its implications for psychological time. Cognition, as Toda (1978) explains, is the internal representation of external cues, and the cognitive system a body of internally structured schemata that serve as a base for organising our behaviour in a meaningful way. I am suggesting that the schemata *and* their sources are in need of elaboration; without it the complexity of time at the level of cognition is impossible to explicate.

German psychology seems to provide the most detailed conceptual distinctions with respect to experiential aspects of time. This is reflected in the many aspects that are being explored. Wendorff (1980: 479–89) cites a whole range of psychological studies of time. Research on *Zeitsinn* covers the sense of time; the ability to estimate time in terms of intervals, durations, rhythms, and sequences. It also includes the knowledge that humans beings are biological clocks tuned to the rhythms of the earth. Studies on *Zeitbewusstsein* incorporate aspects of awareness ranging from the tacit to the explicit and rationalised. Investigations into *Zeitwahrnehmung* deal with the immediate perception of motion and change-continuities. Analyses of *Zeiterleben* concentrate mainly on the subjective and qualitative experience of past, present, future, or now in relation to earlier and later, whilst those of *Zeiterfahrung* focus on socio-historically mediated form of *Zeiterleben* (time experience). Examinations of *Zeitkenntnis* comprise the time aspects of cognition, knowledge, and thought whilst those of the *Zeitperspektive* establish the primary orientation of individuals and categories of people to the past, present, and future. Enquiries of the *Zeitgitter* examine people's orientation within the socio- temporal structure and the breakdown of that orientation is often associated with insanity and mental illness (Adam 1991; Melges 1982; Schaltenbrand 1963). Lastly, studies of the *Zeithorizont* seek to establish the range of the temporal extension with reference to the identity of individuals and categories of people as well as their horizon of decision making, planning, and rootedness in the past. The time horizon also forms a focus for sociological studies where the extent of the horizon is related to class, subcultural attitudes, age, race, sex, and different professions.

The diversity of 'fine distinctions' of this body of research demonstrates the power of reflective awareness and conceptual thought but not its isolation from its sources or its location in the human mind. The studies themselves cannot be our focus here; only their treatment of time is of relevance to our search for the distinctiveness of human time. However, there emerges a problem. To study the experience of duration, the estimation of an interval, people's orientation within horizons, or the timing, sequencing, and coordinating of behaviour, is to *define time* as duration, interval, passage, horizon, sequencing, and timing. This conceptualisation is in turn imposed on the studies. I am therefore suggesting that time does not 'emerge' from these studies, but is pre-defined in the very aspects that are being studied. What does emerge from even this very brief glance at some psychological studies is the implication of time in every aspect of our psyche: brain function, consciousness, experience, cognition, communication, language, identity, development, maturation, social interaction, even our sanity. To a sociologist these aspects are of course inseparable from social being. We therefore need to turn to the social studies of time in order to complement the work of psychologists and to complete this overview of studies of human time.

Time budgeted

For the most comprehensive review of sociological studies of time I would refer to Bergmann's (1983) excellent essay. However, since we are not interested in the studies per se but the assumptions they entail with respect to time, our emphases and organisation of the material will be different from Bergmann's classification into time orientations, temporal order, the evolution of time-consciousness and social change. We shall focus on studies of time use, enquiries into attitudes and orientations towards time, research concerned with organisational aspects of time, and investigations of the life cycle and ageing.

In sociology the oldest and most established studies of time are known as time-budget studies. These are investigations into people's use of time in their daily lives. Analogous to the early psychological studies on the perception of duration, time-budget studies were initially not concerned with content but only with studying *how much* time was allocated for the family, work, and leisure. This information was, and still is, used as an indicator of particular lifestyles and the quality of people's lives: quality being measured by the amount of free time available (Staikov 1982). During their many years of existence, time-budget studies, like the psychological perception studies, have generated a proliferation of research which has largely continued along a one-dimensional track. These studies are characterised by their quest for precision, with time as a resource being expressed by numerical specification of both the duration and the frequency with which activities were carried out. Focusing on one chosen aspect of time within a specified range, they *exclude* all the other aspects of time that might simultaneously have a bearing on people's lives, and that people relate to, at any one moment.

The Jahoda et al. (1932) study *Die Arbeitslosen von Marienthal* (The unemployed of Marienthal) was an early exception to this approach. It showed the quantitative measure to be meaningless if it failed to take account of the experience of time. The focus of the Jahoda study has thus shifted to the content of the experience a quarter of a century before a similar change occurred in psychology. The study did, however, remain an exception until the 1960s when time became a renewed focus for sociological investigation with such studies as Moore's (1963) *Man, Time, and Society*, and Roth's (1976) *Timetables*. Today, Young and Schuller's (1990) Greenwich (London) study of recently retired people serves as an example for an approach that seeks to retain the sort of complexity first highlighted by Jahoda and her colleagues.

Regardless, however, of whether the focus is on time budgeting or on time management, or whether it is on time used or time filled, as in the research on the unemployed and retired, all these studies are dealing with clock time only. This is the case irrespective of whether or not they focus on how this clock time is experienced, structured, passed, rationed, or allocated. This also applies to organisational sociology and, for example, Blyton's (1985) *Changes in Working Time*, where clock time is assumed without question. Clark (1982: 5) shows sociologists of organisation to be using five different concepts of time which, he suggests, nevertheless 'all share the unitary framework of time associated with the calendar and the clock'. What these studies have in common is their use of the symbolised form of clock time only. Theirs is an 'in time' analysis where clock time provides the boundary within which life is enacted, without cognizance of the constitution of time or the embedded time in events, processes, and organisation. He therefore urges social scientists to recognise that time is *in* events and that this event-time too is used as an organising device in contemporary society. Clark (1982: 14) suggests an understanding not of time but times where chronological time is no longer 'treated as an overlayer which systematically and coercively shapes all other times'. Probing further we find that these studies share a second, less obvious, time characteristic. All conceptualise time as a quantity. Unlike the mathematical quantity of physics, however, this social quantity is viewed as a resource – scarce or plentiful depending on the circumstances – that may be used, allocated, sold, or controlled. As such it merits further exploration in relation to aspects of social control and relations of power. We shall therefore look at time as a resource in the next chapter on industrial time and power.

Orientations and perspectives

Moving to the third group of time studies we find that, to a large extent, the studies of temporal orientation and temporal perspective also share the framework of analysis encountered above. Whether these are carried out by anthropologists or sociologists, the symbolised form of time as clock or calendar time is either used for the study directly or as a norm against which societies are compared and found lacking. Utilised as both a measure and a comparative tool, clock time is once more the unquestioned assumption.

LeShan's (1952) pioneering work on 'Time orientation and social class' initiated a whole range of empirical investigations into the relationship between time orientation and class, sex, age, and deviance. The studies that followed linked deferred gratification and the length of future orientation to social success. Time here is a spatial measure of length and again the measure in calendar time units is assumed to be constant. Kastenbaum (1961) and Lüscher (1974) developed this approach further. The former found the concept of the future orientation in need of differentiation. He identified coherence, density, direction, and extension as integral aspects of future orientation, whilst the latter wanted their subjective and objective aspects distinguished.

In Evans-Pritchard's (1969) study of *The Nuer* the tribe's understanding and reckoning of time is delineated in its difference from the Western use of time and orientation in time, theirs being conceptualised as both ecological and socio-structural. Ecological time is Evans-Pritchard's concept for the Nuer's view of the relation between social activities and natural events such as the rainy and dry seasons; structural time is his term for kinship relations and periods of time reckoning that extend beyond one seasonal cycle. Whorf's (1956) very different linguistic analysis of the Hopi's understanding of time is conducted on the basis of very similar assumptions. Whorf concludes that the Hopi do not have a word for time, not even a tensed language, and that they therefore see the world differently. Evans-Pritchard and Whorf implicitly assume a clock time standard against which they construct the time of the other society. Their backcloth, in other words, is not explicated and theorised. It remains a one-dimensional part of their common-sense understanding of everyday life. 'Those who have written about time in history or time in nonwestern cultures,' Hägerstrand (1985: 5) points out, 'have almost exclusively dealt with symbolic time. The time-perspective hidden in nature or in work itself or the products of work – in other words aspects of embedded time – have been largely ignored.'

Leach's (1968) essays form an exception here. Whilst being called 'Two essays concerning the symbolic representation of time', they link the symbol to its sources and look at the embedded aspect of time. Leach's (1968: 27) concern is with 'what the significant social categories are, not with what they ought to be'. He then asks how we come to have a verbal category such as time at all, and how this might link with experience. He thinks that time embraces two logically distinct experiences: repetition and irreversibility. All other aspects, he proposes, are derivations from these. 'I am inclined to think that all other aspects of time, duration for example or historical sequence, are fairly simple derivatives from these two basic experiences: a) that certain phenomena of nature repeat themselves b) that life change is irreversible' (Leach 1968: 125). This is not the place to discuss Leach's polarisation of time into experiences of reversibility and repetition. That particular dichotomy will be examined later. At this point we merely need to appreciate in what way Leach's approach differs from that of Evans-Pritchard or Whorf, for example, and how studies which elaborate on Leach's work use different aspects of time. Thus Horton (1967) found East African societies to be emphasising aspects of recurrence and order in contrast to societies who value change and progress. Other aspects of time orientation that have been studied in this vein relate to past, present, and future emphases. These orientations have not only been researched in individuals as members of specific groups and societies, but in whole societies.

With a focus on peoples' primary time orientation – be this on order or change, or on the past, present, and future – clock time *ceases* to be the only or the dominant imagery. Despite this difference, however, the classical strategy of polarisation is retained. In other words, to investigate whether change is valued more than repetition or vice versa is merely a variant of the classical order–change dichotomy of social science perspectives. Time here is still conceptualised as either repetition or change, circle or line, as a phenomenon of life or of nature: an understanding that has emerged from the previous chapter as inadequate.

A number of sociologists have investigated approaches and orientations to the future and, to a lesser extent, the present and the past. Hohn (1984), Huber (1972), Luhmann (especially 1982b, c), Kaufmann (1970), and Nowotny (1985) in their contemporary studies, and Mannheim (1972) in *Ideology and Utopia*, have related a focus on the future to social planning. Clock time is an important aspect of these studies but no longer the only one. Both historicity as the recognition that people make history in conditions outside their control and the vision of an open future are seen here as the historical pre-condition for planned, pragmatic, or revolutionary change. Contemporary Western societies, it is argued in these studies, create their futures as a continuing affair in the present, be it through utopian or pragmatic practices. The future is no longer merely predicted, it is actively constructed. This means, writes Huber (1972: 31), 'defining a new set of long range goals to orient present action'. Nowotny (1985) extends this argument further when she suggests that the future is being eliminated and replaced by an extended present. In a present overloaded with choices, she proposes, the future is determined now. We shall return to her work later to discuss these ideas. Contemporary approaches to the future are frequently contrasted with the pre-Enlightenment practice of learning from the past (Koselleck 1985) or traditional societies' recreation of the past (Giddens 1979, 1981). Green's (1985) study of the temporal attitude of four very different contemporary Negro cultures notes the similarity of approach to time – past, present, and future – and locates that correspondence in traditional West African cosmology. Bergmann (1983: 472) shows how a whole range of such orientations are used for the contrast of overall stereotypes such as primitive versus modern, agrarian versus industrial, or mythical versus historical. Other favoured dichotomies are cyclical and linear approaches linked to cosmologies and religion (Yaker 1972).

Where sociologists have studied orientations to the future, past, or present they no longer use the clock time quantity exclusively but conceptualise time as a societal dimension to be recreated, constructed, learned from, or eliminated. In the previous chapter the past, present, and future were established as fundamental to life. To have a relationship to them as a condition of one's existence, however, seems to be irreducibly human. The relationship to those aspects of time will therefore be the focus of attention in Chapter 6 on human time and transcendence.

The life cycle

The life cycle is a further area for studies of social time. This research entails a concern with people's development, their ageing, their maturation, and their status passages. With reference to ageing we find that psychologists distinguish between biological and mental age whilst sociologists delineate the social aspect of ageing. 'Age, being basically a function of time,' writes Moore (1963: 60), 'should move at a steady rate. Yet, "physiological age" or "social maturity" may differ from chronological age and from one person of the "same" age to another. Thus a person may be flattered as "mature beyond his years" or degraded as "old before his time". Aside from these variations, the relations of events to time requires the concept of rate to refer to the fast, normal, or slow pace at which individuals experience events as they get older.' In all their meanings, these processes are associated with the irreversible direction of time and with the knowledge that we all live our lives from an unremembered birth towards an unforseen death. Whilst the direction is given, the process is understood as both structured and punctuated by socially marked stages. Biological development is symbolically transformed into biographical statuses. Our identity, suggests Weigert (1981), is built up as we live our lives along 'time tracks' with careers, and as we pass through several statuses. Through it, he argues, individuals are locked into their social institutional contexts. Statuses and careers are, however, not only rigidly staged and sequenced but can also run concurrently. One can simultaneously be mother, student, wife, barmaid, daughter, Aikido Dan, grandmother, and much else. Yet the living through the status passages themselves will not have been simultaneous but sequenced. Like passing through stations, we may have become a wife, a mother, a grandmother; we may have enrolled at university and graduated; have taken the black belt of a first Dan, and learned to serve drinks. Thus, while there is order, sequence, and unidirectional process, the order of the sequence is not predetermined but open to a wide range of variation.

All organisms and bodies age, the meaning of that ageing, however, is socially relative. 'A human life course,' explains Weigert (1981: 216), 'is based on the biological processes of bodily ageing, to be sure, but each of us also passes through intricate networks of overlapping sociotemporal processes which constitute the total experience of ageing in everyday life.' Piper (1978) postulates the category of 'social age' which he conceptualises as analogous to Sorokin and Merton's (1937) 'social time'. Chronological age, he argues, may not correspond with the social categorisation of age. At the age of thirty a university professor would be classified as young, whilst an industrial blue-collar worker of the same age would not be classified as such. Thus, to be categorised a child, a youth, an adult, or an old-age pensioner depends on social criteria which may not correspond with chronological ageing. Chronology, however, must not be confused with natural time but needs to be recognised as a social construction. As we shall see later it has to be understood in relation to aspects of transcendence and power, and not, as Sorokin and Merton (1937) argued, as physical and therefore inadequate for social analysis.

Irreversible time dominates in studies of the life cycle. This applies irrespective of whether the life cycle is conceptualised as a cumulative

develpment of growth and decay or in terms of unidirectional successive
stages; whether time is understood as internal or external to the system;
whether a 'time in' or an 'in time' approach is used; whether we theorise
life as being lived along time-tracks or whether we analyse social age. The
relation between these approaches, however, is never theorised; it has yet
to be established. Despite the emphasis on moments of return,
irreversiblity and change are central to the cycles of life since no
repetition is the same in its recurrence. Traditionally, time has been
associated with change and the historical dimension (Heirich 1964;
Martins 1974) and not with the life cycle or issues of social order. Yet it is
clear that time is centrally implicated in all these social dimensions. Our
next two categories of studies therefore cover investigations that are
explicitly concerned with change and order. Since, however, the time in
change may vary widely we need briefly to concern ourselves with those
differences.

Social change and order

When the Lynds (1929) studied the changes of Middletown and Stacey et
al. (1975) those of Banbury, the changes were plotted between two fixed
chronological points. In the Middletown study the (then) contemporary
life of the 1920s was compared and contrasted with conditions of the
same town thirty years earlier, the difference being conceptualised as the
measure of change. This 1890 baseline was also used as a source to the
Middletown of the 1920s and causal links were established so that the
past could serve as an explanation for the present. A later study (1937)
did not deviate from this approach. The second study of Stacey et al.
(1975) focused on the changes that had taken place in Banbury since the
late 1940s when Stacey conducted her first investigation of post-war
changes in that town. Both the Lynds' and Stacey's initial and follow-up
studies were intended as explorations of structure and process. Yet such
chapter headings as 'The changing face of Banbury: 1951–66' would have
been more correctly entitled 'The *changed* face of Banbury' since the
analysis occurred on a 'before and after' basis and was not focused on the
processes of change. Theirs is a static analysis where calendar time was
retrospectively imposed as a reference grid. This time constitutes the
structure that defines the points at which the difference is being assessed.
It is an analysis that de-temporalises change since it excludes what Mead
had defined as essential: the moment of becoming. In contradistinction
to these studies, the irreversible, temporal aspects of change are the
focus of evolutionary approaches in social science. Such an understanding is based on the awareness that the present, to use

Leibnitz's famous phrase, is 'charged with the past and pregnant with the future'. The idea of progress (or decline) is integral to it and stages of succession often play an important role. In Marxist and interactionist writings change is further understood as being constituted in interaction. In these social science traditions the focus is on the production of change rather than on the difference between earlier and later states and their measurement. Once historicity becomes central to the analysis past, present, and future come to be recognised as constituted.

Time can thus be variously implicated in change. It can be conceptualised as calendar time which in turn provides the chronologically based points between which differences are established and measured. Here time is conceived as a parameter within which social events succeed each other. The study of change within a parameter of retrospectively fixed points has to be distinguished from studies that focus on the process of change. Both, however, conceive of stages and linear progressions. This produces an imagery of a linear time. In nine out of ten of Moore's (1974: 36) diagrammatic representations of theories of the direction of change, time is represented as a line. It is expressed as a dimension along which the changes are taking place. For both types of conceptualisations clock time provides the measure, and in both the past serves as the source from which to explain the present and predict the future. Mead (1959) and Luhmann's analyses differ from these since both explicitly conceptualise time as constitutive of, and constituted in, the present.

In contradistinction to emphases on change, Moore (1963), Schöps (1980), and Zerubavel (1979, 1981), for example, focus their studies on organisational aspects of time. All three are concerned to sensitise social scientists to the temporal order of social life. In these studies the focus is on how individuals and groups of people co-ordinate, synchronise, and sequence specific actions; when these are to take place; how long they are to take; how often and within what length of time span they are to happen; and in what order of priority they are to be selected. Whilst Moore focuses on time as a parameter, resource, and order, Zerubavel emphasises regularities, schedules, and the evolution of the abstract concept of time in relation to its usage as a commodity. Both Zerubavel and Schöps point to the importance of the symbolic dimension and the normative aspects of all human social temporal regularities. For these theorists time is not change but an organising principle.

The social study of timing, planning, and organisation of actions involves aspects of time we have already encountered in the organisation of living beings, machines, and clocks. It involves duration, sequence, synchronisation, rate, and periodicity and it depends on open rhythmic interaction and interdependence. What distinguishes the human organisational aspects from those of machines, suggests Schöps (1980), is their context-dependent, normative character, norms in social science being traditionally associated with the role structure of societies and with the ability to apply sanctions. I would disagree with Schöps's idea that the normative aspect of the temporal order sets humans apart from other animal species. Roles, norms, and sanctions, I propose, form an integral aspect of all social organisation. Only their content, source, and speed seem to differ, as studies on ants (Wilson 1971), bees (Michener 1974), and primates (Lawick-Goodall 1971), for example, quite clearly demonstrate. In so far as time structures and provides norms for the life of individuals and groups, it has been proposed to be a 'social fact' by Durkheim (1915), Sorokin and Merton (1937), and other sociologists writing on the topic of 'social time'. I would agree with defining time in social terms, but cannot follow social theorists in claiming that dimension exclusively for the human realm. The evidence presented here corroborates Mead's (1959) conceptualisation of sociality as a principle of *all* nature and not merely of human social life. Sorokin and Merton's (1937: 621) statement that 'the system of time varies with social structure' needs to be recognised, therefore, as applying equally to the social organisation of all life forms.

Where time is seen as a social ordering principle, with timing of social action a necessity of all social life, I want to propose that it is neither the principle of sociality nor the normative aspects of time structuring alone that set humans apart from the rest of nature. To have a relationship to the conditions of one's existence and to use time as a resource and a commodity, it seems, constitute an irreducible difference, as we shall see in the following chapters.

Reflections

Several important points emerge from this overview of studies on social time. People budget their time. They plan, use, and allocate it on a daily basis within the parameter of their lifetime and even beyond. This, however, does not apply to all people. Anthropologists have studied societies for whom time is not a resource and historians have shown the use of time as resource and commodity to be a recent phenomenon of Western, industrialised societies. The attitude and relationship to 'time as such' also emerges as a recent development of such societies. Whilst all humans seem to have a relationship to their birth and death, to ponder their origins and destiny, and have a relationship to the past, present, and future, not all societies conceptualise time and the past, present, and future in our abstracted form. In other words, not all societies have names for the modalities but they do make distinctions between *Bew-*

irktes and *Bewirkendes*; between that which has been and is thus beyond influence and that which is still to come and therefore open to influence. It also seems probable that all societies reckon time in some way.

From the psychological studies time has emerged pre-defined as duration, passage, sequence, interval, timing, and horizon regardless of whether this referred to the study of experience, estimation or behaviour. To a limited extent this also applies to empirical studies in the social sciences where time appears as something that people budget, use, allocate, plan, spend, sell, or save. Instead of being merely estimated, time is reckoned and measured as well as being used as a measure. It is filled or passed, and constituted in ageing and history. It is experienced not only as short or dragging but as a horizon for orientation and a parameter within which everyday life is organised and structured. In social science time is therefore pre-defined as a quantity to be measured and a resource to be used and controlled. Whilst the scope has widened, the time principles of organisation and those of the mechanical clock time have re-emerged in the studies of human social time. The meaning of those aspects, however, has once again changed with the different context. Where psychologists argue that emotions, consciousness, cognition, and language have to be taken account of in any understanding of human time, some social scientists insist that values, norms, and structures of power need to be fundamentally included in the conceptualisation of human social time.

The studies of human time merit detailed analysis in their own right. In this treatise, however, they form an integral but very small part of a wider exploration. Our focus is on the bearing of a comprehensive understanding of social time on social theory. This necessitates being highly selective, picking out a few peaks from which to survey the landscape rather than detailed studies of any one. The peaks I have in mind are going to be explored through the key concepts of power and transcendence.

5

Industrial Time and Power

As the tempo of modern life has continued to accelerate, we have come to feel increasingly out of touch with the biological rhythms of the planet, unable to experience a close connection with the natural environment. The human time world is no longer joined to the incoming and outgoing tides, the rising and setting sun, and the changing seasons. Instead, humanity has created an artificial time environment punctuated by mechanical contrivances and electronic impulses: a time plane that is quantitative, fast-paced, efficient, and predictable. (Rifkin 1987: 12)

In this chapter I shall explore this very specific character of social time in contemporary industrial societies, using Britain and West Germany as examples for description and analysis. I shall investigate what role the clock and calendar play in such societies and what happens to the more traditional ways of organising social life. This entails examining the implications of understanding time as a quantity, of relating to that quantity as if it were the only time, and of using it as a resource that may be budgeted, wasted, allocated, sold, or controlled.

Timed social life

Once we become aware of it, we are left in no doubt that the largest part of Western industrial everyday life is timed. During the week, for example, adults working away from home and school children get up at a specific time. If they do not, then their getting up is conceptualised as being either late or early. Their morning routine, their departure from the home, their arrival at the place of work or study are carefully timed; so are their work, their rewards and sanctions, their achievements, their careers, their time at school or work, and their time off.

Even the most cursory look at contemporary school life reveals that everything is timed. It demonstrates that the activities and interactions of all its participants are choreographed to a symphony of buzzers and bells, timetables, schedules, and deadlines. Layer upon layer of such schedules form the structure of our education system. Not only are the lessons for the day timetabled, but so are the subject contents: physical geography for the first six weeks of the term, agricultural systems of Asia for the following four weeks and so forth. The beginning and end of lessons, the term, the school year, and the dates and times for tests and exams are some of the fixed points within which subjects, teachers' activities and pupils' expected progress are programmed (Ball et al. 1984; Delamont and Galton 1986). Within the overall structure of finite time resources and nested timetables, activities are scheduled for pre-set durations. They are structured to follow certain sequences and to happen at a specific rate, at a particular time in the children's lives, over a fixed period, and for a set number of times. In addition to being synchronised and co-ordinated into the structure of the school, the education system, and the socio-political system of the country as a whole, those school activities are allocated, prioritised, and selected on a *zero sum* calculation of the time resources of teachers and their pupils. 'School life is organized by and into complex temporal sequences,' write Ball et al. (1984: 43), 'The daily institutional reality of the school takes its experiential form from these sequences, and it is their finite length which constrains activity and provides the basis for the setting of priorities and making of allocations.' The rate at which the activities are planned to proceed and progress largely relates to actual achievements in relation to both the long term and the single lesson goals. Each single timing, synchronisation, and allocation is in turn nested within a multiplicity of others, from an 'educational plan' down to the didactic detail of the time structure of individual lessons. The daily timetable seems to play a particularly important role in school life. It provides all the participants with a regular routine within which the carefully scheduled learning, teaching, examination, assessment, management, administration, cleaning, cook-ing, eating, and playing can proceed in an orderly and predictable manner. 'Pupils and teachers are bound into a regular routine,' write Delamont and Galton (1986: 138), 'so that for the pupil there are fixed points of arrival, registration, assembly, lessons, break, lessons, lunch, lessons, break, lessons, home, every day whether it is Tuesday or Wednesday.' And the timetabled routine further ensures, we could continue their argument, that geography is taught to class 3A every second lesson on a Monday and to class 3D every last lesson on a Thursday. It makes certain that assembly is always on Mondays, Wednesdays, and Fridays but never on Tuesdays and Thursdays.

The regularity of this routine is further enhanced by the bell. Like the bell that first structured the lives of the brethren of the Benedictine order during the sixth century (McCann 1970; Rifkin 1987, Zerubavel 1981), the school bell separates and sections one activity off from another and it ensures that everyone begins their activities together. Like the monastery bell, the school bell secures conformity to a regular collective beat. Unlike the monastery bell, however, the school bell structures secular time, a time that no longer belongs to God but to a human collective. It gives physical expression to the contemporary standardised abstraction within which the education of our children is organised. The school bell delineates the French teacher's time from that of the Geography teacher's, study time from play time, and school time from private time. It binds staff and pupils into a common schedule, within which their respective activites are both paced and timed. When the Benedictines first introduced the custom of having fixed and pre-set times for each of their order's activities, marked and separated by the ringing of a bell, this was a revolutionary practice. Today it is neither questioned as a practice nor doubted as a principle: it is simply taken for granted. Without alternative vision and choice the participants surrender to the bureaucratically organised institutional beat.

Focusing on timetables of contemporary life, we find that a strict temporal order is particularly pertinent for rationalised, bureaucratically structured organisations. Here human activities are orchestrated to the collective beat of machine time and regulated to a standardised and predictable precision. 'Synchronization, sequence, and rate of activities,' explains Moore (1963: 10), 'operate within narrow tolerable limits. Moreover, present actions must be taken in order to assure the outcome of future events, often over a considerable period.' It is interesting to note that this temporal organisation of our socially created bureaucracies is not only structured around clock time but also resembles the nature and quality of the created machine time in a most extraordinary way. Both feature duration, sequence, synchronisation, periodicity, and rate. Even more importantly, both are designed to the *ideal of invariability*. In both, Prigoginian fluctuations would be perceived as a threatening disruption to the smooth running. The extreme fluctuations that characterise the processes of life would pose a severe threat to the time structure of bureaucracies; they are conceived as a 'rocking of the boat' where too much rocking represents drowning and almost certain death.

Daily time structuring through schedules and timetables, argue Delamont and Galton (1986), is one of the characteristics by which school, work, and institutional life generally, may be separated from the daily routine of those on holiday and those no longer at work. Before we find out to what extent their lives could be considered to be organised without institutional timetables, we need to add to this list the vast group of full-time carers who are at home with their charges. People who are at

home all day certainly have more discretion with respect to the organisation of their time; yet it would be wrong to assume that the timing of their
activities is free from the constraints and influences of the timetables of
the society in which they live and the persons and institutions with whom
they interact. People at home are influenced in their timing by their own
habits and those of the people around them. They are constrained by the
opening hours of banks, shops, health centres, libraries, cinemas, and
pubs; by their association memberships; and by their leisure activities.
They cannot extricate themselves from the institutional timetables
imposed on other members of their family. The timing of activities of
those who are at home on a full-time basis is therefore structured around
the institutional timetables of school hours, the schedule of those
working outside the home, the opening hours of amenities and the
timetables of public transport. Whether we are affected in a primary or
secondary way, we cannot escape the clock time that structures and times
our daily lives. Even on holiday the timing of our activities can never be
purely voluntary since it too depends on externally based social timings:
the timetables of the hotel, organised leisure activities, public transport,
and the opening hours of local amenities. As long as we remain part of a
society that is structured to the time of clocks and calendars our activities
and interaction with others can only escape its pervasive hold to a very
limited extent.

Organisation within a time-grid of calendars and clocks facilitates
precision and it potentially eliminates the reliance on interpretation. The
extent to which this opportunity is seized, however, is context dependent.
A brief excursus on punctuality will illustrate this point. In industrialised
and industrialising countries activities must not only be synchronised,
but the synchronisation itself has become embedded in a clock-time-grid.
Thus, it is not enough for teachers and pupils, for example, to arrive
together in the allocated space, merely to synchronise their arrival for
their common activity. Their scheduled arrival must be with reference to
an allocated clock and calendar time. If they were all to arrive at 9.10 am,
they would all be late if the lesson had been timetabled to begin at 9.00
am. Essays and course work too do not only have to be done collectively
at the same time, but have to be handed in at the 'right' time as defined by
clock and calendar time units; and if the teacher is 'late' in the handing
back of the work, this may affect both the timing and the success of the
revisions for the examinations. To be punctual is to be 'on time' as
defined by an external, common time reference. The standardised clock
time is to date the most precise and most widely used time reference by
which to achieve punctuality. However, despite the widespread existence
and availability of calendars and clocks, punctuality does not only carry
different meanings for different societies, but it is also differently

evaluated in different cultures. Levine and Wolff's (1985) description usefully illustrates this point.

When Levine, an American professor of psychology, took a visiting professorship in Brazil, he went with his own culture's assumptions about punctuality with respect to lecture attendance. Giving his first lecture in Brazil, he was puzzled by the low attendance, only to find a steady stream of 'late comers' to trickle in throughout the duration of his two hour lecture. But, unlike their American counterparts, the Brazilian students neither sneaked in quietly nor offered apologies. They just greeted all their friends and smiled at the lecturer. Nothing in their behaviour suggested that they might have been unpunctual or late, or that their arrival was in any way requiring an apology to the speaker. Even being as much as one-and-a-half hours late, for a scheduled two hour-lecture, did not seem to merit apology. When the two hours were finished by the clock, only a few students left. Levine was to learn later that students roughly stayed for the duration of a two hour lecture. Only the point of starting and finishing was defined rather more flexibly than he was accustomed to. After he completed some comparative studies on punctuality, he summed up his findings with the suggestion that Brazilians are more flexible in their definitions of early and late than Americans, and that they expressed less regret over being late because they rated punctuality as less important (Levine et al. 1980: 541). There is no need however to go as far as Brazil to appreciate the difference of interpretation of what it means to arrive 'on time'. There is a significant difference even between the very similar societies of Northern Europe. Being invited to a party for 8 o'clock means quite different things in West Germany and Britain, as many unwary visitors to either country may have experienced. In Britain this specified time can mean that persons are expected any time between 9 o'clock and the closing time of the pubs. In Germany it means 8 o'clock; any deviation requires an apology and an excuse for being early is always more acceptable than one for being late. In Britain, arrival before the specified time seems invariably to cause embarrassment for hosts and guests alike. In Germany, lateness within the range of 15 minutes may be blamed on the traffic. Anything longer requires more profound reasons. Lateness in excess of one hour is excusable only by a sudden death in the family, an accident, or some other major disaster. Whilst the above description of attitudes to punctuality may have focused on the extremes of the vast variations that occur within countries and between different contexts, it does, however, highlight the tightly normed aspects of timed behaviour in social life.

All social life is timed. It has a time-based order. Synchronisation and 'time-structuring' are fundamental to any collective order as we have seen in the previous chapter. They are principles that apply equally to the simplest organism and to contemporary human social life. The form this timing takes as well as the respective meanings of it, however, may differ fundamentally. Punctuality is one form of synchronising collective action. It has therefore to be recognised as a specific case within the overall principle of timing and synchronisation. Punctuality depends on the shared meaning of an external time reference. Punctuality, as distinct from mere synchronisation, implies some objective frame of reference by which those who meet and expect each other may be judged to be 'on time'. Whether this point is defined by the rising sun, the time of the apple blossom, the first Monday in the month of May, the combination of clock and calendar as 5.30 am on the 4.5.1990 or 0530/04051990, they are all socially generalised reference points. What counts as punctual, however, is fundamentally context dependent.

There is a further difference in the nature of the reference points themselves. We therefore need to distinguish between the clock and calendar reference and the natural markers such as the sun, the moon, and the tides. As an aspect of the rhythmicity of nature, the latter are marked by recurrence with variance. As a human creation, the former are characterised by the explicit design goal of invariant precision. It is the difference between time as a property of nature (or God and gods) and of people that is of importance for an understanding of the control of time in contemporary industrialised social life. I suggest that it is only with our relating to the human creation of calendar and clock time *as* time, that time became a receptacle to be filled, a resource to be used and allocated, and a commodity to be sold and exchanged on the labour market. Only with the conceptualisation of the created time *as* time does it become necessary to ground our understanding of social time in the relations of power.

Thus far our social time has merely been shown to be highly structured. This structuring of social life should, however, not be thought of as a neutral fact. Once we ask who structures whose life, what rules are being adhered to, and how these processes occur, then timed social life becomes fundamentally embedded in an understanding of the structural relations of power, normative structures, and the negotiated interactions of social life. For the purpose of our investigation, however, such questions and their implications will only be taken to be significant if their time aspect contributes something new to existing sociological knowledge. I shall therefore refrain from discussing work that demonstrates first that powerful members of society control the timing, planning, pacing and the goals of those who are structurally weak and, secondly, that this depends on the collusion of those whose time is being controlled. The task of this chapter is to explore aspects of time that lead beyond work that integrates studies of time control into existing sociological knowledge on control and power.

Social time controlled

Humans are time binding, time transcending and time controlling beings. Whilst the control of the time-infused conditions of existence is a universal human characteristic the control of time *per se* is not. It is a recent historical phenomenon and needs to be associated with the conjuncture of industrialisation and the development of calendars and clocks. We need to differentiate the control of time as such from the generalised control over the time aspects of our existence. I propose therefore that the former is best understood in conjunction with relations of power and the latter with reference to transcendence.

The control over the entropic processes of decay, over the decline of our bodies, over artefacts and social institutions is an endeavour we share with all human societies and so too is the control over the timing and synchronisation of collective action and the structuring of our social relations, our daily activities, and our futures. Through taking control over the time aspects of their living conditions humans have consistently transcended the times of their own existence. As Gurvitch (1963: 174) explains, 'no society, no class, no structured group (local, professional, family, or other) can live without trying to control these social times, which is quite a different thing from conceptualizing them and even more different from quantifying them!' Symbolic language, artefacts, technologies, and institutions are the major means by which we attempt this control. Hägerstrand (1985: 10) identifies culture with this process and suggests that it 'can be viewed as a system of major modifications of naturally embedded time in the material world.' What is of interest to us at this point is the relationship between the universal human search for transcending time and the time control associated with relations of power: between the control of the time aspects of the conditions of existence and the control of time *per se*. Not the substantive evidence of the multiple control of social and personal time, therefore, but the conceptual issue of how to understand that control is being pursued here. In other words, empirical evidence of the control of time is not of interest in its own right but as an illustration in support of the conceptual argument.

In the previous discussion on timed social life we have seen that pupils, for example, have little control over the time structuring of all those aspects of their lives that are connected to school life. The sequencing of their learning, the pace of their studies, the choice over priorities of action, their breaks from work, their starting and finishing time, are all outside their own control. Whilst industrial societies compulsorily control the largest proportion of the waking hours of their school children and all of the time of their prisoners and mental patients, employers achieve this control by buying the time of their workers. In the realm of employment such control becomes more visible since the time structuring of work is not merely controlled but bargained for. Not labour but labour time is being exchanged in that relationship. In other words, labour is exchanged for money in a mediated form and time is the medium through which labour is translated into its abstract exchange value.

Time is contested in disputes, and fights over time control can be observed through the history of strikes where the duration of the working day, week, year, and working life, the pace of work and break times, overtime and time off, holidays and paid leisure time are at the centre of the arguments (Blyton 1985; Keenoy 1985; Rinderspracher 1985; Starkey 1988). The Factory Acts of 1830 and 1840 in Britain bear witness to this. Subsequent Acts have steadily reduced the statutory maximum length of the working day. This long period of fights *over time*, as both Hohn (1984) and Thompson (1967) have pointed out, was preceded by fights *against* time. These earlier disputes are argued to characterise the turbulent transition period to industrial labour. Workers were resisting the imposed standardised clock time discipline as an alien rhythm that no longer took account of either qualitative variability or the natural rhythms of activity and rest. Historians suggest that the appearance of disputes over the length, pace, intervals, and sequencing of work coincides with the establishment of work rhythms based on clock time. With clock time accepted as the norm, fights against time get replaced by those *about* time. 'The first generation of factory workers were taught by their masters the importance of time,' suggests Thompson (1967: 86), 'the second generation formed their short-time committees in the ten-hour movement; the third generation struck for overtime or time-and-a-half. They had accepted the categories of their employers and learned to fight back with them. They had learned their lesson that time is money only too well.' We could add a fourth and fifth generation that fought for paid 'time out' and 'time in'. The Britain, the 1984–85 strike of the miners and the 1986 strike of the Fleet Street journalists at Wapping exemplify strikes for 'time in'. In other words, not the amount of time off, but to have the chance to work in exchange for money was at the base of these and many other recent strikes.

Thompson (1967), Giddens (1981), and Hohn (1984) concur in their interpretations of industrial time. It is, they argue, a historically novel and distinct expression of industrial capitalism. It has all the characteristics of clock time and it is in this form that it is being used as a bargaining medium between worker and employer. Disputes are centrally about duration, intervals, sequencing, synchronisation and pace, the key elements of clock time which is divisible into standardised units and beats to the uniform rhythm of the metronome. Industrial wage labour separated what used to be inextricably linked in meaning and practice: working time and free time. But, as Hohn (1984: 11) points out, the division goes further still. The very form of time has been chopped up into uniform, repetitive clock time units. Work rhythms based on clock time are no longer context dependent. This means that there is no longer a way to take account of specific conditions and particular needs. One outcome of this change is the need for external normative and legislative protection which has to impose socially meaningful boundaries on these endlessly uniform strings of time units. Contemporary industrial work organisation has to have its rhythms artificially superimposed on the standardised, metronomic beat of clock time. Because of this exclusion of natural rhythms in social situations timed by the clock, Hohn (1984: 159) proposes that the participants have to be protected by normative breaks and a reduction in working hours.

Labour time as quantity and abstract exchange value is no longer something that is merely used, passed, or filled. It has become an integral component of production, a quantity that helps to mediate exchange. It has become a commodity. Here the control is not only over the time structuring of the activity but also over the commodity itself. Once created as a commodity, time has become an ineradicable aspect of industrial social life which in turn affects the control of the timing and even the temporality of that life. Social science owes to Marx the understanding of industrial time in terms of commodified time and it is as an extension to Marx's understanding that both Giddens and Hohn present their discussion of this topic. The creation of clock time, as a time that is standardised, context free, homogeneous, and divisible into infinitely small units, is seen by both as fundamentally implicated in the historical development towards commodified time. Where before the capacity of a person to work a piece of land in one day would be the determinant of the measure, now 'man-hours' are calculated on the basis of universally applicable units of clock time. In industrial societies time has become the measure of work where work was the measure of time in earlier historical periods. The German *Tagwerk* (day[s]work) used to be such a measure: variable and context dependent. It entailed the knowledge that a prime piece of land is easier to work than one on a stony hill. The *Tagwerk* as a measure thus varied with the quality of the land in a similar way that temporal hours used to vary with the seasons. The calculation of 'man-hours', on the other hand, like the clock time units on which it is based, is an invariable, standardised measure that can be applied universally regardless of context. This time is a context-

independent phenomenon. It is no longer based on events, processes and
tasks, or on the 'time proper to them' but on clock time units.

> Work and time are "cleansed" of orientations and meanings which are
> antithetical to the capitalist work-discipline. In the process of industrialisa-
> tion the cycles of work and relaxation, which formerly accompanied the
> nature and task-bound rhythms, attain their own metric dynamic and
> gradually become indifferent towards traditional contexts of meaning and
> significance. (Hohn 1984: 150; transl. E. King and B. Adam)

It is this process of de-contextualisation which makes Giddens (1981: 9,
134) argue that clock time – as measured duration, freely exchangeable
with all other time – is the 'very expression of commodified time'. In
societies where time is exchanged as a commodity, not merely time but
life and work become divisible into a multiplicity of units. Working time
becomes separated from break time and leisure time, sleeping time from
waking, eating or working time, production time from that of the market,
the patients' time from that of their doctors. Because time is not only
stratified but also used as an abstract medium for exchange, the time of
some members of such a society may be deemed more important or costly
than that of others. Thus it is important to recognise that it is not time
per se that is being paid for, that it is not *having* time in quantitative
terms but the money value that is being put on it which matters. This in
turn relates to its use and the extent to which the control over such usage
is discretionary or imposed.

Despite this inextricable link between time and money, the relation is a
complex one to untangle. Time as money, argues Thompson (1967: 95), is
a new development which has to be understood in relation to the
'marriage of convenience' between puritanism and capitalism and their
concomitant socialisations towards time-thrift and time-discipline. The
time-management in industry known as Taylorism serves as a prime
illustration. It exemplifies the monetary attitude to time as something
that needs to be spent and allocated with scientific precision. Every
second of the workers' time has to be used to its fullest potential. Over a
long period of industrial conflict, members of industrial socities have
been socialised into treating time like money, in other words, not to waste
and squander it. We have taken on board the Protestant ethic and
accepted, albeit to varying degrees, that it is our (Christian) duty to be
frugal with it, to use it to the full, and to manage it with the utmost
diligence (Weber 1989: 157). On closer inspection, however, we discover
that time is not at all like money. Whilst time passes outside our control,
money can be consumed at an intentional pace or it can be left to
accumulate. Depending on our framework of analysis, time is constituted
or a quantity to be used, allocated, or exchanged. As a quantity it can

only be used up; unlike money it cannot be saved or stored, with the exception of 'time off' which can be accumulated within one year in the form of holidays. Hohn (1984: 157) suggests that the idea that time is money is only meaningful in its reversal, namely that money is time. The unemployed, for example, have a lot of time at their disposal which is of little money value to them whilst the possession of money enables people to buy the time of others. Hohn not only reverses the idea that time is money but links the value of time to its usage and to whether or not a money value can be put on it. However, whilst the value of money stands in a direct relation to quantity – the more the better – this relation is far more paradoxical with respect to time. It is always desirable to have more time when one has *not* got any; yet having time decreases its value. As the situation of prisoners, unemployed people, and others with 'plenty of time on their hands' shows, time abundance is accorded a low social value and scarcity a high one. The less time we have the more precious it becomes. Time is like a currency. Its value fluctuates with supply and demand. Apart from scarcity, its value seems further related to status, wealth, and authority. The professionals' time is more important than that of their clients and the time of service givers is usually valued more highly than that of their recipients except in cases where the status, wealth, or authority of the latter exceeds that of the former. In these situations the recipient may buy the time of the professional or be conceived as having the right to structure or dispose over the time of the service giver. More generally, the wealthy can buy the labour, service, and skills of others *as* time, whilst agents of the state and persons in a position of authority have the right to time-structure the lives of those under their control. We can, for example, buy health service time to get immediate attention. In such a case money reverses the importance of the time of the doctor to that of the recipient of the service. Governments have the right to legislate opening times of social amenities, the minimum age for getting married, and the number of years young people are to be compulsorily educated. Teachers have a legal right to structure and control the time of the pupils, and employers set out their rights of multiple time controls over their employees in legally binding contracts of employment.

It has thus become apparent that time control may be bought and sold on the labour market, that it may be implied in social roles, or legislated for as a statutory right, and that conflict situations in industry make the nature of that control more visible. But, what is it we 'own' to use, allocate, buy, sell, save, budget, fill, lose, or kill when we 'have time'? Regardless of how we apply these ideas, they seem invariably to relate to a quantity: to minutes, hours, days, weeks, months, years, or to stretches of our life-time and our social past and future. Whilst the created clock time is the common denominator there is, however, a need to further distinguish between its use as a resource and that of a commodity. Giddens therefore wants us to differentiate between commodified time and time as a resource. He wants the latter understood in relation to our finitude of existence and the former as a mediator between goods and labour. He suggests that commodified time, like all other commodified aspects of our lives, is characterised by a double existence: lived and commodified, with the latter being dominant in our society today. Where Giddens stresses the double existence, others emphasise multiple clusters as being characteristic of industrial time. It is these, and the question of power, to which I shall now turn.

Many writers suggest that time as a tool for social control has to be conceptualised through a cluster of characteristics, that one aspect or a duality will not suffice. Thompson (1967), in a classic essay on 'Time, work-discipline, and industrial capitalism', suggests that industrial time is to be understood in conjunction with paid employment, the division of labour, and a social stratification into roles. Where these conditions prevail the task-orientation has been replaced by that of measured time. 'This measurement,' writes Thompson (1967: 61), 'embodies a simple relationship. Those who are employed experience a distinction between their employer's time and their "own" time. And the employer must *use* the time of his labour, and see it not wasted: not the task but the value of time when reduced to money is dominant. Time is now currency: it is not passed but spent.' His work thus supports the above analyses on the commodification of time. Like Weber and many others, Thompson (1967) suggests that it was the puritan ethic in conjunction with the capitalist mode of production that utilised clock time in this character- istic way. What is important to appreciate here is that the existence of *clock time on its own is not enough* to bring about work relations that are characterised by time-thrift and time-discipline. This is demonstrated by Needham's (1981, 1988) work on past Chinese societies where time was measured with the aid of the clock without being related to as an independent reality to be sold and exchanged on the labour market. Where Thompson stresses the division of labour, paid employment, and social roles, Heinemann and Ludes (1978) emphasise the process of abstraction and severance from context. They show how abstract clock time forms a coherent part of our contemporary social system where social relations have become context free and anonymous. They argue that clock time has to be understood as part of a wider severance from concrete events and contexts, as a shift from a personal to an abstract economic exchange.

Thus, in the first place trust is transferred to trust in the value constancy of
certain materials (e.g. gold). Eventually money/currency becomes an
abstract unit of calculation, the trust in persons or substances is replaced by
the trust in the functional capacity of the economy of the social system.
Money becomes neutral as regards people and things. There follows a
severance of the motivation from the assumption of purpose for action and
therefore a generalisation of the motivational background, which engenders
a uniform motivation, effective for all to participate in the system's economy.
(Heinemann and Ludes 1978: 222; transl. E. King and B. Adam)

To characterise our contemporary Western social relations, they use the
triple imagery of 'de-materialisation' of interactions; severance, of social
relations from their contexts; and event-free chronology with a focus on
an open future. None of these, they insist, must be seen in isolation. Their
approach is underlined by Hohn's (1984) historical investigation which
shows this process of abstraction to be generalised across the range of
social relations in our society. Hohn's evidence suggests further that this
development is accompanied by a separating, stratifying, and breaking
into uniform component units of what used to be inseparable. His work
shows how labour, production, and market time, for example, have
become differentiated and how the work rhythm, after having been
broken down into discrete units, is replaced by an abstract, context free,
uniform metronomic beat. Hohn thus confirms both Thompson's (1967)
and Heinemann and Ludes's (1978) analyses when he argues that the
capitalist work-discipline abstracts both work and time from their
contextual meanings and imposes an independent metric dynamic.
Nowotny (1975) adds a further dimension to these thoughts by suggesting
that such a freeing from meaning and content is achievable only through
expression in number values. Mathematical expression allows for both
its ability to be divided and translated. The abstract measure, she
suggests further, has to be understood in conjunction with time being
valued both in its own right and for its economic value. Luhmann's
(1982c) conceptualisation of world-time needs to be added here since it
overlaps with many of the aspects of time which have just been
elaborated with reference to industrial time. To Luhmann, the abstract
measure in conjunction with the objectified time-frame which he
classifies as chronology is a very recent historical development. He
identifies a change from an indistinguishable fusion of events and time –
time in events – via objectification and abstraction to the linear
conceptualisation of world-time. For world-time, Luhmann (1982c: 302)
argues, content is irrelevant and 'the connection between what lies in the
past and what lies in the future becomes in principle contingent.' He
identifies this world-time with four features: independence from context
and content; a chronological dating and timing grid; translatability,

namely a transivity that allows comparisons of non-simultaneous stretches of time; and mental reversibility by which we are able to repeat what is fundamentally irreversible. World-time and industrial time converge.

What emerges as significant here is the need to recognise industrial time as a resource with both a use and an exchange value. As such it forms an integral part of societies where the social interactions and exchanges have generally become independent of context and content, and where the time structuring is based on standardised, invariable units. Time in such societies has become stratified and separated into family, work, leisure, production, and market time, to name just a few. Chronological calendar and clock time, related to as being time *per se*, in terms of an independent, objective reality, forms the central link between all these aspects. Only in this compound form, I want to suggest, is it meaningful to speak of the control of time.

Giddens's analysis, whilst corresponding with aspects of those of Thompson, Heinemann and Ludes, Hohn, and Nowotny, simultaneously cuts across these. He has different foci, asks different questions, and ends up with a fundamentally different understanding of industrial social time. Giddens's distinction between relations of high presence or absence and the concomitant time-space distanciation, seem closely related to Heinemann and Ludes's conceptualisation of a historical development towards context and person independence. Both are historical interpretations of a historical process along very similar lines. Giddens argues here that in contradistinction to traditional small communities modern social relations can be conducted in the absence of persons. In small traditional communities, he suggests, time is not separated from the substance of activities, and social relations are conducted with co-presents on the basis of kinship relations and tradition. Modern social relations, on the other hand, no longer depend on such a high presence availability. The combination of writing and other forms of stored information, abstract exchange values, and abstract, quantitative time *per se*, allow for interactions with absent persons across time and space. In other words, it enables interactions with peoples of the past and the future and with contemporaries half-way across the globe, thus vastly increasing the 'time-space distanciation' of modern societies.

Giddens wants us to understand this stretching across spatial and historical distance in relation to power, and he locates the source of this power in the increased storage capacity of information. In modern society, Giddens argues, this power rests with the state because the conjunction of increased 'time-distanciation' and increased storage capacity of information constitutes the basis for the state's capacity for surveillance. In this context Giddens relates time to stored information.

This in turn is conceptualised as power, based on the capacity for surveillance. Time here is conceptualised as a kind of receptacle that may be filled with storable information whilst simultaneously serving as a quantitative measure of power based on what Giddens calls the 'authoritative resources' of a society. The degree of time-space distantiation, he suggests, stands in a direct relation to power and the reproduction of structural relations of domination. This, however, is not the only way Giddens links time to relations of power. In addition to time-space distantiation and authoritative resources, Giddens theorises the relation of time and power through 'allocative resources' and the 'reproduction of structural relations of exploitation'. Whilst Foucault's work plays an important role in Giddens's focus on domination, it is Marx's work on commodification on which he draws for his analysis on time and power relations based on allocative resources. Since Marx plays such a dominant role in the analysis of both Giddens and Hohn it is not surprising that their interpretations of this particular aspect of social time largely coincide. Giddens, however, specifically stresses the *mediating* role of time over and above Hohn's emphasis on abstraction and context independence. Time as a mediating link between goods and labour is crucial to Giddens since it is the units of time that make values of commodities divisible and quantifiable, and permit their common existence as interchangeable commodities. He distinguishes with Marx between surplus production and the production of surplus value. Only in the latter, Giddens (1981: 119) suggests, do commodities exist in the exchange, not in their own right, however, but as mediated exchange values, which in turn depends upon the temporal equation of units of labour. Giddens's triple imagery is one of commodified form of production, commodified labour, and commodified time. This time, like all other commodities, he suggests, is characterised by the double existence of the lived aspect and that of the abstract, pure value. His formulation of the relation of this double existence to clock time merits quoting at length.

Time as lived time, as the substance of the lived experience of *durée* of Being, becomes 'formless duration'. With the expansion of capitalism, this is what time seems to *be*, just as money seems to be the universal standard of value of all things. Time as pure duration, as disconnected from the materiality of experience, comes to be perceived, in direct opposition to the actual state of things, as real, 'objective' time, because like money it is expressed in a universal and public mode. This universal and public mode, again like money, is nothing other than its own quantification as a standard measure standing at the axis of a host of transformation/mediation relations. The commodification of time, and its differentiation from further processes of the commodification of space, hold the key to the deepest transformations of

day to day social life that are brought about by the emergence of capitalism.
(Giddens 1981: 131)

Focusing on the main features of Giddens's approach to time and power,
we note that unlike the other theorists he does *not* conceptualise time as a
resource in this connection. He sees time as neither an authoritative nor
an allocative resource. With respect to time-distanciation and the
reproduction of domination, information is the authoritative resource
exploitable for surveillance and the domination of people. Time here
serves as a measure, in terms of chronological distance and stacked
information, of domination by which we can differentiate societies. In the
case of commodified time, the allocative resources are conceptualised as
being natural materials, technology, and artefacts on the one hand
(Giddens 1981: 51), and capital and labour on the other (p. 118). All may
be possessed individually or collectively, and stored for the production of
surplus. Again time is *not* understood as a resource but as mediator of
surplus value between the resources. Only as *Dasein*, as 'being unto
death', is time given the status of a resource. But Giddens's analysis of
power does not extend to this resource. Only when time seems to be a
quantitative formless resource like money or currency, when it appears to
be an 'objective reality', does he connect it to social relations of power.

As both measure and mediator Giddens's time conceptualisation thus
does not transcend the dominant, common-sense conceptualisation, the
very aspect he sets out critically to analyse. His linkage of time-
distanciation and power, for example, only becomes meaningful in a
society like ours where time has become separated from the activities, the
temporality, and the timing of social life: where it is conceptualised as a
quantity. Time-space distanciation as a measure of a society's 'stretching
over time' entails the prior understanding of time as a quantitative
measure and as a boundary within which life is enacted. It is meaningless
in a society without such objectified time and therefore an inappropriate
tool for understanding any but our own contemporary, industrial society.
Like Marx, Giddens presents a critique of the 'seeming independence' of
time as an objective reality, unconnected to events and activites. But,
unlike Marx, he leaves it as a statement and does not connect this
reification explicitly to the relations of power. He makes the points
without making them a coherent part of his theory, with the result that
he, like the nineteenth-century economists that Marx set out to criticise,
does not get beyond the quantitative aspects of commodity production.
He fails to make explicit the commodification–reification–alienation–
power connection which was central to Marx's analysis of commodification and which emerges strongly from this exploration.

Whilst Giddens provides by far the most interesting, sophisticated, and

novel analysis of time and power, there are niggling gaps at the very
points where, to me, connections would be most interesting. Many
aspects are left implicit where an explication would have been highly
illuminating. One can only speculate that this is due to his deliberately
not focusing on time, not seeking a theory of time as a pre-condition to
his social theory, but merely using aspects of it when and where they
apply.

Historical and anthropological research, for example, have shown that
time *per se* is only conceptualised as a resource in societies like ours;
societies which have not only created clock time, but relate to that creation
as *being* time and organise their social life by it. In other words where clock
time in all its aspects has permeated the conceptualisations, experiences,
and organisation of social life. *Dasein* appears thus not to be a time
resource in all societies, but only those that have reified time. It is the
reified time that I want to conceptualise fundamentally in terms of
relations of power. This leads back to my suggestion that it is not in the
aspect of control, not even externally imposed control, that we should seek
to understand contemporary industrial social time as intimately tied to
power, but in the extent to which clock time has become reified,
internalised, and imposed. In other words, social time needs to be
conceptualised in terms of relations of power to the extent that clock time
as time has become an independent, context-free value, a social and
economic reality that structures, controls, disciplines, and provides norms
for our social life. Only in that form, I want to suggest, does it become
meaningful to locate power in the capacity to dominate the time of others.
The question of who controls the time of whom can only be posed after
time has become conceptualised as something we can use, allocate, spend,
or fill. In societies that do not conceptualise time *per se*, interactions and
phenomena are subject to social control as well, and these may have time
embedded within them, but it would be meaningless to speak in such a
context of the control of people's time. As transformative capacity, I
would argue, these aspects are better conceptualised in terms of
transcendence, keeping the power relations with respect to time restricted
to societies organised primarily through clock time. Where control over
the time aspects of social life is attempted rather than over time as such,
transcendence is going to be used as the more appropriate key concept
through which to understand such human endeavours.

Before turning our attention to issues of time transcendence, however,
we shall explore the phenomenon of waiting. So far the focus has been a
wide one. I have investigated a diversity of timing and time control in a
multiplicity of situations. In the next few pages the focus narrows to a
single phenomenon to examine once more the time aspects discussed so
far and to foreshadow those that are to follow.

Waiting

Our awareness of the complexity of social time beyond the symbol and the quantitative measure can be enhanced by focusing on the phenomenon of waiting. In our society waiting entails the knowledge of things, processes, and the time structures of nature; the implicit acceptance of values, norms and relations of power; and an awareness of the transcendence of personal life-spans and of species-specific time.

> The essential temporality of everyday life means that humans experience not only the passing of time, but also the necessity to wait until one temporal process has run its course in order for another to begin. All humans wait, and in the fullest sense of the term, only humans wait. Waiting is an experience based on the interpretation and understanding of the temporal structures of events and human desires. If you or I wish to brew a cup of coffee, each of us must wait until the water heats, passes through the coffee grounds, gathers in a cup, mixes with the cream and sugar, and cools sufficiently. The poorest pauper and the most powerful politician must each wait for the coffee to brew! To want a cup of coffee is to subordinate yourself to the time required to brew one. It does not matter if you will miss your plane or lose your job, the coffee brews on its own schedule, and you wait. (Weigert 1981: 227)

The waiting described here is about knowledge and expectancy. It demonstrates that we know the unique time-scale of natural things, artefacts, and their processes. It shows that we know what physicists express in the second law of thermodynamics. We know, proportionate to the amount in the kettle, how long it will take for the water to come to the boil. We know the time-scale of the brewing cycle, and that of the cooling. We know that the successful execution of brewing a cup of (real) coffee depends on the appropriate sequence and timing of all the necessary actions. Knowing it, we can even use that period of waiting for another activity. Far from being incessant, undifferentiated flux depending on humans to get together and structure them, natural processes have an inherent rhythmic time-structure. If they did not have time embedded in them, a time proper to them which is demarcated by beginnings and ends, much of human and animal waiting would not exist. Our exploration of natural time has shown the idea that only humans wait to be misplaced anthropocentrism.

Knowing the time of things and processes forms an integral part of our everyday living. We know the time-scale of our own and our pets' pregnancies, of the winter cold, the moon's cycle, the train journey between Cardiff and London, and (in principle at least) the first-class letter. Taking natural rhythms as basic, Gurvitch (1963) argues the need to extend this knowledge to all 'things social', and the necessity for sociologists to take note of it.

> The sociologists cannot ignore indeed that each society, each social class, each particular group, each microsocial element (e.g., each We and each relation to others) or further, each level in the depth of social reality (from the morphological base to the collective mentality) – indeed, every social activity (mythical, religious, magical, or economic, or technological or juridical, or political, or cognitive or moral or educational) has the tendency to operate in a time proper to itself. (Gurvitch 1963: 174)

Knowing it we can anticipate, and we wait.

Knowing the times proper to things, processes, and events is, of course, fundamental to human time-reckoning systems. We have to know those times before we can recognise them as regular and consistent in relation to others that are faster or slower. It is not their regular, rhythmic occurrence, however, but their consistency and the recognition of the latter that matters. Cooking rice, for example, is not a regular occurrence but a process that is consistent with reference to other processes and as such is used as a measure for a short time-span in many rural rice-growing communities. Thus it is the time proper to processes, their consistent beginnings and ends, that provide us with standards against which other processes, actions, and events can be compared, planned, assessed, and measured. It is against this time measure that the clock time has to be understood. The latter relates no longer to any time proper to things and processes, but beats its own created, independent time. With the invention of the pendulum clock all context dependence has been transcended, a new human time has been created and this machine time, as I have argued above, has come to be identified as *being* time, as time *per se*.

The knowledge of the time-scale proper to the processes of nature, society, machines, and the clock needs to be distinguished from knowing the *right* time for action. Both may involve waiting, but whilst we wait in the former for processes to take their course, in the latter we wait for the appropriate moments so that we may interact with them. Thus, to know the right time to plant potatoes, to harvest apples, to swim in the lake, to wean the baby, to teach the child to read, or to send the Christmas parcel, means we can successfully act, interact, and function in our daily lives. Waiting for the right time may, however, not only refer to species-specific times and the time *in* situations, but also to the socially created units of clocks and calendars. Thus, the right time to go to the bank in Britain is during its opening hours between 9.30 am and 3.30 pm; and the right time to celebrate Christmas and open presents is on the 24th or 25th of December, depending whether you are German or British. This right time is not only fundamentally context dependent but in many cases also socially normed. What constitutes the right time to take A-level exams is not an invariable date on the calendar and time on the clock, but the specific time and place set by the appropriate examination board. For members of societies that are not structured by the clock, the right time to be at the healer with a sick child, to arrive at a wedding or funeral is socially defined in relation to other collectively known time references in the environment. Waiting for the right time is also a component of communication. Over and above the synchronisation, timing and pauses without which there could be no transmission of meaning, waiting takes yet another form. Meaning cannot be communicated if everybody speaks at once; it depends on people taking turns in speaking and listening since communication is a serial, single-order medium. Taking turns here does not only serve a utilitarian purpose, but it relates to what we encapsulate in the concept of tact. Small children have to learn to wait their turn and the appropriate, tactful timing of their communications and actions. We are not born with this ability but have to acquire it as part of growing up.

Waiting in relation to the shortage of time and 'structural overload' is a contribution to the understanding from systems theory. Only so many possibilities, it is argued there, can be actualised in any co-ordinated interaction between systems. In systems theory, waiting is not only conceptualised as a problem of synchronisation but as an aspect of the need to prioritise actions according to their urgency and value which, in turn, may be accelerated or delayed by similar considerations of others. The more complex the social organisation, argue Luhmann (1971), Bergmann (1981a: 166–171), and Moore (1963: ch. 2) from a different theoretical perspective, the higher the proportion of enforced waiting. Conceptualised as a zero sum, only so much is possible in one working day, for example; the rest has to wait. The waiting and the perceived shortage of time, however, are recognised as standing in direct relation, not to that which can be done, but to that which we feel should be achieved or would like to be able to accomplish. It thus relates to both potentialities and the whole interaction network within which we are fundamentally located.

Thus, we wait because things, beings, and institutions operate in a time proper to themselves, and we wait for the right time to interact with them. The interactions then entail that we wait to take our turn, and that we wait because not everything is possible all at once. Yet waiting is not a neutral phenomenon as we shall discover when we investigate who waits for whom for how long. This aspect is most easily recognised in situations as waiting for the doctor, the solicitor, or the local member of parliament, where, if we were to let them wait, an apology would be necessary. Here, a certain inequality enters those interactions of mutual dependence, and the question of who waits for whom becomes important. In these situations waiting is intimately bound up with social status and power, and can be understood as a ritualised expression of asymmetrical social relations (Schwartz 1979: 842–9). In such waiting situations power may be linked to the immunity from waiting through the possession of such resources as money, influence, or expertise. Alternatively it may be associated with who determines waiting for whom, the right to impose waiting, and the duty to wait.

Frankenberg's (1988) writing on the symbolism of healing serves as an example here. He describes medicine as a waiting culture, where the asymmetry between the patients' and the doctors' time is of deep symbolic significance and where the severity of the treatment is reflected in the length of time patients have to wait. Making persons wait may not only signify the importance of the one, but also signal the disregard for the other. Social security offices, law courts, and job centres serve to illustrate this point. Looked at in this way waiting becomes expressive of relations of power. Schwartz (1979: 841) proposes that 'the distribution of waiting time coincides with distribution of power'. In waiting, he argues, usable time is transformed into a resource that expresses the value of the service. As such it can be allocated, controlled, and saved. Frankenberg and Schwartz thus seem to agree that waiting is expressive of the scarcity of a resource and that waiting time is proportional to its social value. It is further suggested by both Schwartz (1979: 860–7) and Lauer (1981: 99) that in situations where waiting time is transformed into a resource it serves to validate and legitimate existing power relations. By making people wait, the power of the person, the service, or the role is maintained and enhanced.

Power of a different kind enters into waiting for some future benefit and doing something now for reward at some later period. Such deferred gratification forms an integral part of growing up and becoming socialised. Children must learn to postpone pleasure now for success and reward in the future. This entails a certain trust, knowledge, and expectancy of the future; in other words, the future has first to attain reality status. Cottle and Klineberg's (1974: 73–7) work shows this to be a very slow incremental development in children. They further demonstrate a link between deferred gratification patterns and occupational classes. Deferral, they argue, is most likely to occur when future rewards are both reasonably certain, and to some degree under a person's control. However, they suggest that such conditions are rarely found among those who live in poverty (pp. 187–95). Hohn (1984) presents a particularly powerful argument here that gives depth to the more neutral results of studies which establish that the poor and members of the lower classes are less future orientated. In agreement with the studies he begins his analysis by showing that those who hold the long-term future perspective and who value this type of waiting are the structurally strong classes. He then argues that deferred gratification entails that one is in a position to have a trusting relationship to the future and he differentiates the idea of security from that of need and necessity. Hohn (1984: 157) contrasts the securely based relation to the future, built on capital and the fixed rules of finance and credit, with the fundamental uncertainty of the labourer who remains linked to the life-long satisfaction of immediate needs. The distinction is an important one. It separates the capacity to be concerned with the security of the future from the situation where some people are forced to attend to the most pressing needs because their resources are limited to their labour power. Hohn grounds the deferred gratification debate firmly in modern capitalist societies and provides a powerful twist to the studies that focus merely on class differences.

> To be concerned therefore always implies the capacity of disposal over time. The concern about future income and the need to exchange work for a wage are not exhausted by a contrast between the long- and short-term planning perspective. The difference is not merely about the potential for planning the future and designs for present action, but corresponds generally to the articulation of the basic temporal pattern of capitalist industrial societies, which emerges with the allocation of labour power on the free market. This basic pattern is founded on power secured by the social structure. . . (Hohn 1984: 149; transl. E. King and B. Adam)

Hohn agrees with Heinemann and Ludes (1978: 238) that this time-based, structurally secured power forms both the most important and most normatively binding synchronisation mechanism of our contemporary social activity. We need to be aware, however, that the social meaning and evaluation of this type of waiting do not necessarily extend to other societies since it is particularly culture specific. It is, argues Weigert (1981: 229–30), a 'culturally valued type of waiting', by which persons are assessed in their self-control, morality, and even their humanity.

Reflections

As the central aspect of contemporary Western life, time in its multiple expressions needs to be understood not only with reference to clocks and calendars but also to norms, values, and social control; whilst the quantitative, reified measure and the commodity have to be appreciated in conjunction with social relations of power. To seek control over the conditions of existence seems to be integral to human life generally. Through it humans extend their temporal horizons and transcend their species-specific, biological aspects of time. Whether such control is to be conceptualised in terms of transcendence or relations of power, however, seems to be dependent on specific contexts. Not whether time is under the control of self or others but whether clock time has become related to as *being* time seems to determine whether or not time itself is controlled. Power only becomes the irreducibly human time-aspect where this reification has become both condition and outcome of social life, where the creation has come to be related to as real and subsequently gets used as a quantity, a measure, a resource, and a commodity.

Waiting entails knowledge of time. But, as our brief exploration has demonstrated in concentrated form, it entails a knowledge that bears little relation to traditional and contemporary conceptualisations of social time. It affirms that time is not exhausted by its symbolic formation and expression. It demonstrates that the time proper to things, events, and processes as well as their time structuring is fundamentally taken account of in social life. It shows that the source of what constitutes the right time may range from the most purely physical to the most exclusively cultural. It makes us recognise that some of that knowledge is deeply sedimented and taken for granted, that the shared meanings are not neccessarily available to us at a discursive level of consciousness. It allows us to see that order, organisation, control, power, resource, commodity, concept, measure, horizon, external frame, and internal age are *not* available choices that may be abstracted for study on an either/or basis. They are all simultaneously implied in any one aspect on which we have focused. This realisation impresses on us once more that the social sciences' exclusion of natural time and the time of 'dead things'; their abstraction of bits, and choices on the basis of dualisms and even multiple dualities are highly unsuitable for a conceptualisation of human social time. It leaves us in no doubt that human social time extends far beyond the time of clocks and calendars: that it is a fact of life and fundamental to existence. As such, however, it is not merely accepted but constantly transcended.

6

Time Transcended

Human time is characterised by transcendence and this is expressed in many distinct ways. All human action, for example, is embedded in a continuity of past, present, and future, extends into the past and future; and constitutes those horizons whilst binding them in a present. Habits and traditions, goals, wishes and intentions, values and meanings, even pragmatic action, are only possible with such temporal extensions. Through our symbolic, artefactual, and technological creations we have transcended our species–specific link with space, time, and motion. We relate to each other on the basis of timeless values and meanings and actively seek the permanent, the enduring and even the time-reversible. In contemporary Western societies we passed the boundaries of our planet and colonised the hours of darkness. This human transcendence of time, I suggest, has to be sought in the relationship to our own transience and finitude. Before exploring the implications of our conceptual journey in the final chapter, we shall therefore need to investigate the human relationship to the temporality of *Dasein* and to time as past, present, and future and to examine our findings with reference to widely accepted social science views such as the association of linear and cyclical time perspectives with traditional and modern societies respectively.

Life unto death and beyond

All rhythmically organised beings, as we have seen earlier, extend beyond the present. In human beings this natural principle is centrally linked to our relationship to the finitude of existence; a relationship that varies with individuals, societies, and historical periods. In the encounter with death, we have not merely realised the extension of our present within the birth–death horizon but postulated an existence beyond death. We have constructed our being eternally and surrounded ourselves with symbols

of permanence. The awareness of finitude, the conscious search for
transcendence, and the construction of immutability have therefore to be
conceptualised as coeval.

Death unites us with all living things. The foreknowledge of death we
seem to share with only a few of the 'higher' animals such as elephants
and, according to our current knowledge, we are the only beings that
express that knowledge symbolically. Our life is lived in relation to our
finitude. This is what Heidegger is referring to when he proposes that
transcendence is the essence of *Dasein*. As concern, resolve, anticipation
and projection towards our own possible existence, Heidegger understands human existence as 'being ahead of itself'. To him transcendence is
the ultimate basis of all human knowing and behaving. *Dasein's* total
penetration by birth and death and the concomitant fear of non-existence
are our ontological condition.

Knowledge of finitude, however, changes the nature of being. 'No
doubt death had been something familiar to man all through the long
ages of prehistory,' writes Dunne (1973: 15), 'but in the first age of
recorded history he began to strive against it, he began to strive for
immortality. The failure of this striving led him to a much deeper
awareness of his mortality; it tempered his spirit.' Dunne goes on to
suggest that once death has been encountered and a relationship to it
developed, life too is no longer purely lived. It becomes an achievement.
This implies that once death is related to, direct and unmediated
existence is no longer possible. Having a relationship to death thus marks
a departure from the way other species appear to us to encounter death.
In the relationship to mortality and the cycle of life, both death and
existence are transcended. It is in that relationship, Dunne further
argues, that we have to find the human spirit. Not a thing or essence, but
more like Elias's fifth dimension, this human spirit, as the relationship to
all aspects of our existence, may be conceptualised as part of the process
of imposing meaning. Thus, neither in the fact that we are aware that we
have to die nor in our experiencing death in others and the recognition of
our own finitude, but in our having to reflect on it, having a relationship
to it, imposing meaning on it, and in having to take an attitude to it, do
we find the source of transcendence and human time.

Because of its centrality to human being, death has played a central
role in ancient cultures. It provided the pivotal point between earthly
existence and its transcendence, between finitude and the continuity of
being in a different realm. In the mind, death can be endured and through
it the meaning of life revealed. This idea is basic to human thought and
underlies the ancient practices of rituals and meditation through which
death can be experienced without dying (Dunne 1973: 5–46; Grof and
Grof 1980; 1–33, Pelletier 1982: 224–54). All of them involve a passage

from life to death to new life, and point to the relativity and imperma-nence of the boundaries to our individual being. In the records and reports of those experiences there occur journeys through danger, loss of body and self, and consequent rebirth to a new level of consciousness. These phases apply to the ritual death of ancient Shamans and the descriptions of the passage from death to new life in the Egyptian and Tibetian 'death books' (Evans-Wentz 1957), to A-bomb victims and people who have faced clinical death (Grof and Grof 1980; Hampe 1979; Pelletier 1982), and to some schizophrenic episodes and LSD-induced states (Grof 1985). In the following account, where a woman reports her experience of being involved in a frontal collision of her car with a lorry, all the points raised so far, and those that follow, are united into a whole. It bridges human experience from earliest recorded history to the present. Her account should not however, be thought of as an isolated example. It has been chosen as one amongst many because it typifies experiences that people undergo in the face of death (Hampe 1979; Heim 1892; Kübler-Ross 1986; Moody 1977; Noyes 1971, 1972; Osis and Haraldsson 1982).

During the several seconds that my car was in motion, I had an experience that seemed to span centuries. I rapidly moved from sheer terror and overwhelming fear for my life to a profound knowledge that I would die. Ironically, with that knowledge came the deepest sense of peace and serenity that I have ever encountered. It was as though I had moved from the periphery of my being – the body that contained me – to the very centre of myself, a place that was imperturbable, totally quiet and at rest. The mantra that I had previously been using in meditation sprang into my consciousness and revolved automatically, with an ease that I had never before known. Time seemed to have disappeared as I watched sequences from my life passing before me like a movie, quite rapidly, but with amazing detail. When I reached the point of death, it seemed that I was facing an opaque curtain of some kind. The momentum of the experience carried me, still completely calm, through the curtain and I realized that it had not been a point of termination, but rather of transition. The only way that I can describe the next sensation is to say that every part of me, whatever I was at that moment, felt without question a far-reaching and encompassing continuum beyond what I had previously thought of as death. It was as though the force that had moved me toward death and then past it would endlessly continue to carry me, through ever-expanding vistas.

It was at this point that my car hit a truck with great impact. As it came to rest, I looked around and realized that by some miracle I was still alive. And then, an amazing thing happened. As I sat in the midst of the tangled metal, I felt my individual boundaries begin to melt. I started to merge with everything around me – with the policemen, the wreck, the workers with crowbars trying to liberate me, the ambulance, the flowers on a nearby hedge, and the television cameramen. Somewhere, I could see and feel my injuries, but they did not seem to have anything to do with me; they were merely part of a rapidly expanding network that included much more than my body . . .'. (quoted in Grof and Grof 1980: 10–11)

This particular death experience not only corroborates the thousands of reports that are collated in contemporary research and Jung's studies of the unconscious, but matches the descriptions in myths, ancient death books, and mystic experiences of enlightenment. It reveals the relativity of our individual boundary and our embeddedness in an existence of different temporal dimensions. Whilst Heidegger's conceptualisation of *Dasein* provides us with a theory of the transcendence of the present *within* the boundary to individual existence, research into death experiences shows the transcendence of these personal delineations. This theoretical research, Jung's psycho-analytical work, Grof's (1985) empirical exploration into psychedelic states and his experimental work with holotropic therapy, point to the existence of a collective unconscious that connects individuals to all humanity, other life forms, and the cosmos. From this understanding, *Dasein* as the permeation of our individually based, finite past and future in the present becomes only one aspect of being. Spiritual and cosmic transcendence emerge as equally fundamental to that of individual existence, whilst admittedly being less accessible to us in our everyday lives.

If we allow ourselves to take such accounts seriously, we are faced with conceptual difficulties. Taken on board they cannot be merely added to existing knowledge. Accepting them as valid radically alters our understanding of reality as I shall show later. At this point I want to give merely a first glance at this necessary shift in understanding by picking out two aspects that are common to all the descriptions, experiences, and rituals of death: the suspension of time and the loss of identity as the individual merges with the whole. I see the two as inextricably linked. That which we know ourselves to be – individuals that are delineated against others and the environment with boundaries of space, time, and matter – gets absorbed and enfolded back into the whole. This physically and temporally bounded being, which we conceptualise as a material entity, emerges as neither separate nor separable from the whole that constitutes it. The cosmic whole in turn reveals itself not as timeless but time*full*. It seems to encompass all of time, space, and matter, to unite all the infinite, defining boundaries into one. Once absorbed back into this whole, individuals with their species-specific time lose their meaning. Their being, however, appears not lost but absorbed in its totality, enfolded back because the boundaries no longer apply. Such transcendence poses problems for a Newtonian, Cartesian cosmology. It is not easily integrated into an understanding of reality based on single, isolated bits in motion and mutually exclusive dualities. Clocks and steam engines are inappropriate metaphors with which to grasp such dissolution of individual boundaries and their enfoldment in a cosmic whole. The irreconcilable paradoxes dissolve, however, with the contemporary natural science understanding I outlined earlier. Being, as it is revealed in those encounters with death, is not only consistent with the cosmology of some leading contemporary physicists but also with that of Eastern mysticism and mythological cosmologies, be they contemporary or ancient ones. With modern science beginning to converge with the rest of the world's cosmologies, meaning has become potentially global.

We are united as humans in our experiences of death and its existential paradoxes, but we are separated by the way we relate to these. How we differ cannot be the focus here, but a brief look at our Western approach to death seems warranted since it will help us better to understand the distinctiveness of our contemporary Western social time. In our society we treat *Dasein* as a resource and death as something to be averted and controlled. Where the dominant aim is the extension of life rather than a transcendence of death, fear more than anything else seems to mark the attitude to the death–life unity through which living beings extend their present and ensure continuity of their existence. We associate death with the end of time and with such words as always, absolute, final, forever, and no return. Our practices suggest that death, for any but the extremely old, is something to be averted, avoided, cheated, controlled, refused, and shunned.

> The dominant modern response to the relentless approach of death is massive denial. Ban the word from our everyday conversation and death is no longer a social reality. Hide dead bodies from public view by keeping them inside hospitals, funeral 'homes', or beautifully landscaped country scenes like cemeteries, and death is no longer a public event. Eliminate all public displays of mourning by survivors, like black clothes, flowers or ribbons on the door to the deceased one's home, or periods of isolation, and death is no longer commemorated in our lives. Finally, when the dead body must be handled, let specialists do all in their power to make it look alive and be the centre of a bureaucratically and commercially transformed exercise in the multimillion dollar industry dedicated to the American way of death. (Weigert 1981: 235)

Today's dying have to be re-defined and re-placed. They get taken from the community to places for the sick. Where in earlier times a clear knowledge of impending death was essential for a proper and dignified death, today it is deemed unkind and inconsiderate to tell the dying that they are dying. Aries (1976) describes how death used to be not only organised by the dying persons themselves, but also a very social and public ceremony. This is no longer the case. In our contemporary society, dignity has come to be associated with life and health whilst dying is seen as the process in which the integrity, unity, and wholeness of the person disintegrates. Dying represents helplessness, loss of control, and failure. It has become a source of shame and embarrassment for all involved: for the dying, those that surround them and especially for the experts whose vocation it is to prevent death from occurring. The modern medical ethic is about preserving and prolonging life. Death, as that which is incurable, finds no proper place within such an ethic. We have entrusted doctors with the control of disease and created the myth of their power over death. To Illich it is the shift to claiming 'natural death' as a right, which has endorsed new levels of control befitting the industrial age generally. We not merely fear or deny death, we are consumers of it. Treatment has turned into duty and death has become part of compulsory care. 'Any fatality occurring without medical treatment,' Illich (1976: 198) points out, 'is liable to become a coroner's case. The encounter with a doctor becomes almost as inexorable as the encounter with death.' Like Marx, Illich locates the development of commodification in the process of abstraction and the externalisation of the locus of control. In our society this process has progressed to a point where it is no longer the patients who struggle with their own death but doctors who battle with death *per se*. As consumers of health we pay our doctors to control and overcome the inevitable: the finitude of our existence.

Aries (1976) compares this contemporary attitude to that of people of the Middle Ages and he differentiates the two by their respective familiarity and accessibility to death. When death was a regular and familiar occurrence at the intersection of public and private life, he suggests, there was resignation and dignified acceptance rather than fear. Yet, it could be argued that death is far more public today where real and fictional, individual and mass death, of an ordinary and an abrupt nature is presented daily by the media. We can watch victims of earthquakes, revolutions, droughts, and wars dying on our television screens. Hardly a single day passes without some war film promoting the 'just cause' for mass murder; and we are cordially invited to mourn the death of fictional heroes, television personalities, and other VIPs. We are surrounded by a magnitude of death that would have been difficult to encompass for our predecessors of the Middle Ages. The mediated nature of such a familiarisation with death may make the experience less real, less close, and less immediate despite almost instantaneous global coverage but it seems to me that familiarity and accessibility cannot be considered as the key factors that differentiate our contemporary fear of death from earlier resignation and acceptance. Commodification and the desire to control the inevitable seem far more plausible explanations.

One response to the finitude of our existence is the search for permanence in all that is durable: artefacts, institutions, symbols, rules, and traditions. Our cardinal metaphors of space, time, matter, and number, argues the physicist Jones (1983), reflect these deep needs and yearnings. By giving meaning to existence, we can overcome individual finitude. As those cardinal metaphors came to be developed historically into their separate and distinct identities, so the meaning of that which they explain came to be changed. Even our self-understanding is implicated in that conceptual change. 'To the extent that our modern spatial metaphor intensifies our sense of distinctness, uniqueness and unconnectedness,' suggests Jones (1983: 187), 'to that extent the *existential* problems of life, those that concern our *standing out*, have become more paramount and dramatic.' Integral to such an understanding is, of course, the realisation that the cardinal metaphors take on a different meaning if death is not feared but related to as a most revered and important aspect of the eternal cycle of life as is the case in some non-Western societies. Whatever the culturally specific form of our relationship to death, however, it entails universal implications for human time. First, the relationship to finitude is synonymous with a past and future extension beyond the natural cycle of seasons and with our conscious striving for permanence. Secondly, the dual knowledge of *Dasein* and the rhythmicity of nature is a necessary condition for the potential development towards understanding time as a quantity and a resource. Together, that knowledge and relationship constitute the base to the human time we share with all cultures.

The extended present and the myth of eternal return

The conventional way of understanding the time-consciousness of ancient mythical cultures as distinct from modern Western societies is to impose the imagery of cyclical and linear time respectively (Cottle and Klineberg 1974: 160–96; Couch 1984: 309–14; Rinderspracher 1985: 23–33; Russell 1981; Schmied 1985: 144–62; Yaker 1972). Nietzsche can be held responsible for having disseminated this simplification most effectively and pervasively. As a weapon against the prevailing idea of progress, Nietzsche emphasised a time without goal and a curved path of eternity (1980 vol. 3: 649, vol. 10: 107; Cancik 1983: 257–9) which reduced to the contrast between linear and cyclical time. Nietzsche's conceptualisation of course bears little resemblance to the social sciences' distinction between change and sameness as characteristics for linear and cyclical time respectively. His is a non-teleological theory of change, a theory that focuses on rhythmic repetition with variation as a means to explain progress. Like Sheldrake's (1983) theory of form, Klages's (1934) work on rhythmicity, and Heidegger's (1960) conceptualisation of repetition, Nietzsche's (1980) theory of change stresses *renewal* at the moment of repetition.

Social scientists use the conceptualisation of cyclical and linear time for a distinction between 'traditional' and 'modern' societies or ancient and contemporary cultures. Many suggest that members of ancient societies lived in a world of 'eternal return' or, in Giddens's and Lévi-Strauss's terminology, in 'reversible time'; whilst a past and future extension and a sense of history are associated with linear time, a time that has a beginning and an end and is bounded by either nothingness or godly eternity. An understanding of mythical societies as cyclical and therefore 'timeless' demonstrates that the person making that statement identifies time with historical, chronological dating. I have shown elsewhere that this also applies to anthropological studies of contemporary traditional societies (Adam 1992). This means that the social science conceptualisation of the contrast between cyclical and linear time needs to be firmly located in the Western tradition of thought where time has been bifurcated into bounded earth-time and eternal god-time; into immanent and transcendent time. The ideas of 'outside time and space' and of 'timelessness' both belong to this tradition. As such, I suggest, cyclical time is a highly unsuitable conceptual tool for the interpretation of the mythical time-consciousness of ancient peoples and contemporary 'traditional' societies. Whilst there is no question that mythical time is qualitatively different from our modern conceptualisation of historical time, this difference should not be dichotomised into the Western, clock-based, Newtonian conceptualisations of reversible and irreversible or cyclical and linear time.

In addition to the conceptual difficulty, Bourdieu (1979) and Nowotny (1975) present empirical evidence that shows traditional societies to be fundamentally past and future extended and their belief systems to span vast periods of time. Nowotny (1975: 328) insists that there exist no human societies that could be said to 'lack the ability to transcend the immediate present'. To argue that ancient peoples led their lives in a 'perpetual present' or a cyclicality, where the past and especially the future have little bearing on their existence, denies those cultures something that forms and integral aspect of *all* life forms since, as I have shown in previous chapters, past and future extension, foresight and planning are fundamental to all rhythmically organised beings. There is, however, a need to distinguish between *being* one's past and future, having an awareness of it, and relating to this as an existential condition. All living being is fundamentally past and future based but our potential for *relating* to the past and future, as Dunne (1973) and Plessner (1952: 371) point out, has turned the problem of existence into a virtue of living, of living unto the future with the knowledge of the past and reflective monitoring, with creative planning and daring adventure. I have argued that the relationship to death and belief systems are coeval since all known religions share a concern about the finitude of existence. Individually and fused, they entail a time-distantiation beyond the seasonal cycles of nature. We can therefore argue that the relationship to death extends human beings beyond the cycles of nature even when their daily lives are dominated by concerns that do not reach beyond the growth cycle of seasons. To conceptualise ancient cultures in cyclical time – be it a 'timeless' or seasonal kind – denies those societies the human characteristic of a relationship to death and spiritual concerns with transcendence.

With respect to ancient societies we can, of course, only conjecture about the extent of their time extension and the nature of the temporality of their lives. We have only a few relics of their existence from which to reconstruct their present and compile a picture of their temporal extension. Those remains, however, provide a strong case for a past and future extension beyond the cycles of the seasons. They indicate a concern with questions about the cosmos and the transcendence of finitude. Temples, artefacts, and myths are records of past presents. As such they provide us with a basis for interpretation and reconstruction. Bearing in mind that all analyses of ancient cultures can only be conjectures based on reconstruction, I shall focus on myths through the work of Eliade (1959a, b, 1965), and Blumenberg (1979), and on megalithic temples through the studies of Critchlow (1979) and Thom (1967).

Megaliths and myths can be viewed as expressions for the human endeavour to know about the meaning of existence, origin, and destiny. They define the world from the human centre, provide a place for human beings in the scheme of nature, and they give substance, security, and historical continuity to communal life. We can conjecture that megaliths enabled neolithic people to maintain contact with that which transcended their own being, that they directed the people's attention to a metaphysical source of being, and that they unified time, space, and the sacred. With their spatial composition a likely reflection of the complex geometrical patterns of the 'journeys' of the stars, and their material the most permanent available to ancient peoples, the temples reveal themselves as an expression of a time-consciousness that bears little resemblance to the idea that ancient life was lived in a 'reversible time', an eternal now, or the round of seasonal cycles. Critchlow's (1979) 'reading' of megaliths is particularly interesting. To him, the temple was the embodiment of sacred time and space. It was, he proposes (p.22), 'a centre expressing the controlling archetype, a timeless source of time and a spaceless source of space, a centre of the world from which one could find the centre of oneself, the central reality of one's own being.' Critchlow argues that the composition of megalithic temples suggests a time-consciousness that embraces becoming and irreversibility while simultaneously unifying eternity and the now; that it demonstrates a relation to the past and future of daily life, the cosmos, and the sacred; and that it shows an awareness of the harmonious concordance between heaven and earth.

The circle is widely recognised as the most sacred representation but, as I shall show, its meaning and implication cannot be adequately grasped through the identification with repetition of the same. Over and above the recurrence of the same, the full, unending circle is also the most appropriate form to express undifferentiated space and a totality of time (Critchlow 1979: 150). From this interpretation, 'cyclical time' emerges as something in which ancient societies are not merely located, but which they have *chosen* as a tactic to unify the one with the whole and to gather up, in the now, the whole of time. In rituals, as in myths, original moments are reproduced, and in their repetition a reality is created where all of time becomes fulfilled in the present (Dossey 1982: 28–31). In this enfolding of the origin seems to lie the power of creation and the source of all future possibilities. Once more we find an expression of what Heidegger, Klages, and Nietzsche expressed through repetition, rhythmicity, and cyclicality, respectively. Recreating archetypal cycles, perfecting them into a circle, and elevating them to sacred status can thus be understood as an *active creation* of eternity in the present. However, the importance of the circle extends beyond this active closing of the periphery to its centre. 'The centre,' explains Critchlow (1979: 151), 'is the controlling point and represents, by a projection into the third dimension, the ontological axis and is thereby symbolically outside time and space. The centre is simultaneously the non-directional point and the non-measurable moment. Because the centre is indivisible (a-tomic) it symbolically represents the primal unity which is both source and goal of the existent.'

Such an interpretation of the social time of ancient societies has implications for social theory. Quite clearly, the 'outside time' of myths, rituals, and the sacred centre cannot be contrasted in a meaningful way with the 'in time' or 'timefullness' of chronological dating and clock time that underpins social science analyses. Furthermore, people who transformed the changing cycles of nature into the perfect circle, as expressed in their sacred temples and artefacts, had to be aware of temporal time. Making time stand still has therefore to be recognised as *a creative* act rather than the inescapable condition of existence of a 'primitive' people bound by the seasonal cycle and an eternal present.

I want to suggest further that this holding in unchanging form what is moving, changing, and interconnected, is most explicitly realised by our earliest human ancestors through their art. It is here that we also find the first evidence of abstract representation in the form of squares, parallel lines, grids, and rows of dots. Why people painted cannot be the focus here but, regardless of whether it was used for religious, communicative, or mythical reality-creating purposes, the effect on human time was fundamental. Art externalises and fixes beliefs, experiences, expectancies, fears, and hopes in a form that can be shared by many people across generations. Once objectified, the artistic creation not only becomes a source for reflection and understanding, but also a way of passing on culture without the need for either the co-presence or even the existence of those who do the communicating. It is a way of accumulating wisdom outside the body and beyond the knowledge of individual persons. I therefore disagree with theorists who place special emphasis on writing as the distinguishing mark between Lévi- Strauss's 'hot' and 'cold' societies. Giddens (1981: 38–9) suggests that 'in those societies which possess no writing, where there exists no physical "imprint" of past time, the past is contained in the deep impress which tradition holds over the routinisation of daily experiences. But the symbolic mark, writing, is incomparably the most potent means of extending experience in time-space; by the same token, the advent of writing concretises certain basic dilemmas of hermeneutics alien to purely oral cultures.' I propose that it was 'oral cultures' that produced cave paintings and because of it they need to be understood as time-distantiated to a far greater extent than is generally allowed for by social scientists. Furthermore, I suggest that written language ought to be seen as a development from art rather than from spoken language since it shares the human time effects with those of art. Technology too shares these time aspects with art. Its tools and products are a source for reflection and understanding and a supra-individual way of accumulating and passing on knowledge. Thus, technology too fosters a time-distanciation that exceeds seasonal cycles and the life-spans of individuals. From harnessing fire to electricity and nuclear power; from splitting rocks in order to use them as tools to splitting the atom for the use as energy and bombs; from keeping warm by living in caves and being wrapped in animal skins to living in houses with central heating and wearing woollen garments, technology spans the human development and has aided our time-transcending and time-distantiating efforts.

We know that people use their creations as tools for understanding the world. As externalised reflections of reality, the creations become a source for understanding reality. Objectified we can know something with the full complement of our senses, adding several dimensions to the auditory one of speech, and the auditory–visual combination of communication between co-presents. Not only does this change the quality of the knowing but it changes the reality. Objectified, the creations can become what Giddens conceptualises as duality of structure; they become both condition and outcome of action. This makes them a constitutive factor of human reality. As Jantsch (1985: 168) suggests, 'there is not only the symmetry break between the outer world and its symbolic abstraction. The abstraction – we may say, the idea or the vision – superimposes itself over the existing reality and starts the creative process of the transformation of the outer world.' Re-presenting and creating the temporal world in static and permanent form means the reality thus created appears as if it were fixed and immutable. In this static form it facilitates reflectively based knowledge and with it a time-distanciation that far exceeds that of spoken, symbolic language. Since permanence and invariance form such a central aspect of human life it seems to me imperative that we do not choose between temporality and non-temporal time but find a way to embrace their unity in our theories and thus reflect that most human characteristic of human time.

The 'evidence' of this exploration suggests that it is highly improbable that ancient societies lived their lives in 'reversible' or cyclical time, that their experiences were characterised by recurrence of the same, and that their time horizon did not extend beyond that of the natural cycle of the seasons. Change and rhythmicity which entails linearity *and* cyclicality emerge as fundamental, and repetition without change, timelessness, and the perfect circle as a human creation. Humans, it seems, have fashioned their creations mostly in enduring and encapsulated forms. This enables them to reflect the nature of their world and themselves, but it has also resulted in the contemporary tendency to reify the static creations: to think of them as *being* the temporal world. With permanence accepted as the norm and the legitimate goal, temporality has become veiled and to a certain extent invisible. This makes us forget that the created reality, like that of rituals, myths, and cave paintings, can only be maintained by continuous re-creation.

The future: expanded, colonised, and lost

The extension of ancient cultures into a distant future, and their reaching out to connect with a time-transcending principle or god(s) has to be differentiated from an extension into the future in order to eliminate and control its uncertainty. Our contemporary buildings, technological innovations, and such institutions as banking, insurance, and law, all form part of what Hägerstrand (1985) calls the 'colonisation of the future'. He argues that there is a functional similarity between buildings which provide protection for a period yet to come, and all those institutional practices that are located in the sacredness of promise or contract. All have the effect of extending our present to include and secure the future as a resource *now*. Safety, security, and certainty seem to be the motivating forces for the colonisation of the future. Hägerstrand (1985: 12) suggests that a building, for example, is not built merely for the present; it 'reaches into the future as a kind of space-time container which provides protection for a period to come'. Similarly, practices and institutions based on promise allow for the securing of a future event in the present. Thus, in a contract of employment, future holidays can be secured and the potential loss of the job regulated in such a way that time is allowed for finding an alternative. Saving and investing money makes us think that we are securing our future financially. Insuring my life, the house, the car, the car insurance's 'no claims bonus', all seem to level potentially unmanageable future risks into even and manageable proportions for the present. In other words, insurance is about eliminating the consequences of the dangerously unpredictable elements of the future and, as Wendorff (1980: 622) points out, about levelling potential fluctuations to an equable burden. As such, it tames time and colonises the future.

The change from human beings as part of nature or as God's creatures, living in God's time and to God's design, to history makers who construct their future, is shown by Hohn (1984: 49–104) to have occurred during the height of the Middle Ages. He conceptualises this change as one from sacred to profane history. He suggests that out of the unity of present and eternity emerged a goal-orientated, teleological awareness, the foundation for the mercantile time that was to function as an ordering principle for world trade. Market economies were future and uncertainty orientated. With an awareness of the divergence between the past and the future that uncertainty got transformed into a risk factor to be allowed for and calculated; and with the emergence of world trade in conjunction with city states the future became an entity, a quantity to be allocated, budgeted, controlled, and utilised for exchange. It became equated with money.

A further significant change in our relationship to the future occurred at the turn of this century when technologies seemed to offer a 'new world'. Kern (1983: 89–108) shows how the future was enthusiastically embraced on one hand and subject to control on the other. With the burst of major technological inventions not only the long-term but also the immediate future changed. The telephone, for example, required an instant response and eliminated the waiting for a (written) reply. A group of artists identifying themselves as 'Futurists' wrote a manifesto in which they firmly linked their own orientation to the scientific progress of their time. They identified the basis of all that was traditional and set out to create their own innovative future. 'Why should we look back', they wrote in their manifesto, 'when what we want is to break down the mysterious doors of the Impossible? Time and Space died yesterday. We already live in the absolute, because we have created eternal, omnipresent speed' (quoted in Kern 1983: 98). From the historical study of Kern, the turn of our century emerges as an age for planners, and revolutionaries: for new colonialists not just of places but of time.

Our contemporary approach to the future seems to have shifted from colonialisation to something resembling elimination. 'I want the future now' is the slogan on a best-selling T-shirt in London's Carnaby Street. The Temptations sing 'hurry tomorrow I need you now'. Graffiti in Berlin bemoans the fact that 'the future is not what it used to be' (Nowotny 1989: 51). Once more, technology seems to be implicated in this complex change. If telephones, telex and fax machines have reduced the response time from months, weeks and days to seconds, the computer has contracted them down to nanoseconds. The time-frame of a computer relates to event times of a billionth of a second. 'This marks a radical turning point in the way human beings relate to time,' argues Rifkin (1987: 15). 'Never before has time been organised at a speed beyond the realm of consciousness.' When instantaneous reactions are required, the difference between the present and the future is eliminated. Nowotny (1985) argues that different technologies have varying effects, spheres of influence and emphases: time-space technologies on mobility, production technology on time resources, and information technology on flexibility. Western societies having opted for relentless change, seem to seek simultaneously the control of the processes and the consequences of technological change. 'As I see it,' writes Nowotny (1985: 14), 'we are about to abolish the *category* of the future and to replace it with that *of the extended present*.' Stumbling from one correcting measure to another, she views us as unable to get beyond having to cope with the innovative present.

> The future became accessible under the condition of remaining inaccessible. Today, this distance is threatening to collapse. Expectations no longer hold the glittering promise of a horizon that is still to be reached, and experience as the basis from which one wants to extrapolate future expectations, has lost much of its credence. The category of the future is shrinking towards becoming a mere extension of the present because science and technology have successfully reduced the distance that is needed to accommodate their own products. (Nowotny 1985: 15)

In concordance with Schumpeter's analysis of creative destruction, Nowotny (1989: 12) further argues that the increase in the processes of alternating innovation, repetition, and discarding operationalises the future in the extended present. An incessant need for innovation creates obsolescence at an ever-increasing rate which in turn can no longer be absorbed in the present and consequently creates problems for the future that have to be dealt with now. This suggests a porosity and permeability of the boundary between the present and the future, a blurring that makes it almost impossible to establish which time dimension we are dealing with. From that perspective, today's preoccupation with the future is nostalgia, a concern with something which is about to disappear.

With nuclear war technology the future is 'disappearing' in yet another way. Through the invention of the nuclear bomb we have lost the certainty of continuity. With its creation, the human race as a whole has to live with the *potential end in the present* irrespective of whether or not that knowledge forms part of a society's stock of knowledge. It is a potential threat on a global basis. Death, beyond being an integral aspect of every individual person, has become a fundamental aspect of the human race collectively. Even if we were to disarm and to destroy every last bomb on this earth, the knowledge of this tool of potential global extermination is not reversible or erasable. Social time is irreversibly altered because of it since the moment of the end has become part of the immediate present for the whole of the human species, and probably for most life forms on this earth. We can no longer take for granted one of our most fundamental and tacit assumptions: that the following generations will carry on where we will leave off. Continuity through future generations, I suggest, has become a misplaced base assumption.

Schutz and Luckmann (1973: 47) wrote about the personal knowledge of death in relation to the life plan, that 'knowledge of finitude stands out against the experience of the world's continuance'. With respect to the loss of a legitimate expectation of continuity, however, it looks rather as if the experience of continuity permeated our lives to such a pervasive extent that we can contemplate finitude – especially the global one – only at moments when this continunity is fundamentally shattered; namely, when we experience near and actual nuclear disasters in other countries or sudden death and destruction on a massive scale. If we recognise, however, that reality and our consciousness are constituted in repetition, the way I have shown in this treatise; if we realise that experiences need to be repeated before they penetrate the depth of our being; and if we acknowledge our capacity to experience death without the need to die, then is it not a matter of urgency that this knowledge be brought together and this human capacity be utilised to develop a globally based awareness of 'the end in the present'. That way we could begin to take responsibility for our long-term future rather than passively adapting to its potential loss.

The contemporary future seems operationalised in the present and the certainty of continuity no longer guaranteed. With these changes Heidegger's *Dasein* has taken on a new meaning. Today's *Dasein* is no longer bounded and permeated by individual birth and death but by origin and final destruction. With the splitting of the atom the most basic condition of our existence has changed from the part to the whole. It is no longer personal but global, no longer historical but cosmic. Now our consciousness, our frameworks of understanding and our social theories need to become adequate to that existential reality.

The past: possessed, recorded, and constructed

The past preserved in the present is the legacy of our predecessors' transcendence. The thoughts, stories, writings, sacred buildings, and art; the inventions, cosmologies, and institutions; the communication networks that now span the earth and the space surrounding it; all are monuments to past people's relations to their future. Through them our predecessors transcended their own being in a way that is different from leaving a record and from merely having a past. This past is best understood as past future (Koselleck 1985) or as bygone present-futures of practical engagement (Oakeshott 1985). The records of this past future, however, vary and therefore need to be differentiated. We need to distinguish between those that are evidence of the lives of predecessors, and those we keep for use in the present and the future. Social record-keeping, as the second type of record in the form of census, birth and marriage registers, educational, criminal, or production records, is a deliberate rather than a spontaneous outcome. It is quite unlike fossils, the rust on the car, or styles of fashion. Social records are kept for the purpose of storing information which would get lost if it were left to spontaneous processes. Where the past is actively recorded in this way it is always selectively reconstituted for the purposes at hand.

As living and evolved beings we *are* our own past as well as expressions of spontaneous records. As social beings we *have* a past and we relate to it. We also actively preserve what would otherwise be lost in order that we may have a record of the past. The capacity to keep written records and to store information in computers makes our contemporary relation to the past fundamentally distinct from that of Neolithic societies, for example. It is a difference that is not exhausted by the fact that members of contemporary Western societies locate themselves as biographical individuals in a chronological time grid and a social history. Yet, members of all societies are subject to the same condition. Their past and their future can only ever be constituted in the present. Past and future can only be lived, experienced, related to, interpreted, sought out, captured, recaptured, or preserved in the present. Any reality that transcends the present has to exhibit itself in the present. 'Both future and past, then, emerge only in a reading of present,' argues Oakeshott (1985: 8), 'and a particular future or past is one eligible to be evoked from a particular present and is contingently related to the particular present from which it may be evoked.'

Art, writing, printing, and the technological inventions of photography, film, records, and cassette players, have dramatically changed the way we relive past presents. Through them, we can relive moments in externalised form which before were entirely dependent on human memory. Similar to myths, technological inventions suspend the passage of time by trapping it not in the story but in photographs, gramophone records, or on film. Their meaning, their quality, and their feeling, like that of myths, changes with the context. Listening to popular songs of earlier periods allows us to relive experiences of many years ago. We need to recognise, however, that the contemporary reliving is always inclusive of the intervening years, that these years are fundamentally implicated and resonate through the experience. The relived experience is different because of it. The same principle applies whether we read political theory that was written at the turn of the century, watch a Shakespeare play, or look at a photograph album. In other words, the present experience can only be understood through the mediation of the intervening knowledge and historical events. The past is reconstituted in the present, as Mead (1959) asserts, because each moment is recreated, reselected, and re-interpreted, preserved, and evoked afresh in the light of new knowledge. This makes the past revocable and as hypothetical as the future. Again, this is a principle that applies to all human pasts. Only the means by which we revoke and preserve the past have changed, and so have our attitudes and relationships to it. Thus, myths, chronicles, museums, photographs, and newspapers are examples of different strategies for preserving the past.

> Contemplating the more distant past has become a growing scholarly endeavour, contemplating the more immediate past a growing industry. The industry's product is the past not just of any locality but of the world. As world population expands there are ever more people to have news about. The billionfold past is carried into the present by means of newspapers which present each morning such a generous account of the hours just gone by that if all of it were read conscientiously nothing would be done today except keeping up with yesterday. (Young 1988: 209)

Giddens (1981: 91–7) charts a development from verbal to written, printed and, most recently, contemporary computer-based recording of information. In agreement with Foucault, he shows that concomitant with this development is an increased capacity for surveillance and power. In other words, writing appears to have originated as a means to record and store information for the administration of societies. This encoding and preserving of information not only extends our socially based reach, namely our time-space distanciation, but it also increases the potential for social control. 'The keeping of written "accounts" – regularised information about persons, objects and events – generates power that is unavailable in oral cultures', argues Giddens (1981: 95). Whilst the 'keepers of the past' have always held positions of power in society, this power becomes unassailable once it no longer resides in the memory of individual persons but in the institutions of the state. The extension into the past is thus a multifaceted aspect of our being and ought to be reflected as such in our social theories.

There are some further complexities to be explored and I want to contrast these with popular views of social science. I want to investigate these additional distinctions against the background of the idea that all time is social time and against the contention, first formulated by St. Augustine, that the past is 'past remembered' and is therefore an aspect of mind. Oakeshott's (1985: 1–44) work is illuminating and helpful to this task.

Oakeshott distinguishes between encapsulated, remembered, consulted, and message-bearing survivals of the past. His 'encapsulated past' is similar to my understanding of *being* our own past, where that which exists now can be conceptualised as the sum total of the past. This total may then comprise our personal, genetic, and cosmic past, as well as the outcomes of physical and mental processes, of habits, novel actions, and promises. Oakeshott insists that the significance of this 'encapsulated past' needs to be understood as independent from the process of recall. We are our past, he argues, regardless of whether or not we remember or consult aspects of it; and much of this encapsulated past is beyond recall in any case. This is the past of Prigogine's historical T-time and the past of an ecological understanding where it is acknowledged that it depends on our frame of reference whether we understand our earlier being in terms of calendar years and the condition of childhood, or in terms of rocks, algae, or particles in the 'primeval soup'. 'Everybody carries within himself the universal human, and therefore possesses an organ of universal communication,' writes Cupitt (1985: 90) with reference to Jung's work. 'The psyche was retrospectively unbounded, and one could go back through the personal and the collective unconscious into the darkness of the biological and even the mineral life from which we have come forth.' This particular way of understanding Oakeshott's 'encapsulated past' gains further strength once it is linked with the evidence from the previously discussed death and near-death experiences.

Oakeshott locates the 'remembered past' in the continuity of consciousness and identity and suggests that awareness of the past in
memory is always self-awareness. This means that the remembered past
needs to be differentiated from the recalled past that we draw on and
consult for the purpose of action. Analogous to Schutz's distinction
between 'because' and 'in-order-to' motives, Oakeshott differentiates
between a rememberance embedded in the flow of consciousness and one
in a more deliberate and objective mode. Regardless of the content of
that which is being consulted, Oakeshott (1985: 16) suggests that
'recollection here is joining a puzzling or intractable present with a
known and unproblematic past to compose a less puzzling or more
manageable practical present. Here, there is something like genuine
"pensee de derriere", although it is not the pastness of the recalled
experiences (and certainly not their actual situation in our present
experience) which is significant but their familiarity and their relevance
to present circumstances.' Sheldrake's (1985) distinction of the
remembered past in terms of 'when' or 'how' refers to characteristics that
are both similar to and different from Oakeshott's analysis. The memory
of when I fell from my bike locates me in a time-frame in relation to
myself as a continuous being. Remembering how to ride a bicycle draws
on different sources. Like Oakeshott, Sheldrake points to the familiarity
of the past we draw on when we remember to do something. But
Sheldrake goes on to argue that this past is known as a *totality*. What
once was a process of learning and practice that can be located as an
aspect of our personal development - i.e. when we learned to ride the
bicycle - has become fused into a totality of motion, action, and
knowledge that we may draw on for use in the present. As such it forms
an ineradicable part of us and should therefore also be understood in
terms of 'encapsulated past'. What Oakeshott separates emerges as
mutually implicating from Sheldrake's analysis.

I want to propose that this drawing on present survivals of the past - be
they artefacts, records, or theories - for the purpose of future orientated
action in the present needs to be further distinguished from learning from
the past. Koselleck (1985) writes about this in terms of *Historia Magistra
Vitae*, where the past is embued with emancipatory powers as a 'school of
life' that teaches through the mistakes and fortunes of predecessors. He
argues that this was a mode of understanding and relating to the past that
lasted for two thousand years up to the eigtheenth century. Koselleck
(1985: 39) suggests that this history is related to as a schoolmistress of life
and that it sets us free to repeat successes of the past instead of repeating
past mistakes. When fundamental change occurs within generations,
however, the past can no longer provide a suitable model for the future.
Berger's (1984: 12) analysis concurs with that of Koselleck when he

suggests that the role of history has changed since the French Revolution: 'Once it was the guardian of the past: now it has become the midwife of the future. It no longer speaks of the changeless but, rather, of the laws of change which spare nothing.' A historical awareness where the past is re-enacted in order to create the reality of the present is frequently contrasted with historicity. The concept of historicity, evoked in the work of Heidegger, Giddens, and Luhmann, entails the conscious knowledge that we are not only historically formed but are forming history; that history makes us and we make history, if not in conditions of our choice, to use Marx's qualification. Historicity is, as Giddens (1979: 221) points out, 'the active mobilisation of social forms in the pursuit of their own transformation'.

The past which we remember and consult today through records and survived fragments has not merely changed in scale and depth but its multiple expressions coexist. Modern and ancient buildings stand side by side. Home may be a Welsh stone cottage or a high-rise flat built during the 1960's. Meals are cooked on open fires, ranges, electric and gas cookers, or in microwave ovens. While one person walks to work, another goes on horseback. One cycles, another might go by car, while a third may take Concorde to fly to a business meeting. With the invention of photography some 150 years ago, we are now able to know as many as eight generations of ancestors by sight. We can read the thoughts of people who lived as long as two thousand years ago, as well as those that were written only yesterday. We can carbon-date rocks and fossils and 'conclude' ages of hundreds of millions of years. We can study megaliths and burial chambers and speculate about their creator's time-consciousness, their values, or their cosmology. All these surviving records *exist simultaneously* and make up the complexity of the temporal depth of our contemporary existence. They carry within them the meanings of the past, but it is up to us whether we ignore them, treat them as relics, as means for future action, or as meaning bearers of the past.

'Message-bearing survivals' are a further type of record of the past identified by Oakeshott. Similar to his 'encapsulated past', such records do not depend on our knowing or remembering for their existence. As message-bearing survivals, they may be listened to, used, or neglected. As such they form part of the social inheritance of any society and constitute the condition of articulate, practical activity. They are utilised for action but do not in themselves become an object of inquiry. Thus, Oakeshott proposes, not what the fragments mean in terms of having been a future present in the past but only their use value for the present marks their significance.

Finally, our remembrance of the past, our learning from the past and the knowledge that we make our history must not be confused with a historical understanding of the past. All these aspects of our past, outlined above, need to be differentiated from the human activity which completes the survived fragments, relates them to others, constructs them into a meaningful whole, and conceptualises them as past futures. They need to be distinguished from the historical enterprise. Historical understanding entails a relationship to the past that seeks to grasp the past *as* past, and its meaning in terms of past futures. It seeks the past for the meaning it had in the *past* and not for the purpose of action in the future-orientated present.

This brief investigation has shown that the past is preserved in thoughts, artefacts, institutions, books, and computers; in the natural environment through the processes of growth and decay; and in memory, writing, and technological inventions. It thus contradicts the popular conceptions that the past is always socially constituted or that it is an aspect of mind, remembered and reconstructed in the present. It demonstrates that the preserved past can be understood in terms of stored information and that the way this is achieved varies from being a spontaneous process to being a deliberate action. It makes clear that such action may again differ in terms of its aim: to transcend the present, to learn from the past, or to record the past for purposes of administration and social control. For analytical purposes different forms of remembrance and different sources of the past have been distinguished. These in turn have been delineated for their wide variety of usage. We are shown to relive the past and to learn from it; to use it for future action and for making a puzzling present manageable, for creating reality and for changing it, for legitimating existing practices and for personal and social control and power.

Reflections

With the discussion of issues relating to human existence and aspects of time common to humanity, we have once more transgressed the boundaries of sociological analyses. That contravention appears to have been worthwhile, however, since our expanded focus has not only helped to illuminate what is taken for granted in everyday life but also to clarify the assumptions of the various ways of understanding that life and its multiplicity of times. The exploration of social time through the concept of transcendence proved of deep significance to social theory. Classical social science dualisms such as linear and cyclical time emerged as inappropriate for the task of delineating industrial from traditional and ancient societies. The differentiation between natural and social time could not be upheld to distinguish between the times of nature and society. Time, timing, tempo, and temporality emerged as fundamental aspects of both nature and human social organisation. Temporality, rhythmicity, time as measure or parameter, the time aspects of organisation, were all found to be integral to social time generally and to our present reality. It has become apparent, however, that these neutral concepts have to be imbued with particular meanings if they are to be appropriate for the description of specific levels of our being and environment. Transcendence and relations of power have been suggested as possible concepts with which to enrich the neutral terms so that they may become meaningful expressions of human time generally and industrial time in particular. To recognise the significance of this extended view entails that we leave this more substantive conceptual focus and reflect more specifically on the implications of our findings for social theory.

7

Time for Social Theory: Points of Departure

In this treatise we have taken on board the challenging idea that a theory of time is a necessary pre-condition to social theory. To accomplish this task I have allowed our investigation to be guided by the theories, studies, and implicit utilisations of time in the social and natural sciences. Explored in these multiple expressions, time emerged as a fundamentally transdisciplinary subject and necessitated an understanding that is no longer containable within the traditional assumptions and categories of social science. We now need to reflect on the implications of these findings for social theory. This entails refocusing on some issues and re-assessing a few of the classical social theory traditions in the light of our findings. It requires that we spell out the limitations of the classical practice of abstraction and dualistic theorising for an understanding of 'social time' and that we question the tradition of claiming time exclusively for the human realm by locating it in mind, language or the functional needs of social organisation. This involves us in a re-evaluation of the dualistic conceptualisation of natural and social time and the closely related idea that all time is social time. It necessitates further that we explore the role of metaphors and focus explicitly on the social science convention of limiting the time-span of concern to a few hundred years.

Whilst there emerges a strong sense of a new direction for social theory the individual components do not yet fit together to form a cohesive whole. According to Gebser (1986: 375-6) an appreciation of the limits of existing approaches invariably precedes the slow and difficult process towards a new method of understanding. We must not be surprised, therefore, that our extensive reconceptualisation does not culminate in a polished new theory but merely a first step in that direction; it identifies points of departure and indicates the potential for future development.

Social time and natural time revisited

In order to adjust the meaning of social time in the light of this research, we need to remind ourselves of the traditional conceptualisations of natural and social time. Sorokin and Merton (1937) may be said to have provided the 'definitive' classic statement on the distinction between social and natural time. They associate the physical time of diurnal and seasonal cycles with clock time and define this time as 'purely quantitative, shorn of qualitative variation' (p. 621). 'All time systems', Sorokin and Merton suggest further, 'may be reduced to the need of providing means for synchronising and co-ordinating the activities and observations of the constituents of groups' (p. 627).

Whilst social theorists are no longer united in the belief that all time systems are reducible to the functional need of human synchronisation and co-ordination they seem to have little doubt about the validity of Sorokin and Merton's other key point that, unlike social time, the time of nature is that of the clock, a time characterised by invariance and quantity. Despite significant shifts in the understanding of social time, the assumptions about nature, natural time, and the subject matter of the natural sciences have remained largely unchanged. In other words, the development in the conceptualisation of social time has not been accompanied by one of natural time with the result that our understanding of natural time, as this exploration has shown, is grossly out of tune with contemporary natural science understanding. Even where the importance of the physical and biological aspects of time are appreciated for social life, they are not theorised or in any way related to that life (Bergmann 1983; Elias 1982a, b, 1984; Schöps 1980; Schutz and Luckmann 1973). Social time seems defined against 'an other' which appears to be no more than a convenient backcloth against which to describe and define a more complex understanding of social time. Everything social time is thought *not* to be (or not only to be) is classified as 'natural time'.

In contradistinction to social science analyses this research shows that most of what social scientists preserve exclusively for the human realm is generalised throughout nature. It demonstrates that the characteristics identified with natural time are in fact an exclusively human creation. Past, present, and future, historical time, the qualitative experience of time, the structuring of 'undifferentiated change' into episodes, all are established as integral time aspects of the subject matter of the natural sciences and clock time, the invariant measure, the closed circle, the perfect symmetry, and reversible time as our creations. This investigation thus establishes natural time as very different from its social science conceptualisation. Furthermore, it shows that it matters what assumptions social scientists hold about natural time and the subject matter of the natural sciences in general as these not only affect the definition of social time but also the understanding of the nature of 'the social'. Since our traditional understanding of natural time emerged as inadequate and faulty we have to recognise that the analysis of social time is flawed by implication. However, the difficulty extends beyond the need to achieve a more appropriate understanding of natural time since the assumptions associated with this understanding are embedded in the more general theories that social scientists hold about nature.

A brief expansion of these general social science assumptions about nature will clarify this point. Nature as distinct from social life is understood to be quantifiable, simple, and subject to invariant relations and laws that hold beyond time and space (Giddens 1976; Lessnoff 1979; Ryan 1979). This view is accompanied by an understanding of natural time as coming in fixed, divisible units that can be measured whilst quality, complexity, and mediating knowledge are preserved exclusively for the conceptualisation of human social time. On the basis of a further, closely related idea it is proposed that nature may be understood objectively. Natural scientists, explain Elias (1982a, b) and Giddens (1976), stand in a subject-object relationship to their subject matter. Natural scientists, they suggest, are able to study objects directly and apply a causal framework of analysis whilst such direct causal links no longer suffice for the study of human society where that which is investigated has to be appreciated as unintended outcomes of intended actions and where the investigators interpret a pre-interpreted world. Unlike their colleagues in the natural sciences, social scientists, it is argued, stand in a subject-subject relation to their subject matter. In addition to the differences along the quantity-quality and object-subject dimensions nature is thought to be predictable because its regularities - be they causal, statistical, or probabilistic - are timeless. The laws of nature are considered to be true in an absolute and timeless way, the laws of society historically developed. In contrast to nature, human societies are argued to be fundamentally historical. They are organised around values, goals, morals, ethics, and hopes, whilst simultaneously being influenced by tradition, habits, and legitimised meanings. These general social science assumptions, first formulated by leading proponents of the German *Geisteswissenschaften* (human sciences) such as Rickert and Dilthey, inform the social science understanding of social and natural time. Because it is postulated that the physical world is subject to laws, that natural processes entail no element of choice, purpose, or meaning, and that nature can be quantified and studied objectively it is suggested that the past and future are irrelevant and that the B-series of time is therefore the appropriate conceptual tool for the natural sciences.

We can now appreciate that the task is not simply to adjust our understanding of natural time. An extension of focus that includes an understanding of the times of nature necessitates a change in the social sciences' fundamental assumptions about nature or, as Luhmann (1980: 32) puts it, a shift in the base assumptions of sociological theory. The evidence presented in this book supports my proposition that an improvement and widening of our understanding of social time without a radical change in the assumptions that underpin our present scientific knowledge is not enough. It makes clear that natural scientists no longer hold this nineteenth century view of nature. It demonstrates that the social sciences' practice of understanding of the physical and biological realm in contradistinction to the human social world is consistent with, and supportive of, the contemporary dualistic understanding of natural and social time. It affirms that these underlying assumptions are steeped in the Newtonian, mechanistic understanding of nature and natural time, an understanding where particles move in reversible time to invariable laws, within an absolute time that defines our uniqueness. It suggests that this Newtonian understanding is perfectly complemented by the basic assumptions of classical philosophy which had been adopted by social theorists for their various time classifications. The philosophical approach is dominated by Cartesian dualism which separates not just mind from body, but repetition from process, quality from quantity, form from content, subject from object, the individual from the collective, the A-series from the B-series, cyclical from linear time, and traditional from modern conceptualisations and structures of time. Barnes (1971: 545), commenting on the work of Lévi-Strauss, suggests that in order to 'escape from an amusing but ultimately sterile ballet of symbols in which history and anthropology, synchrony and diachrony, consciousness and unconsciousness, continuity and discontinuity, reversible and irreversible time dance endlessly round each other until the audience decides to go home, we have to break down the dichotomies, establish continua and feed in more facts.' When we do, the picture changes and the simplified dualities loose their meaning: thinking in opposites ceases to be a viable theoretical option. As we have seen in the first chapter, social scientists who seek to take account of time in their theories recognise the need and make a commitment to overcome dichotomies and dualisms. They do so, however, without letting go of the assumptions upon which dualisms are built. Thus, the best that can be achieved is a reconceptualisation of dualisms into genuine, mutually defining dualities (Giddens 1981, 1984; Hopkins 1982; Jaques 1982; Lauer 1981). Predictably, the new approaches do not solve the problem but end up with new dichotomies and continue to pose irresolvable difficulties with respect to time, as I have demonstrated throughout this investigation. Recognising time as both condition and outcome, reversible and progressive, *Dasein* and *durée*, quality and quantity, resource and commodity merely shifts the focus from dichotomies to isolated pairs. It provides no means for a conceptualisation of the connections between multiple pairs, their continuity and discontinuity, or their mutual implication. Theories of dualities are impervious to ecological principles or to such ideas as resonance and implication.

We need to recognise further that most dualisms entail an implicit hierarchical evaluation which has remained untouched by the dualism-duality conversion. Dichotomies are usually not value-neutral and thus need to be appreciated as not only fundamentally inclusive of their counterpart but also ranked in order of importance and priority. As scientific classifications these polarities thus read objective over subjective, mind over matter, social over biological or physical time (or vice versa depending on who does the prioritising), modern over traditional time, and commodity over event-based time. Contemporary physicists such as Capra (1976) and Chew (1968) propose that the practice of making one aspect more important than others is no longer tenable and in need of re-evaluation. Capra (1982: 83-9) and Briggs and Peat (1985: 216-7) demonstrate the importance of the idea of 'bootstrapping' for an understanding where issues of fundamentality, priority, and importance are recognised to be relative, a property of the framework of observation.

The Newtonian-Cartesian understanding causes yet another difficulty. Elias insists that we need to understand time as an immense synthesis rather than an abstraction. However, the conceptual tools that are being used to understand this synthesis are, as we have seen, based on an understanding of reality that abstracts bits, particles, aspects, units, events, or periods in order to understand them. It is becoming obvious that the wrong conceptual tools are being used if we seek to grasp and theorise synthesis, qualitative rhythmicity, intensity, and acausal relationships with the aid of Newtonian and Cartesian assumptions. The complexity of social time cannot be understood by focusing on aspects in isolation if that focus excludes an awareness of the bearing of diurnal, seasonal, menstrual, and metabolic cycles; the variety of time structurings; the irreversible exchanges in relations of incomplete autonomy and dependence; the relationship we have to all those time aspects of existence; and the time we have created as an independent reality: all are implicated in any one aspect we focus on. We could think of the difference of approach in terms of focus and isolation. When we are focusing the rest of our visual field is not disappearing in the way it does when we are isolating and abstracting some part or event in order to study it. It is the difference between an embedded understanding where both the thinker and the object of understanding remain an integral aspect of the totality, and one that severs those infinite connections. Our traditional understanding of social time and the convention of claiming for the human social realm what are qualities of all nature are linked to assumptions that separate society from nature and enforce choices on an either/or basis. A different picture emerges, however, once we put the Newtonian and Cartesian understanding aside and concentrate on the infinite connections and relations. With such a shift of focus and emphasis, existing assumptions and classifications begin to become meaningless.

These thoughts lead us once more to a closely related, historically persistent idea, an early version of which was put forward by Durkheim (1915) in *'The Elementary Forms of Religious Life'*. It simply states that all time is social time, meaning human social time. That this assertion, in its social science meaning, is no longer tenable has been amply demonstrated in this treatise. Yet it is worthwhile to look at this idea once more since it may help to shed light on the limitations of current approaches for a comprehensive time-based social science understanding. A summary of this idea may be expressed in the following way. Time is always social time because only humans regulate and organise their lives by time. Only they conceptualise time. Only they use, control, allocate, and sell their time. Only they lead an 'in time' existence and create their own histories and futures.

This research leaves no doubt that there are time aspects which pertain exclusively to human social contexts. But these, as we have seen, need to be distinguished from the more universal principles of time that are to be found throughout nature. Organisational aspects of time, for example, are found at the inorganic, organic, and the human social level, as well as in the design aspects of human artefacts. The organisational principles of time, in terms of sequence, duration, periodicity, rates of change, and synchronisation may be the same for all, but their meaning and expressive form change with the context. The same applies to an 'in time existence', which is led by simple organisms, plants, animals, and humans alike because it relates not exclusively to calendars but to being bounded by external rhythms. The difference here lies in how the being relates to that rhythm or, in the case of Western societies, whether the rhythm has been abstracted from the natural rhythms within which other beings organise their social existences. All beings, it has further become apparent, are their own past, present, and future. The difference lies in the degree to which they are aware of this fact and the way they relate to it. This research suggests that clock time, and the Newtonian time-reversible *t*- coordinate, are the only time aspects that can be exclusively designated human social constructions. All other aspects, irrespective of whether or not they are conceptualised, are also integral aspects of nature. Human time therefore needs to be understood to include the times of nature. In agreement with Mead (1959), we could view time as socially constituted in interaction since the symmetry-breaking process of interaction is one of the sources of time. But Mead's socially constituted time is very different from that of Bergmann, Elias, Durkheim, or Sorokin and Merton. In other words, the idea of time as socially constituted depends fundamentally on the meaning we impose on 'the social', whether we understand it as a prerogative of human social organisation or, following Mead, as a principle of nature.

The idea that time is not separable from the meaning of time, that it always symbolises something that is socially formulated, is a more complex one to untangle. Without getting drawn into the complex philosophical debates about the existence of reality outside language, it can be argued that in instances where language comes to be equated with reality we are no longer in a position to conceptualise a number of things. We are left without bases from which to account for meaning variance, to understand non-language-based nature, and to translate from one system of meaning to another (Giddens 1976: 17–18). Furthermore, it leaves no room for understanding novelty and creativity; and it denies to the rest of nature experience, meaning, and consciousness. In the light of contemporary scientific understandings of reality, Mead's (1959) conceptualisation, and the research presented here, we find that the tradition of equating time with its symbol is no longer tenable. There may be good reasons for such an exclusive stress on the symbol. It is possible, as Hägerstrand (1985: 8–12) points out, that social scientists have linked time so intimately to the symbol of time because this is quite simply the very form on which they have been focusing. More importantly non-symbolic expressions of reality are traditionally understood to be outside the disciplinary boundaries of the human social sciences. These reasons may explain the convention but they cannot justify it. We can accept that for us to be able to talk and think about time necessitates our putting it into words. If this is all that is being expressed, it is not very much; if it equates reality with the symbol, it goes too far. There is no need to deny that all humans formulate meanings symbolically or that this is a fundamentally social process. There is an urgent need, however, to appreciate that time is an aspect of nature, and that nature encompasses the symbolic universe of human society. Once we recognise ourselves as bearers of all the multiple times of nature, and once we allow for nature to include symbolic expression, the gulf between the symbolic knower and nature as an external (unknowable) object can be dispensed with. The mutually exclusive dichotomies of nature and culture, subject and object become irrelevant.

From the evidence presented in the last four chapters we emerge as activity-matter, causal as well as non-local communication networks, biological clocks that beat in 'off-beat' to the rhythms of our earth, and as beings that grow and decay dynamically in interdependence with other systems of change-order. Recognising ourselves as having evolved, and thus *being* the times of nature, allows for the humanly constituted aspects of time to become one expression among the others. Biologists have dispelled the idea that only humans experience time or organise their lives by it. Waiting and timing in nature presuppose knowledge of time and temporality, irrespective of their being symbolised, conceptualised, reckoned, or measured. Yet, once time is constituted symbolically, it is no longer reducible to the communication of organisms or physical signals; it is no longer a mere sensory datum. For a person to have a past and to recognise and know it entails a representational, symbolically based imagination. Endowed with it, people do not merely undergo their presents and pasts but they shape and reshape them. Symbolic meaning thus makes the past infinitely flexible. With objectified meaning we can not only look back, reflect, and contemplate but we can reinterpret, restructure, alter, and modify the past irrespective of whether this is done in the light of new knowledge in the present, to suit the present, or for purposes of legitimation.

Kinget (1975: 43) speaks of a 'living past' and sees our assumptions about it demonstrated in the practice of psychotherapy which is premised on trust in the possibility of reshaping the past in the present. Looked at in this way, time may be viewed as having evolved as an aspect of (Meadian) sociality in the universe. The way humans - as a species or as members of specific societies, groups, and families - symbolise time and relate to it, may then be understood as a specific explicated form of something that is uniquely implicated in all of nature. This understanding was first articulated by Mead shortly before his death. Mead began to formulate what contemporary natural scientists have substantiated for us: the mutual implication of sociality and temporality and its applicability to all of nature. In other words, contemporary natural scientists have provided the substantive evidence for Mead's theory that nature fundamentally includes human social life, and that natural and social time are therefore not mutually exclusive but implicating.

The exclusion of non-symbolic expressions from social science analysis has not only resulted in a highly problematic conceptualisation of nature and natural time but it has also meant the omission of artefacts and technology from social science. As Carlstein (1982: 8-9) points out, 'social scientists have commonly refused to see 'dead things' as social or have left them aside for the natural scientists. Social scientists have also commonly refused to look upon artefacts as social in the sense that they impinge on how individuals interact with each other. These 'dead things' are, at best, seen as symbols and are not considered to be genuine ingredients in social situations and processes.' Yet, with respect to time, it is difficult to see how we can understand society without the time aspects of those 'dead things', those created artefacts and machines that shape our lives and our understanding of reality. There can be no longer any doubt that our conceptualisations of time are deeply influenced by them. Furthermore, our artefacts have become mediators and filters through which we not only live our lives with others in our environment but understand and symbolise that life and ourselves. They have become metaphors. As such they deserve our most careful attention.

Knowing through metaphors

There is strong evidence to suggest that we are self-conscious by virtue of mediation, that we recognise ourselves through an external or externalised 'other'. It is likely that animals, as sentient and mortal creatures that share the world of humans, are one of the earliest sources for questions about the nature of human being. As bases of self-understanding they suggested answers that were consequently formulated in language, expressed in paintings, and encoded in sacred rituals. Animals are both familiar and distinct, and their powers - comparable but never the same as those of humans - a source of quality. Berger (1980: 5) designates that relationship metaphoric since, 'within this relationship what the two terms - man and animal - shared in common revealed what differentiated them. And vice versa.' In our contemporary Western world animals are no longer a dominant metaphor for self-recognition. In the age of machines natural metaphors are, to a large extent, replaced by our own creations.

Every new phase of technological development, it seems, has served as a tool for self-understanding and led to new conceptualisations of reality. During the seventeenth and eighteenth century the clock constituted the prime metaphor. The universe was understood as a giant clockwork and its inhabitants were conceptualised as functioning to its principles. During the nineteenth century the principles of steam technology were embraced as additional sources for self-understanding. The imagery involved people 'letting off steam' and the need for 'safety-valves' to avoid dangerous social explosions. Emotions and social interactions were likened to a steam engine functioning under pressure with a need for the steam to escape in order to avoid disaster. During the last twenty years the computer has been elevated to the position of dominant metaphor. Its principles are used for the conceptualisation of mind and for all operations that involve the transfer of information.

The process from the invention of a new artefact to its use as a metaphor seems to follow a pattern.

> Each technological innovation offers a new kind of human experience. At
> first, it is entirely strange, and difficult to grasp; but we quickly find in it
> sufficient familiar features to act as points of reference, and we then explore
> it, savour it, come to terms with it, and assimilate it into the pattern of our
> everyday life. We learn to live with it. Once it is established in this way, it can
> be the basis of a metaphorical transfer: we then see previously *familiar* things
> in terms of this novelty. We have acquired a new perceptual tool. (Edge 1973:
> 35)

Through metaphors we evoke the inner connections between things but that is not all. We have a tendency to reify metaphors to a point where we loose sight of the human authorship. Frequently the distinction between the metaphor, its source, and its name gets blurred or lost. Reified, metaphors lose their usefulness as a conceptual tool for social science. It is therefore important for us to keep a clear distinction between the tool and that which we grasp with its aid.

Since metaphors play such a central role in our theories it is pertinent for us to learn to 'see' what has thus far been invisible: the design principles of artefacts that guide and structure our understanding. Only once we become fully aware of them can we use the metaphors to our full advantage. The Newtonian machine technology has emerged as a particularly unsuitable metaphor for an understanding where time is allowed to become a prominent feature of social analysis, and much of the discussion in the previous chapters has shown the severe limitations of the machine-clock metaphor. In this last chapter I want to focus briefly on the differences between the technology of lenses and the post-Newtonian technology of holograms so that we may appreciate their respective principles and recognise their existing and potential role for social theory. The purpose of this brief excursus to holography is therefore not to seek the implications for a conceptualisation of social time but to explore the potential for a social theory that takes account of time.

Holography has shifted understanding from causal, sequential, linear connection chains to interference patterns and from mechanical interaction, organisation, and transmission of information of individual parts to mutual implication. Whilst the lens remains a powerful metaphor for an analysis of isolated parts, holography allows an understanding of the sort of interconnectedness and mutual implication we have encountered in Chapters 2–6. The hologram is therefore proving an excellent metaphor for a whole, encoded and implicated in the 'parts', since the information it stores is not located in the individual parts but in their interference pattern. Any one part of a hologram contains, implies, and resonates information of the whole. The focus here is not on individual particles in motion, crossing time and space in succession, but on all of the information gathered up simultaneously. In contradistinction to Newtonian mechanics and geometric optics where the part is different from the whole in an absolute way and where the emphasis is on substance, holography focuses on information gathered from the whole of the object under investigation. It has dispensed with the absolute distinction of wholes and parts. Three aspects of the hologram metaphor are thus initially important for understanding in social science: its non-sequentiality, its individual-whole relationship, and its multiperspective focus.

In order to appreciate the difference between the metaphors we need to explore the principles that underpin their respective designs. With lens-photography an image is created on the plate in such a way that each point on the object corresponds to a single point on the image on the plate. The object stands in a 1:1 relation to the image. In case of the plate being broken, the broken-off part would be missing from the image. 'By thus bringing the correspondence of specified features of object and image into such sharp relief,' writes Bohm (1983: 144), 'the lens greatly strengthened man's awareness of the various parts of the object and of the relationship between these parts. In this way, it furthered the tendency to think in terms of analysis and synthesis.' In holography, laser light beams are fired in phase before being split and sent along different paths. A reference beam goes to the plate directly while the other beam picks up the reflections from the entire object. It illuminates the object 'in the round' and from all aspects. Once the light beams are reunited on the plate they are no longer in phase but interfere with each other and thus produce an interference pattern on the plate. This pattern in no way resembles the object but has its features encoded. In contradistinction to the photographic plate each region of the holographic plate carries the encoded information of the whole. If part of the holographic plate gets damaged, no part of the image gets lost. Briggs and Peat (1985: 271) explain the difference. 'The pattern is not in 1:1 correspondence with the object because the phase information from each region of the object is recorded throughout the holographic plate. Thus, if a portion of the plate is lost, the total image is retained.' Because the memory is distributed over the whole of the holographic plate, each part contains the whole *Gestalt*. From the encoded pattern a three-dimensional image can then be recreated by shining the reference beam onto the plate and viewing it from the other side. The object is thus recognised in its totality rather than having its individual features matched piece by piece. The principle of splitting light-waves that are in phase, thus creating both a reference beam and another beam carrying multiperspectivist information, appears to be very similar to the process by which we recognise ageing, growing, and change of any kind since one way to know change is by reference to something relatively unchanging, or something that changes more slowly. If all processes occurred 'in phase' we could not know them in relation to each other. We would have no basis from which to recognise change.

Derived from the Greek 'holo' which means whole and 'gram' which means to write, a hologram 'writes the whole' (Bohm 1983: 145). This encoding of the totality in every tiniest aspect of itself represents a departure from all previous Western, science-based understandings of the relationship of parts to wholes. Here the sum can neither be said to be more than the part nor can it be argued to determine the part as in the case of organic holism. The language of causal determinism is misplaced in a holism where the connections are simultaneous and where everything implies everything else. Simultaneity, mutual implication, and complexity, the time aspects that pose such insoluble difficulty for traditional social theory, appear manageable for a theory based on holographic principles. Holographic principles are therefore eminently more suitable than the technology of clocks and lenses for an understanding in which time is allowed to play a central part. Understanding through opposites, abstraction, analysis, and synthesis seem no longer to be the only options for social theory.

Whilst holography is more suited to an understanding that takes account of the multiplicity of times than any of the mechanically based metaphors, it must be noted that it too is dominated by our sense of sight, thus emphasising stability and spatiality. Its principles, however, apply to all wave phenomena from light and water to sound and electromagnetic energy. Contemporary holography therefore provides merely the first visually based step in the direction of this particular way of understanding. The potential of the holographic principles are explored, studied, and conceptualised in physics, biology, neurophysiology, acoustics, and in brain and consciousness research, to name just a few areas. Only social science, it seems, has so far ignored the theoretical potential of this metaphor. This book is not the place to begin this task in earnest. To grasp the full implications for social theory is beyond the capability of one person; it needs the effort of many theorists. At the present, merely the potential is apparent for a time-sensitive, truly contemporary social theory. In the absence of such a post-Newtonian framework of meaning the 'level-approach' emerges as superior to that of classical Cartesian dualisms and Newtonian mechanics.

Resonance and non-hierarchical levels

From this research, all the times we have encountered so far emerge as implicated in our contemporary social time. We *are* time and this fact unites us with all other rhythmically organised beings. Together with plants and animals we *are aware* of time and experience it. As human beings we *have a relationship* to time and we reckon time. As members of Western industrial societies *we create time* as a resource, as a tool, and as an abstract exchange value. We thus express what is separated in academic disciplines: the times of the different realms of being. A conceptualisation in terms of levels seems therefore well suited to explain and theorise the multitude of times entailed in contemporary life. To think of these times as expressions of different levels of our being avoids the need to discuss one aspect at the expense of all others. It means that we do not need to chose on an either/or basis. It encourages us to see connections and not to lose sight of the multiplicity while we concentrate on any one of those multiple expressions.

Despite these important advantages, however, there are difficulties associated with the conceptualisation of social time in terms of levels. These relate to our tendency to reify the levels, to conceptualise them hierarchically, and to postulate clear cut-off points between them. The three, as we shall see, are closely interconnected. Beginning with the problem of reification, we must recognise that we do not live, as Schutz and Luckmann (1974: 47) suggest, '*in* all those dimensions simultaneously', and that the levels do not, as Elias (1982b: 1000) proposes, stand in relation to each other. It is our understanding in terms of levels that is in need of being connected and related. *Dasein* (and nature in general) can be conceptualised in terms of levels because we *are* oscillating molecules and rhythmically organised beings with identities as well as beings that constitute, know, measure, and create time. A second difficulty relates to our understanding each 'higher' level expression of time as containing the one 'below' which means that we inadvertently create a hierarchy from simplicity to complexity, from the earlier to the later development, and from the lower to the higher number. This may be an immensely useful way to conceptualise both the continuities and irreducible differences of the times relevant to the physical, biological, and human social realm but our traditional usage gets in the way when we want to explain resonance and mutual implication; when we want to express the idea that any new order changes not only the meaning of that which precedes it but the old order itself. Level, as descriptive metaphor for the multiple times of our existence, thus needs to be applied in a way that does not suppose any fundamental mode of description. It needs to allow for everything to be connected and implicated without a claim of pre-eminence of any one. I refer the reader back to the idea of bootstrapping, where physicists insist not merely that none of the properties of any part of the web of interconnections are elementary but accept no fundamental entities whatsoever: no fundamental laws, equations, or principles. Physicists, like the phenomenologists before them, insist that reality is not revealed to us in some pure form; that we do not observe nature *per se* but nature exposed to our method of questioning. The 'observed' hierarchy needs therefore to be recognised as part of the framework of observation and as soon as it gets in the way of conceptualising mutually implicating connections we need to discard it and replace it with a non-hierarchical conceptual framework.

The recognition that our observations are framed by our questions and theoretical assumptions applies equally to 'level' approaches that postulate clear 'cut-off' lines and conceptualise levels analogous to physical, tiered structures. Korzybski's (1924) three 'time binding levels', Lovejoy's (1960) four 'levels of being', and Fraser's (1982, 1981b) six 'time levels of existence' are examples of theories of discontinuous levels. Thus, Korzybski characterises the human, animal, and vegetable realms in terms of their synthesis-forming capacity as time-, space-, and energy-binding, respectively, whilst the physicist Fraser proposes six stable, integrative time levels of nature: three for the physical universe, one for life forms, and two for the human realm. Not the number of levels or their content are at issue here since these might be varied according to the degree of the analysis' generality but their static developmental stages where the level 'below' is denied aspects that characterise the level 'above'. In other words, whilst theories of time levels are theoretically of interest and echoed in many subsequent social science conceptualisations - including those of Sorokin (1964) and Elias (1982a, b, 1984), for example - they deny to non-human nature what we have found to be central: the importance of past, present, and future extension; of history, creativity, temporality, time experience, and time norms. If time differences are conceptualised with reference to stable, integrative levels then this prevents any understanding in terms of resonance and feedback loops. With discrete, unidirectional levels, consciousness cannot be shown to resonate throughout all of nature; and what we think of as 'human time' stays falsely imprisoned at that level. I have not yet found a satisfactory way of coping simultaneously with hierarchical nesting and implication, with enfoldment and resonance. In the meantime, however, a cautiously applied conceptualisation in terms of levels is to be preferred to an understanding of social time where mutually exclusive choices have to be made.

I have contended repeatedly that it matters how we understand, for example, the invention of clocks or the standardisation of world time in relation to what preceded them. Conceptualised as successors they replace; as additions they leave everything else intact. The findings of this exploration, however, cannot be encompassed by either of these solutions since each new development appears to affect what exists already. Let us take clock time as an example.

Once this created time is related to as a resource to be used, allocated, controlled, spent, or sold it affects our relationship to death, the timing of our activities, our institutions, our technology, our understanding of reality, and our practices of work, leisure, and even sleep. Our environment, too, and even our bodies, are different because of it. It is open to our daring how far we extend this principle to all of nature. There certainly does not seem to be any one obvious point after which it could be argued to no longer apply. Taken to its full extreme it would mean that we understand self-reflective consciousness, language, clock time, and the atom-bomb, for example, as part of nature, and every aspect of our present world as different from what this world was before their evolution and invention. Such an understanding, it seems to me, is in the spirit of Mead's approach in '*The Philosophy of the Present*' where he presents his alternative to scientific positivism and Cartesian dualism. It appears closely related to Mead's conceptualisation of the past, present, and future, of temporality, and of his principle of sociality. To show the links and make this connection more visible it will be helpful to outline Mead's position once more but this time with a special focus on the issue under discussion, namely, that the novel is never a mere addition but changes the whole.

Mead creates a sense of levels, but his levels appear fluid without clear edges or cut-off points. His principle of sociality, as the 'capacity of being several things at once' (1959: 49), and as the process of adjustment that occurs at the conjunction and interpenetration of old and new, is also understood as both the source and essence of consciousness. Mead sees the genesis of an organism's ability to be in different perspectives and times at once in the capacity of interpenetration. A sense of level emerges when Mead conceptualises this consciousness in its 'lowest' form as a kind of plant and animal 'feeling' in conjunction with purposive action, and in its 'highest' form as human ideation (1959: 140-75). We can see here how Mead understands consciousness as a continuum grounded in emergence and the principle of sociality, displaying different char-actersistics in plants, animals, and humans. In similar fashion he conceptualises a progression of meaning from the physical world of signals via an ever-widening gap which, in turn, allows for interpretation and translation between those signals, right 'up' to the human world of symbols. To Mead everything has its own organism-, species-, and level-specific time framework. Humans are not exempt from this and, on the basis of this understanding, he allows for no overarching universal time standard since beings can only know from within their perspective. The fact that a world-wide community has created a particular abstracted time and uses it as a universal measure and absolute framework for dating, he suggests, does not make it any less part of the perspective of that community. Mead clearly argues for an environment-, level-, and perspective-specific time for all beings and the fluidity of his 'levels' can therefore only be appreciated in conjunction with his writings on the ontological status of the past, present, and future (1959: 1–67). To Mead the past is irrevocable to the extent that events cannot be undone, thoughts not unthought, and knowledge not unknown. In this irreversible form, he contends, the past is unknowable since the intervening knowledge continuously changes the meaning of that past and relentlessly recreates and reformulates it into a new and different past. He argues this on the basis of the proposition that only emergence in the present has reality status. He does not accord the past and future such a status because they are real only with respect to their relation to the present. In Mead's thought the past changes with respect to our experiencing it in the present and the meaning we give to it. In contradistinction to the past, he conceptualises the reality of the present as changing with each emergence. When Mead (1959: 65) writes that 'emergent life changes the character of the world just as emergent velocities change the character of masses', his analysis is consistent with contemporary approaches in physics and biology and with the findings of this exploration: it recognises that each emergence irreversibly affects everything else. At this point, however, we encounter in Mead's work the same unresolved limitations I described above with reference to the conceptualisation of hierarchically nested time levels. The difficulty occurs when we seek to bring together Mead's idea of irreducible, unidirectional, inclusive levels with his theory of sociality and his proposals that the emergent does not merely change the meaning of all past and future, but all of present reality and its possible futures.

Bearing in mind the conceptual difficulties and limitations of the level approach, we can see that an understanding through levels achieves a number of things. It emphasises the complexity of time and imposes order on the multiple expressions. It prevents us from focusing on one or two aspects of time at the expense of others. In addition to the more obviously social components, it establishes the centrality of the physical, living, technological, and artefactual aspects of social time. It stresses and affirms connections and relationships. It brings to the surface both the continuities and the irreducible aspects of social time. It helps us to avoid confusing the time aspects of our social life with those of nature and machines. It enables us to see the connection between transcendence and the human creations, between the creation of time and its control, and between the reification of clock time and relations of power. In the absence of more appropriate theoretical frameworks the level approach appears a useful conceptual tool and preferable to an understanding based on stages of succession and mutually exclusive or inclusive dualities.

Simultaneity and extended time-spans

We now need to extend the level-based understanding of social time by incorporating an awareness of the simultaneity of multiple time-spans. This research shows that theoretically relevant rhythms span the spectrum from neural to cosmic ones, from the imperceptibly fast to the unimaginably slow. These time-spans seem to be paralleled by a division of labour in the sciences with quantum physics at one end of the scale, astronomy at the other, and the social sciences and history occupying the middle ground. Each discipline thus seems not only to have its own bounded sphere of competence but a concomitant subject-specific time-scale. In contradistinction to the status quo, this exploration demonstrates that the discipline specific boundaries to the human time-scale are major limiting factors to our understanding since the entire range of rhythms have a bearing on human social time. It impresses on us the need to extend the time-scale not only to the micro and macro dimensions, but also to both the past and the future. It suggests further that the multiple time-spans have to be conceptualised simultaneously.

Giddens's work moves us closer towards this goal, even though his time-scale of analysis does not transgress the middle range of traditional social science. It presents a strong case for the need to recognise that *durée, Dasein*, and *longue durée*, his three planes of temporality, bear on any one moment of structuration simultaneously. The social science focus on any one, Giddens (1981: 19–20) argues, must therefore always imply the others. To him these time planes of daily life, life-time and history are bound by the structural practices of social systems and this may well be one of his reasons for remaining firmly located in the middle-range time-scale of the social science tradition. But could we not regard science and technology as social structural practices? If this were considered reasonable, then even by Giddens's own criteria the time-span of social science analyses would need to be enlarged to an evolutionary scale. Such an extension would not conflict with his antipathy towards evolutionary approaches in social science since he is objecting to the inherent determinism and not the magnitude of the time-scale. Giddens's (1981: 21-3, 1984: 228-44) arguments against evolutionism provide no grounds against either a conceptualisation of the influence of our evolved biological being on present social existence or an extension of our time-scale of understanding. Thus, when I stress the importance of extending the time-scale in order to include evolutionary considerations and beyond, it is not the apparent determinist mechanisms of change I want to stress as important but those silent, sedimented aspects of our socio-biological being that have come to be taken for granted. I am suggesting that the time of our body is not exhausted by our finitude but carries within it our entire evolutionary history. To accept the importance of our evolutionary past for the present is no different in principle from accepting that our history forms an ineradicable part of our social being. This study shows the significance of the evolutionary aspects of social life and questions the validity of their systematic exclusion from social analyses. Contemporary thinkers from a wide range of fields arrived at an understanding that recognises the implication of our past in the present; in other words, that our personal and social history forms an ineradicable part of us. I can find no good reason why we should exlude our biological and cosmic past from the acceptance of this general principle. In death experiences, as we have seen, these connections are revealed and the established boundaries of scientific understanding challenged.

There is yet another reason for extending the traditional time-scale of social science. If biologists recognise that their time-scale of understanding needs to be vastly extended so that they may conceptualise whole networks of feedback loops and symphonies of rhythms, then time-scales of an even greater magnitude ought to be encompassed by the science that seeks to understand a species that has created artefacts that outlast it for thousands of years. We need theories that are adequate to our scientific, technological world with its vast past and future extension. When global telecommunication, nuclear technology, and space travel form an integral part of reality, we can no longer act, research, think, and theorise as if we were still part of a pre-industrial world or the pre-nuclear reality of the founding fathers of our discipline. This is not merely a restatement of the moral point presented earlier where I argued that the time-scale of concern and responsibility ought to be equal to the life-time of our creations and their effects but an argument about social science analyses. I am proposing that we need to take on board the time-scales of our technologies if our theories are to become adequate to their subject matter: contemporary industrialised, science-based technological society. Giddens's concept of time-space distanciation might prove useful here despite its association with the storage capacity of information which makes the present application of the concept primarily past, rather than past and future orientated. There seems to be no reason why the concept of time-space distanciation, with its link to power, could not be exploited to theorise influences on the long-term future. Such an extension would allow us to understand the present as present past and present future, where each change affects the whole.

To emphasise time-space distantiation, the past and future extension and its constitution in the present is, however, not enough. We also need to engage with the natural scientists' understanding of physical reality and grasp the principles entailed in contemporary technologies in order that our creations may cease to control our destinies. Computers and nuclear power are technologies that operate in time-frames outside the capacity of our conscious experience. Nanoseconds, life-times of particles and the life-time of radioactivity can be calculated mathematically but they cannot be known experientially. Yet these technologies are used on a national and global basis. They actually and potentially affect humanity as a whole but our conventional conceptual tools are not adequate to the task of understanding their implication. As Rifkin (1987: 15) correctly points out, 'when many of the decision-making activities of society take place below the threshold of human consciousness, social time, as measured by the clock, becomes irrelevant.' To grasp the mathematical abstraction which affects our lives so deeply requires different theories. It demands post-Newtonian and Cartesian frameworks of meaning. It entails that we begin to understand the principles that underpin our theories and that we recognise the relativity of our frameworks of observation. It necessitates that we shed our reifying tendencies, that we learn to look at the structures of our own thinking and to treat them like empirical data. Furthermore, our contemporary technological, science-based world requires theories that unify and relate what has been separated for over three hundred years. A brief return to the division of cyclical and linear time will help to illustrate the point.

It is a central tenet of this treatise that cycles and lines are artefacts of observation and that their separation into independent entities is intimately tied to Newtonian scientific understanding. Oscillations, rhythmicity, and cycles of recurrence have been shown not to exist in isolation but as unidirectional outcomes of the divisions of cells, combinations of molecules, chemical interactions, social transactions, and relationships of incomplete interdependence between beings, their environments, and other beings. Even the most repetitive action entails asymmetry and direction both within it and in the relation to its environment. Washing-up, the ultimate monotonous activity, serves as a good example. As a directional activity it has a beginning and an end. Its hot water cools. Dirty dishes get clean and the water dirty. The repetition of movements cleans different articles and, although the sequence of the action may always be repeated in the same order - glasses, cutlery, plates, pots - the action in its repetition can never be the same. Everything involved in it has irrevocably changed in the intervening period. Whether we understand such an activity as primarily linear or cyclical does not depend merely on the aspect that has been isolated for observation, but also on the time distance from which the observation takes place. The action could be viewed as linear whilst the act may be considered as cyclical. Observation of the activity over a period might reveal it as cyclical whilst a historical perspective is likely to show up its directional linear changes. Whether we are dealing with habits, routine actions or rituals and myths, reality is constituted as stability through change through their performance. We therefore need to recognise the separation of linearity and cyclicality as relative to the focus and the framework of observation and not locate it with Leach (1968: 125) in logically distinct experiences. Curvature, folding back upon itself, completing cycles but never returning to exactly the same starting point, these are principles of nature; and absolute perfection, the closing of the circle rather than the continuity of cycles, the human endeavour; whilst the separation of cycles from lines, repetition from transformation, history from evolution, and nature from society is an expression of classical science and post-Enlightenment thinking. Only when the distinction between natural cycles, the perfected circles, and the conceptual separation of repetition and change have been made explicit, however, is it possible to relate natural time to social time; chronology, calendar, and clock time to both the rhythms of nature and relations of power; the resource to the experience; and the commodity to the measure. This way of understanding is also necessary before Giddens's (1979: 31) statement that 'life passes in transformation' becomes compatible with his preoccupation with routine; and before we can establish a relation between his (1981: 51) insistence that 'the transformative capacity of human action lies at the heart of power', and his (1981: 134) argument that the 'clock is the very expression of commodified time'. None of these statements, however, can be related in a meaningful way to the idea of 'reversible time'.

The conceptualisation of social life in terms of reversibility makes no sense when even physicists concede that repitition of the same is a mathematical possibility only. In 1896 Boltzmann calculated the *Wiederkehrzeit* (recurrence time) of $1cm^2$ of air as $10^{1000000000000000000}$ years. This means that the likelihood for one cubic centimeter of air to return in exactly the same composition is calculated as ten to the power of ten trillion years; a mathematical expression for 'as good as never' (Eigen

1983: 37-41). Thus, it can be argued that only in conjunction with the recognition of its *idealised* basis in Newtonian physics, and the consequent conceptualisations of reality in terms of it, does 'reversible time' become a meaningful theoretical tool. If physicists have calculated that it takes that long for just one cubic centimetre of air to repeat itself in the same composition, then the idea of repetition of the same should most certainly be considered meaningless for a human social activity or event. This applies even more so to 'reversible time'. There can be no un-living, un-knowing, un-thinking or un-doing. We cannot grow younger, and it is quite clearly impossible to separate a cooked apple pie back into its ingredients of whole apples, sugar, water, butter, and flour. When physicists regard the mere repetition of the same virtually impossible within the existence of our earth, then surely it is safe for social theorists to discard the concept of 'reversible time' as inapproriate for the explanation of the social world.

At the end of this study, time is still a fact of life but it has emerged as a multi-layered, complex fact of life; multiple in its forms and levels of expressions. As time, timing, tempo, and temporality we can recognise some of the complexities of that which is ultimately indivisible. As measure, sense, boundary, resource, and commodity we may know some of the functions which time fulfils in our lives. Through entropy, ageing, and growth we may grasp time as irreversible and directional. Through its rhythmicity life becomes predictable. Thus, the focus on time helps us to see the invisible. It makes our seeing and understanding transparent and shows that the physical reality of our creations underpins our theories. It reveals that technology and artefacts not only shape our lives but our knowledge; that the dead things which are so conscientiously excluded from social analyses are not only implicated in our daily existence but constitute our social theories. They therefore need to be moved to the centre stage of social theory. We need to allow the implications of contemporary living to penetrate the depth of our understanding, to connect the complexity of our being to the meanings we impose on it, and to recognise our existing social theories as relics of a bygone age. The focus on time helps us to identify points of departure. As such it is no longer a luxury; it has become both a necessity and our destiny.

References

Adam, B. E. 1987: *Time and Social Theory*. PhD thesis, University of Wales, Cardiff.

Adam, B. E. 1988: Social time versus natural time, a traditional distinction re-examined. In M. Young and T. Schuller (eds), *The Rhythms of Society*. London and New York: Routledge, 198–226.

Adam, B. E. 1989: Feminist social theory needs time. Reflections on the relation between feminist thought, social theory and time as an important parameter in social analysis. *The Sociological Review*, 37, 458–73.

Adam, B. E. 1991: Time and health implicated, a conceptual critique. In press *Time and Society*.

Adam, B. E. 1992: Perceptions of time. Forthcoming in T. Ingold (ed.), *Humanity, Culture and Social Life*. London: Routledge.

Archer, M. S. 1982: Morphogenesis versus structuration: on combining structure and action. *British Journal of Sociology*, 33, 455–83.

Aries, P. 1976: *Western Attitudes toward Death. From the Middle Ages to the Present*, transl. P. M. Ranum. London: Marion Boyars.

Aschoff, J. (ed.) 1965: *Circadian Clocks*. Amsterdam: North Holland.

Aschoff, J. (ed.) 1981: *Biological Rhythms*. Handbook of Behavioural Neurobiology, vol. IV. New York: Plenum Press.

Aschoff, J. 1983: Die innere Uhr des Menschen. In A. Peisl and A. Mohler (eds), *Die Zeit*. Munich: Oldenburg Verlag, 133–44.

Atkinson, P. 1981: Time and cool patients. In P. Atkinson and C. Heath (eds), *Medical Work, Realities and Routines*. Westmead, Hants: Gower, 41–54.

Ballard, E. 1975: 'Alms for oblivion'. An essay on objective time and experienced time. In P. H. Bossert (ed.), *Phenomenological Perspectives. Historical and Systematic Essays in Honour of Herbert Spiegelberg*. The Hague: Martinus Nijhoff, 168–87.

Ball, R. S. 1892: *Time and Tide. A Romance of the Moon*, London: Society for Promoting Christian Knowledge.

Ball, S., Hull, R., Skelton, M. and Tudor R. 1984: The tyranny of the 'Devil's Mill': time and task at school. In S. Delamont (ed.), *Readings on Interaction in the Classroom*. London: Methuen, 41–57.

Barnett, L. 1957: *The Universe and Dr. Einstein*. New York: William Sloane.

References 171

Barnes, J. A. 1971: Time flies like an arrow. *MAN*, (NF) 6, 537–52.
Bateson, G. 1980: *Mind and Nature: A Necessary Unity*. Glasgow: Fontana/Collins.
Becker, E. 1973: *The Denial of Death*. New York: Free Press Macmillan.
Berger, J. 1980: *About Looking*. London: Writers and Readers.
Berger, J. 1984: *And Our Faces, My Heart, Brief as Photos*. London: Writers and Readers.
Berger, P., Berger, B. and Kellner, H. 1974: *The Homeless Mind*. Harmondsworth: Penguin.
Bergmann, W. 1981a: *Die Zeitstrukturen Sozialer Systeme: Eine systemtheoretische Analyse*. Berlin: Duncker & Humblot.
Bergmann, W. 1981b: Zeit, Handlung und Sozialität bei G. H. Mead. In *Zeitschrift für Soziologie*, 10, 351–63.
Bergmann, W. 1983: Das Problem der Zeit in der Soziologie : Ein Literaturüberblick zum Stand der 'zeitsoziologischen' Theorie und Forschung. *Kölner Zeitschrift für Soziologie und Socialpsychologie*, 35, 462–504.
Bergson, H. 1910: *Time and Free Will*. London: Swan Sonnenschein.
Blumenberg, H. 1979: *Arbeit am Mythos*. Frankfurt am Main: Suhrkamp.
Blyton, P. 1985: *Changes in Working Time: An International Review*. London: Croom Helm.
Bohm, D. 1983: *Wholeness and the Implicate Order*. London: ARK.
Booth, N. S. Jr. 1975: Time and change in African traditional thought. In *Journal of Religion in Africa*, 7, 81–91.
Bossert, P. H. 1975: *Phenomenological Perspectives. Historical and Systematic Essays in Honour of Herbert Spiegelberg*. The Hague: Martinus Nijhoff.
Bourdieu, P. 1979: *Algeria 1960*. Cambridge: Cambridge University Press.
Bourke, V. J. (ed.) 1983: *The Essential Augustine*. Indianapolis: Hackett.
Braudel, F. 1980: *On History*, transl. S. Matthews. London: Weidenfeld and Nicolson.
Briggs, J. P. and Peat, F. D. 1985: *Looking Glass Universe. The Emerging Science of Wholeness*. London: Fontana.
Brown, F. A. Jr., Hastings, J. W. and Palmer, J. D. 1970: *The Biological Clock*. New York: Academic Press.
Buckely, P. and Peat, D. F. 1979: *A Question of Physics. Conversations in Physics and Biology*. Toronto: University of Toronto Press.
Buckley, W. 1967: *Sociology and Modern Systems Theory*. New Jersey: Prentice Hall.
Burger, H. (ed.) 1986: *Zeit Natur und Mensch*. Berlin: Berlin Verlag.
Cancik, H. 1983: Die Rechtfertigung Gottes durch den 'Fortschritt der Zeiten'. Zur Differenz jüdisch-christlicher und hellenisch-römischer Zeit- und Geschichtsvorstellungen. In A. Peisl and A. Mohler (eds), *Die Zeit*. Munich: Oldenburg Verlag.
Capek, M. 1971: *Bergson and Modern Physics*. Dordrecht, Holland: Reidel.
Capra, F., 1976: *The Tao of Physics*. London: Fontana.
Capra, F. 1982: *The Turning Point*. London: Wildwood House.
Carlstein, T. 1982: *Time Resources, Society and Ecology. On the Capacity for*

Human Interaction in Space and Time, vol. I: Pre-Industrial Societies. London: George Allen & Unwin.

Carlstein, T., Parkes, D. and Thrift, N. (eds) 1978: 3 volumes: I. *Making Sense of Time*, II. *Human Activity and Time Geography, III. Time and Regional Dynamics*. London: Edward Arnold.

Chew, G. F. 1968: 'Bootstrap': a scientific idea? *Science*, 161, 762–5.

Clark, P. A. 1982: *A Review of the Theories of Time and Structure for Organisational Sociology*. Birmingham: The University of Aston Management Centre, Working Paper Series.

Cloudsley-Thompson, J. L. 1961: *Rhythmic Activity in Animal Physiology and Behaviour*. London: Academic Press.

Cloudsley-Thompson, J. L. 1980: *Biological Clocks. Their Functions in Nature*. London: Weidenfeld & Nicholson.

Cloudsley-Thompson, J. L. 1981: Time sense of animals. In J. T. Fraser (ed.), *The Voices of Time*. Amherst: University of Massachusetts Press, 296–311.

Conrad-Martius, H. 1954: *Die Zeit*. Munich: Kösel.

Coser, L. A. and Coser, R. L. 1963: Time perspective in social structure. In A. W. Gouldner and H. P. Gouldner (eds), *Modern Sociology. An Introduction to the Study of Human Interaction*. London: Rupert Hart-Davis, 638–51.

Cottle, T. J. and Klineberg, S. L. 1974: *The Present of Things Future. Explorations of Time in Human Experience*. New York: Free Press, Macmillan.

Couch, C. J. 1984: *Constructing Civilisations*. London: Jai Press.

Critchlow, K. 1979: *Time Stands Still. New Light on Megalithic Science*. London: Gordon Fraser.

Crook, J. H. 1980: *The Evolution of Human Consciousness*. Oxford: Clarendon Press.

Cupitt, D. 1985: *Only Human*. London: SCM Press.

Dawe, A. 1981: The Two Sociologies. In K. Thompson and J. Tunstall (eds), *Sociological Perspectives*. Harmondsworth: Penguin Education, 542–54.

Delamont, S. and Galton, M. 1986: *Inside the Secondary Classroom*. London: Routledge & Kegan Paul.

Denbigh, K. G. 1981: *Three Concepts of Time*. Berlin: Springer-Verlag.

Dossey, L. 1982: *Space, Time and Medicine*. London: Shambala.

Dunne, J. S. 1973: *Time and Myth. A Meditation on Storytelling as Exploration of Life and Death*. London: SCM Press Ltd.

Durkheim, E. 1915: *The Elementary Forms of Religious Life. A Study in Religious Sociology*, transl. J. W. Swain. London: George Allen & Unwin.

Eames, E. Ramsden 1973: Mead's concept of time. In W. R. Corti (ed.), *The Philosophy of George Herbert Mead*. Winterthur, Switzerland: Amriswiler Bücherei, 59–82.

Edge, D. O. 1973: Technological metaphor. In D. O. Edge and J. N. Wolfe (eds), *Meaning and Control*. London: Tavistock, 31–59.

Eigen, M. 1983: Evolution und Zeitlichkeit. In A. Peisl and A. Mohler (eds), *Die Zeit*. Munich/Vienna: Oldenburg Verlag, 35–57.

Eliade, M. 1959a: *Cosmos and History. The Myth of Eternal Return*, transl. W. R. Trask. New York: Harper & Row.

Eliade, M. 1959b: *The Sacred and the Profane*, transl. W. R. Trask. New York: Harper & Row.

Eliade, M. 1965: *The Two and the One*, transl. W. R. Trask. London: Harvill.

Elias, N. 1982a: Über die Zeit, transl. H. Fliessbach and M. Schröter. Merkur, XXXVI, 9, 841–56.

Elias, N. 1982b: Über die Zeit (Part 2), transl. H. Fliessbach and M. Schröter. *Merkur*, XXXVI, 10, 998–1016.

Elias, N. 1984: *Über die Zeit*, transl. H. Fliessbach and M. Schröter. Frankfurt a. M.: Suhrkamp.

Evans-Pritchard, E. E. 1969: *The Nuer* (first published 1940). Oxford: Oxford University Press.

Evans-Wentz, W. Y. (ed.) 1957: *The Tibetan Book of the Dead*. Oxford: Oxford University Press.

Feather, N. 1959: *An Introduction to the Physics of Mass, Length and Time*. Edinburgh: Edinburgh University Press.

Fischer, R. 1981: Biological Time. In J. T. Fraser (ed.), *The Voices of Time*. Amherst: University of Massachusetts Press, 357–82.

Folkard, S. and Monk T. (eds) 1985: *Hours of Work. Temporal Factors in Work Scheduling*. Chichester: John Wiley.

Fraisse, P. 1979: Time in psychology. In F. Greenaway (ed.), *Time and the Sciences*. Paris: UNESCO, 71–84.

Frankenberg, R. 1988: Your time or mine? An anthropological view of the tragic temporal contradictions of biomedical practice. In M. Young and T. Schuller (eds), *The Rhythms of Society*. London and New York: Routledge, 118–153.

Franz, M.-L. v. 1970: *Zahl und Zeit. Psychologische Überlegungen zu einer Annäherung von Tiefenpsychologie und Physik*. Stuttgart: Ernst Klett Verlag.

Fraser, J. T. 1975: *Of Time, Passion and Knowledge. Reflections on the Strategy of Existence*. New York: George Braziller.

Fraser, J. T. (ed.) 1981a: *The Voices of Time. A cooperative survey of man's view of time as expressed by the sciences and the humanities*, sec. edition. Amherst: University of Massachusetts Press.

Fraser, J. T. 1981b: Towards an Integrated Understanding of Time. Introduction to the Second Edition, *The Voices of Time*. Amherst: University of Massachusetts Press, xxv–xlix.

Fraser, J. T. 1982: *The Genesis and Evolution of Time*. Brighton: Harvester Press.

Fraser, J. T. 1987: *Time the Familiar Stranger*. Amherst: University of Massachusetts Press.

Fraser, J. T., Haber, F. C. and Mueller, G. H. (eds) 1972: *The Study of Time I*. Berlin: Springer-Verlag.

Fraser, J. T. and Lawrence, N. (eds) 1975: *The Study of Time II*. Berlin: Springer-Verlag.

Fraser, J. T., Lawrence, N. and Park, D. (eds) 1978: *The Study of Time III*. Berlin: Springer-Verlag.

174   *References*

Fraser, J. T., Lawrence, N. and Park, D. (eds) 1981: *The Study of Time IV*. Berlin: Springer-Verlag.

Friedlander, E. 1965: *Psychology in Scientific Thinking*. New York: Philosophical Library.

Fröbe-Kapteyn, O. (ed.) 1952: Mensch und Zeit. *ERANOS Jahrbuch XX*. Zurich: Rhein-Verlag.

Fromm, E. 1980: *The Fear of Freedom* (first published 1942). London: Routledge & Kegan Paul.

Gale, R. M. (ed.) 1978: *The Philosophy of Time*. Brighton: Harvester Press.

Gardner, M. 1982: *The Ambidextrous Universe. Mirrors, Asymmetry and Time-reversed Worlds*, 2nd edn. Harmondsworth: Penguin.

Gebser, J. 1986: *Ursprung und Gegenwart*, 3 volumes, 2nd edn. Munich: Deutscher Taschenbuch Verlag.

Geiger, T. 1970: *Vorstudien zu einer Soziologie des Rechts*. Berlin: Luchterhand.

Geyer, R. F. and Zouwen J. van der, (eds) 1978: *Sociocybernetics: An Actor Orientated Social Systems Approach*. The Hague: Martinus Nijhoff.

Giddens, A. 1976: *New Rules of Sociological Method*. London: Hutchinson.

Giddens, A. 1979: *Central Problems in Social Theory. Action, Structure and Contradiction in Social Analysis*. London: Macmillan.

Giddens, A. 1981: *A Contemporary Critique of Historical Materialism. Power, Property and the State*. London: Macmillan.

Giddens, A. 1984: *The Constitution of Society. Outline of the Theory of Structuration*. Cambridge: Polity Press.

Giddens, A. 1987: Time and social organisation. In *Social Theory and Modern Sociology*. Cambridge: Polity Press, 140–65.

Glaser, B. G. and Strauss, A. L. 1980: *Awareness of Dying*. New York: Aldine.

Gorman, B. S. and Wessman, A. E. (eds) 1977: *The Personal Experience of Time*. New York: Plenum Press.

Grant, J. and Wilson, C. (eds) 1980: *The Book of Time*. Westbridge: Westbridge Books.

Greenaway, F. (ed.) 1979: *Time and the Sciences*. Paris: UNESCO.

Green, H. B. 1972: Temporal attitudes of four Negro subcultures. In J. T. Fraser, F. C. Haber and G. H. Mueller (eds), *The Study of Time* I. Berlin: Springer-Verlag, 402–17.

Grof, S. 1985: *Beyond the Brain. Birth, Death, and Transcendence in Psychotherapy*. Albany, NY: State University of New York Press.

Grof, S. and Grof, C. 1980: *Beyond Death. The Gates of Consciousness*. London: Thames and Hudson.

Gunnell, J. B. 1968: *Political Philosophy and Time*. Middletown, Conn.: Wesleyan University Press.

Gurvitch, G. 1963: Social structure and the multiplicity of times. In E. A. Tiryakian (ed.), *Sociological Theory, Values, and Sociocultural Change*. London: The Free Press of Glencoe, 171–85.

Gurwitsch, A. 1922: Über den Begriff des embryonalen Feldes. *Archiv für Entwicklungsmechanik*, 51, 383–415.

Hägerstrand, T. 1975: *Dynamic Allocation of Urban Space*. Farnborough: Saxon House.

Hägerstrand, T. 1985: Time and culture. In G. Kirsch, P. Nijkamp and K. Zimmermann (eds), *Time Preferences: An Interdisciplinary Theoretical and Empirical Approach*. Berlin: Wissenschaftszentrum, 1–15.

Hamner, K. C. 1981: Evidence for the Biological Clock. In J. T. Fraser (ed.), *The Voices of Time*. Amherst: University of Massachusetts Press, 281–95.

Hampe, J. C. 1979: *To Die is Gain. The Experience of One's Own Death*, transl. M. Kohl. London: Darton Longman & Todd.

Hawking, S. W. 1988: *A Brief History of Time. From the Big Bang to Black Holes*. London and New York: Bantam Press.

Hegel, G. W. F. 1952: *Phänomenologie des Geistes* (first published 1807). Hamburg: Felix Meiner Verlag.

Hegel, G. W. F. 1967: *The Phenomenology of Mind*, transl. J. B. Baillie. New York: Harper and Row.

Heidegger, M. 1960: *Sein und Zeit* (first published 1927). Tübingen: Max Niemeyer Verlag.

Heidegger, M. 1972: *On Time and Being*, transl. J. Stambaugh. New York: Harper & Row.

Heidegger, M. 1980: *Being and Time* (first published 1927), transl. J. Macquarrie and E. Robinson. Oxford: Blackwell.

Heim, A. 1892, Notizen über den Tod durch Absturz. *Jahrbuch des Schweizer Alpenklub*, 27: 327.

Heinemann, G. (ed.) 1986: *Zeitbegriffe. Ergebnisse des interdisziplinären Symposiums 'Zeitbegriff der Naturwissenschaften, Zeiterfahrung and Zeitbewusstsein'*. Freiburg: Karl Alber Verlag.

Heinemann, K. and Ludes P. 1978: Zeitbewusstsein und Kontrolle der Zeit. *Kölner Zeitschrift für Soziologie und Sozialpsychologie*, Sonderheft 20/78, 221–43.

Heirich, M. 1964: The use of time in the study of social change. *American Sociological Review*, 29, 386–397.

Hildebrandt, G. (ed.) 1976: *Biologische Rhythmen und Arbeit*. Berlin: Springer-Verlag.

Hoagland, H. 1981: Some biochemical considerations of time. In J. T. Fraser (ed.), *The Voices of Time*. Amherst: University of Massachusetts Press, 312–29.

Hohn, H.-W. 1984: *Die Zerstörung der Zeit. Wie aus einem göttlichen Gut eine Handelsware wurde*. Frankfurt a. M.: Fischer Alternativ.

Hopkins, H. 1982: *The Subjective Experience of Time with Particular Reference to Time-Bound Institutions*. PhD thesis, University of Lancaster.

Horton, R. 1967: African traditional thought and Western science. *Afrika*, 37, 176–9.

Huber, B. 1972: Some thoughts on creating the future. *Sociological Inquiry*, 44, 29–39.

Husserl, E. 1964: *The Phenomenology of Internal Time Consciousness*, transl. J. S. Churchill. The Hague: Martinus Nijhoff.

176   *References*

Illich, I. 1976: *Limits to Medicine*. London: Marion Boyars.
Infeld, L. 1953: Albert Einstein. In *Makers Of Modern Science*. New York: Charles Scribner.
Ingold, T. 1986: *Evolution and Social Life*. Cambridge: Cambridge University Press.
Jahoda, M., Lasarsfeld, F. P. and Zeisl, H. 1978: *Die Arbeitslosen von Marienthal* (first published 1932). Frankfurt a. M.: Suhrkamp.
Jantsch, E. 1985: *The Self-organizing Universe. Scientific and Human Implications of the Emerging Paradigm of Evolution*. Oxford: Pergamon Press.
Jaques, E. 1982: *The Form of Time*. London: Heinemann.
Joas, H. 1985: *G. H. Mead. A Contemporary Re-examination of his Thought*, transl. R. Meyer. Cambridge: Polity Press.
Jones, R. S. 1983: *Physics as Metaphor*. London: Abacus.
Kalmus, H. 1981: Organic evolution and time. In J. T. Fraser (ed.), *The Voices of Time*. Amherst: University of Massachusetts Press, 330-52.
Kastenbaum, R. 1961: The dimensions of future time perspective. An experimental analysis. In *Journal of General Psychology*, 65, 203-18.
Kaufmann, F.-X. 1970: *Sicherheit als soziologisches und sozialpolitisches Problem*. Stuttgart: Enke.
Keenoy, T. 1985: *Invitation to Industrial Relations*. Oxford: Blackwell.
Kerenyi, K. and Jung, C. G. 1970: *An Introduction to the Science of Mythology*, transl. R. F. C. Hull. London: Routledge & Kegan Paul.
Kern, S. 1983: *The Culture of Time and Space 1880-1918*. London: Weidenfeld & Nicolson.
Kinget, G. M. 1975: *On Being Human. A Systematic View*. New York: Harcourt Brace Jovanovich.
Klages, L. 1934: *Vom Wesen des Rhythmus*. Kampen auf Sylt: Kampmann.
Korzybski, A. 1924: *Time-binding: The General Theory*. Lakeville, Conn.: The International Non-Aristotelian Library.
Koselleck, R. 1985: *Vergangene Zukunft. Zur Semantik geschichtlicher Zeiten*. Frankfurt a. M.: Suhrkamp.
Kübler-Ross, E. 1971: *Interviews mit Sterbenden*. Stuttgart: Kreuz Verlag.
Kübler-Ross, E. 1986: *On Death and Dying*. London: Tavistock.
Landes, D. S. 1983: *Revolution in Time. Clocks and the Making of the Modern World*. Cambridge, Mass.: Harvard University Press.
Landsberg, P. T. (ed.) 1982: *The Enigma of Time*. Bristol: Adam Hilger.
Larson, D. B. 1965: *New Light on Space and Time*. Portland Oregon: North Pacific.
Lauer, R. H. 1981: *Temporal Man. The Meaning and Uses of Social Time*. New York: Praeger.
Lawick-Goodall, J. van 1971: *In the Shadow of Man*. Boston: Houghton Mifflin.
Lawrence, N. 1978: Levels of language in discourse about time. In J. T. Fraser, N. Lawrence and D. Park (eds), *The Study of Time* III. Berlin: Springer-Verlag, 22-52.
Leach, E. A. 1968: Two essays concerning the symbolic representation of time. In E. A. Leach, *Rethinking Anthropology*, London: Athlone Press, 124-36.

Leonard, G. 1981: *The Silent Pulse*. New York: Bantam.

LeShan, L. L. 1952: Time orientation and social class. In *Journal of Abnormal and Social Psychology*, 47, 589–92.

Lessnoff, M. 1979: *The Structure of Social Science*. London: George Allen & Unwin.

Levine, R. V., West, L. J. and Reis, H. T. 1980: Perceptions of time and punctuality in the United States and Brazil. *Journal of Personality and Social Psychology*, 38, 541–50.

Levine, R. V. and Wolff, E. 1985: Social time: The heartbeat of culture. To understand a society, you must learn its sense of time. *Psychology Today*, 1985, 29–35.

Lévi-Strauss, C. 1966: *The Savage Mind*. London: Weidenfeld & Nicolson.

Lévi-Strauss, C. 1978: *Structural Anthropology*. Harmondsworth: Penguin.

Lewis, J. D. and Weigert, A. J. 1981: Structures and meanings of social time. *Social Forces*, 60, 433–62.

Lifton, R. J. 1969: *Death in Life*. New York: Vintage.

Lifton, R. J. and Olson, E. 1974: *Living and Dying*. New York: Praeger.

Lovejoy, A. O. 1960: *The Great Chain of Being. A Study of the History of Ideas* (first published in 1936). New York: Harper.

Lovelock, J. E. 1979: *Gaia. A New Look at Life on Earth*. Oxford: Oxford University Press.

Lucas, J. R. 1973: *A Treatise on Time and Space*. London: Methuen.

Luce, G. G. 1977: *Body Time. The Natural Rhythms of the Body*. St. Albans, Herts: Paladin.

Lüscher, K. K. 1974: Time: a much neglected dimension in social theory and research. *Sociological Analysis and Theory*, 4, 104–17.

Luhmann, N. 1971a: *Politische Planung. Aufsätze zur Soziologie von Politik und Verwaltung*. Opladen: Westdeutscher Verlag.

Luhmann, N. 1971b: Die Knappheit der Zeit und die Vordringlichkeit des Befristeten. In *Politische Planung*. Opladen: Westdeutscher Verlag, 143–64.

Luhmann, N. 1978: Temporalization of complexity. In R. F. Geyer and J. van der Zouwen (eds), *Sociocybernetics. An Actor-Orientated Social Systems Approach*. London: Martinus Nijhoff, 92–113.

Luhmann, N. 1979: Zeit und Handlung – Eine vergessene Theorie. *Zeitschrift für Soziologie*, 8, 63–81.

Luhmann, N. 1980: *Gesellschaftstruktur und Semantik. Studien zur Wissenssoziologie der modernen Gesellschaft*. Frankfurt a. M.: Suhrkamp.

Luhmann, N. 1982a: *The Differentiation of Society*, transl. S. Holmes and C. Larmore. New York: Columbia University Press.

Luhmann, N. 1982b: The future cannot begin. Temporal structures in modern society. In *The Differentiation of Society*. New York: Columbia University Press, 271–89.

Luhmann, N. 1982c: World-time and system history. In *The Differentiation of Society*. New York: Columbia Universtiy Press, 289–324.

Lukes, S. 1978: Methodological individualism reconsidered. In A. Ryan (ed.), *The Philosophy of Social Explanation*. Oxford: Open University Press, 119–29.

Lyman, S. M. and Scott, M. B. 1970: *A Sociology of the Absurd*. New York: Appleton-Century-Crofts.

Lynd, R. S. and Lynd, H. M. 1929: *Middletown. A Study of Contemporary American Culture*. New York: Harcourt, Brace.

Lynd, R. S. and Lynd, H. M. 1937: *Middletown in Transition. A Study of Cultural Conflicts*. London: Constable.

Mandelbaum, M. 1978: Societal facts. In A. Ryan (ed.), *The Philosophy of Social Explanation*. Oxford: Open University Press, 105–118.

Mannheim, K. 1972: *Ideology and Utopia* (first published 1936). London: Routledge & Kegan Paul.

Marcuse, H. 1966: *Eros and Civilisation. A Philosophical Inquiry into Freud*. London: Allan Lane.

Martins, H. 1974: Time and theory in sociology. In J. Rex (ed.), *Approaches to Sociology. An Introduction to Major Trends in British Sociology*. London: Routledge & Kegan Paul, 246–96.

Mbiti, J. S. 1985: *African Religions and Philosophy* (first published 1969). London: Heinemann.

McCann, J. 1970: *The Rule of St. Benedict*. London: Sheed and Ward.

McTaggart, J. M. E. 1927: *The Nature of Existence*, vol. II, book V. Cambridge: Cambridge University Press.

McTaggart, J. M. E. 1968: Time. In R. M. Gale (ed.), *The Philosophy of Time*. Brighton: Harvester Press, 86–98.

Mead, G. H. 1959: *The Philosophy of the Present* (first published 1932), A. E. Murphy (ed.), Preface by J. Dewey. La Salle, Ill.: Open Court.

Mead, G. H. 1962: *Mind, Self and Society. From the Standpoint of a Social Behaviourist* (first published 1934), C. W. Morris (ed.). Chicago: University of Chicago Press.

Mead, G. H. 1967: *The Philosophy of the Act* (first published 1938), C. W. Morris (ed.). Chicago: University of Chicago Press.

Melbin, M. 1978: City rhythms. In J. T. Fraser, N. Lawrence and D. Park (eds), *The Study of Time* III. Berlin: Springer-Verlag, 444–70.

Melbin, M. 1987: *Night as Frontier. Colonizing the World after Dark*. New York: Free Press, Macmillan.

Melges, F. T. 1982: *Time and the Inner Future. A Temporal Approach to Psychiatric Disorders*. New York: Wiley.

Merlau-Ponty, M. 1962: *Phenomenology of Perception*. London: Routledge & Kegan Paul.

Michener, C. D. 1974: *The Social Behaviour of the Bees*. Cambridge Mass.: Harvard University Press.

Michon, J. A. and Jackson, J. L. (eds) 1985: *Time, Mind, and Behaviour*. Berlin and New York: Springer-Verlag.

Michon, J. A. 1985: The compleat time experiencer. In J. A. Michon and J. L. Jackson *Time, Mind, and Behaviour*. Berlin and New York: Springer-Verlag, 20–52.

Mitford, J. 1963: *The American Way of Death*. New York: Fawcett.

Moody, R. 1977: *Leben nach dem Tod*. Reinbek: Rowohlt.

Moore, W. E. 1963: *Man, Time and Society*. New York: John Wiley.

Moore, W. E. 1974: *Social Change*. New York: Prentice Hall.

Needham, J. 1981: Time and knowledge in China and the West. In J. T. Fraser (ed.) *The Voices of Time*. Amherst: University of Massachusetts Press, 92–135.

Needham, J. 1988: Time and Eastern Man. *Cultural Dynamics*, 1, 62–75.

Neisser, U. 1976: *Cognition and Reality. Principles and Implications of Cognitive Psychology*. San Francisco: W. H. Freeman.

Nichols, H. 1891: The psychology of time. *American Journal of Psychology*, 3, 453–529.

Nietzsche, F. 1980: Kritische Studienausgabe in 15 Bänden, G. Colli and M. Montinari (eds). Munich: Deutscher Taschenbuch Verlag.

Nowotny, H. 1975: Time structuring and time measurement. On the interrelation between timekeepers and social time. In J. T. Fraser and N. Lawrence (eds), *The Study of Time* II. Berlin: Springer-Verlag, 325–42.

Nowotny, H. 1985: From the future to the extended present: time in social systems. In G. Kirsch, P. Nijkamp and K. Zimmermann (eds), *Time Preferences: An Interdisciplinary Theoretical and Empirical Approach*. Berlin: Wissenschaftszentrum, 1–21.

Nowotny, H. 1989: *Eigenzeit. Entstehung und Strukturierung eines Zeitgefühls*. Frankfurt a. M.: Suhrkamp.

Noyes, R. 1971: Dying and mystical consciousness. *Journal of Thanatology*, 1, 25–58.

Noyes, R. 1972: The Experience of dying. In *Psychiatry*, 35, 174–203.

Oakeshott, M. 1985: *On History and Other Essays*. Oxford: Blackwell.

Ornstein, R. 1972: *The Psychology of Consciousness*. San Francisco: W. H. Freeman.

Ornstein, R. 1975: *On the Experience of Time*. New York: Penguin Books.

Osis, K. and Haraldsson, E. 1982: *Der Tod: Ein Neuer Anfang. Visionen und Erfahrungen an der Schwelle des Seins*. Freiburg: Bauer Verlag.

Ouspensky, P. D. 1959: *Tertium Organum*. New York: Knopf.

Pattman, R. 1985: *Concepts of Time and Labour in Marxism, 19th Century Political Economy and Reformation Protestant Theology*. Unpublished paper.

Payk, T. R. 1979: *Mensch und Zeit. Chronopathologie im Grundriss*. Stuttgart: Hippokrates Verlag.

Peisl, A. and Mohler, A. (eds) 1983: *Die Zeit*. Munich: Oldenburg Verlag.

Pelletier, K. R. 1982: *Unser Wissen vom Bewusstsein*, transl. W. Stifter. Munich: Kösel Verlag. (Originally published 1978, *Toward a Science of Consciousness*. New York: Dell.).

Petri, H. and Zepf, I. (eds) 1982: *Geht uns die Zeit verloren? Beiträge zum Zeitbewusstsein*. Bochum: Studienverlag Dr. N. Brockmeyer.

Phipps, E. W. J. 1980: Bodytime. In J. Grant and C. Wilson (eds), *The Book of Time*. Westbridge: Westbridge Books, 128–60.

Piper, M. 1978: *Erwachsenenalter und Lebenslauf: Zur Soziologie der Lebensstufen*. Munich: Kösel Verlag.

Pirsig, R. M. 1979: *Zen and the Art of Motorcycle Maintenance*. London: Corgi.

Plessner, H. 1952: Über die Beziehung der Zeit zum Tode. In O. Fröbe-Kapteyn (ed.) *Eranos Jahrbuch 1951. Band XX. Mensch und Zeit.* Zurich: Rhein Verlag, 349–86.

Popper, K. R. 1979: *The Poverty of Historicism.* London: Routledge & Kegan Paul.

Portmann, A. 1952: Die Zeit im Leben der Organismen. In O. Froebe-Kapteyn (ed.), *Eranos Jahrbuch 1951. Band XX. Mensch und Zeit.* Zurich: Rhein Verlag, 437–58.

Powers, J. 1982: *Philosophy and the New Physics.* New York: Methuen.

Prigogine, I. 1980: *From Being to Becoming. Time and Complexity in the Physical Sciences.* San Francisco: W. H. Freemann.

Prigogine, I. and Stengers, I. 1984: *Order out of Chaos. Man's New Dialogue with Nature.* London: Heinemann.

Rammstedt, O. 1975: Alltagsbewusstsein von Zeit. *Kölner Zeitschrift für Soziologie und Sozialpsychologie,* 27, 47–63.

Rawlence, C. 1985: *About Time.* Based on the Channel 4 Television Series. London: Jonathan Cape.

Reinberg, A., Andlauer, P., DePrins, J., Malbecq, W., Vieux, N. and Bourdeleau, P., 1984: Desynchronisation of the oral temperature. Circadian rhythm and intolerance to shift work. *Nature,* 308, 272–4.

Ridley, B. K. 1980: *Time, Space and Things.* Harmondsworth: Penguin.

Rifkin, J. and Howard, T. 1985: *Entropy. A New World View.* London: Paladin.

Rifkin, J. 1987: *Time Wars. The Primary Conflict in Human History.* New York: Henry Holt.

Rinderspracher, J. P. 1985; *Gesellschaft ohne Zeit. Individuelle Zeitverwendung und soziale Organisation der Arbeit.* Frankfurt a. M.: Campus Verlag.

Rosen, R., Pattee, H. H. and Somorjai, R. L. 1979: A symposium in theoretical biology. In P. Buckley and D. F. Peat (eds), *A Question of Physics. Conversations in Physics and Biology.* Toronto: University of Toronto Press, 84–123.

Roth, J. A. 1976: *Timetables. Structuring the Passage of Time in Hospital Treatment and other Careers.* Indianapolis: Bobbs-Merrill.

Russell, J. L. 1981: Time in Christian thought. In J. T. Fraser (ed.), *The Voices of Time.* Amherst: University of Massachusetts Press, 59–77.

Rutenfranz, J. 1978: Arbeitsphysiologische Grundprobleme von Nacht- und Schichtarbeit. *Rheinisch-Westfälische Akademie der Wissenschaften,* Vorträge N 275. Berlin: Westdeutscher Verlag, 1–50.

Ryan, A. 1979: *The Philosophy of the Social Sciences.* London: Macmillan.

Saussure, F. de 1960: *Course in General Linguistics,* C. Bally, A. Sechehaye and A. Reidlinger (eds). London: Peter Owen.

Schaltenbrand, G. (ed.) 1963: *Zeit in nervenärztlicher Sicht.* Stuttgart: Ferdinand Enke Verlag.

Schmied, G. 1985: *Soziale Zeit. Umfang, 'Geschwindigkeit' und Evolution.* Berlin: Duncker & Humblot.

Schöps, M. 1980: *Zeit und Gesellschaft.* Stuttgart: Ferdinand Enke Verlag.

Schon, D. A. 1963: *Displacement of Concepts.* London: Tavistock.

Schuller, T. 1984: *A Chronosociological Approach to Employee Participation.* Unpublished paper.

Schuller, T. 1986: *Serving Time: 60,000 Hours at Fords.* Unpublished paper.

Schutz, A. 1971: *Collected Papers. Vol. I, The Problem of Social Reality*, M. Natanson (ed.). The Hague: Martinus Nijhoff.

Schutz, A. and Luckmann, T. 1973: *The Structures of the Life-World*, transl. R. M. Zaner and H. T. Engelhardt Jr.. London: Heinemann.

Schwartz, B. 1979: Waiting, exchange and power: the distribution of time in social systems. *American Journal of Sociology*, 79, 841-70.

Shallis, M. 1983: *On Time. An Investigation into Scientific Knowledge and Human Experience*. Harmondsworth: Penguin.

Sheldrake, R. 1983: *A New Science of Life*. London: Paladin.

Sheldrake, R. 1985: Collective memory, time and evolution. In C. Rawlence (ed.), *About Time*. London: Jonathan Cape, 194-202.

Sheldrake, R. 1986: A new approach to biology. In S. Kumar (ed.), *The Schumacher Lectures Vol. II*. London: Sphere, 202-18.

Simmel, G. 1980: The problem of historical time. In *Essays on Interpretation in Social Science*, transl. G. Oakes. Manchester: Manchester University Press, 127-45.

Spengler, O. 1926: *The Decline of the West*. New York: Knopf.

Sorokin, P. A. 1964: *Sociocultural Causality, Space and Time. A Study of Referential Principles of Sociology and Social Science*. New York: Russell & Russell.

Sorokin, P. A. and Merton, R. K. 1937: Social time: A methodological and functional analysis. *The American Journal of Sociology*, 42, 615-29.

St. Augustine 1978: Some questions about time. In R. M. Gale (ed.), *The Philosophy of Time*. Brighton: Harvester Press, 38-55.

Stacey, M., Batstone, E., Bell, C. and Murcott, A. 1975: *Power, Persistence and Change. A Second Study of Banbury*. London: Routledge & Kegan Paul.

Staikov, Z. (ed.) 1982: *It's About Time*. Sofia, Bulgaria: Bulgarian Sociological Association.

Starkey, K. 1988: Time and work organisation: a theoretical and empirical analysis. In M. Young and T. Schuller (eds), *The Rhythms of Society*. London and New York: Routledge, 95-117.

Stegmüller, W. 1969: *Hauptströmungen der Gegenwart*. Stuttgart: Alfred Körner Verlag.

Stüttgen, A. 1988: *Heimkehr zum Rhythmus*. Munich: Friedrich Pfeil.

Sudnow, D. 1967: *Passing On. The Social Organisation of Dying*. Englewood Cliffs, NJ: Prentice-Hall.

Teilhard de Chardin, P. 1959: *The Phenomenon of Man*. London: Collins.

Tiryakian, E. A. 1970: Structural sociology. In J. C. McKinney and E. A. Tiryakian (eds), *Theoretical Sociology. Perspectives and Developments*. New York: Appleton-Century-Crofts, 111-36.

Thom, A. 1967: *Megalithic Sites in Britain*. Oxford: Oxford University Press.

Thompson, E. P. 1967: Time, work-discipline, and industrial capitalism. *Past and Present*, 36, 57-97.

Thrift, N. 1985: Review article, A. Giddens: The constitution of society. *Sociology*, 19, 609-24.

Toda, M. 1978: The boundaries of the notion of time. In J. T. Fraser, N. Lawrence and D. Park (eds), *The Study of Time III*. Berlin: Springer

Verlag, 370–90.

Vester, F. 1979: Time and biology. In F. Greenaway (ed.), *Time and the Sciences*. Paris: UNESCO, 53–70.

Waddington, C. H. 1957: *The Strategy of Genes*. London: Allen & Unwin.

Waddington, C. H. 1959: *Towards a Theoretical Biology*. Edinburgh: Edinburgh University Press.

Walker, R. C. S. 1982: *Kant*. London: Routledge & Kegan Paul.

Weber, M. 1989: *The Protestant Ethic and the Spirit of Capitalism* (first published 1930), transl. T. Parsons. London: Unwin Hyman.

Weigert, A. J. 1981: *Sociology of Everyday Life*. London: Longman.

Weiss, P. 1939: *Principles of Development*. New York: Holt.

Weiss, P. 1973: *The Science of Life*. Mount Kisco, NY: Futura.

Wendorff, R. 1980: *Zeit und Kultur. Geschichte des Zeitbewusstseins in Europa*. Wiesbaden: Westdeutscher Verlag.

Wendorff, R. 1984: *Dritte Welt und Westliche Zivilisation. Grundprobleme der Entwicklungspolitik*. Wiesbaden: Westdeutscher Verlag.

Wessman, A. E. and Gorman, B. S. 1977: The emergence of human awareness and concepts of time. In B. S. Gorman and A. E. Wessman (eds), *The Personal Experience of Time*. New York: Plenum Press, 1–58.

Wever, R. 1979: *The Circadian System of Man*. New York: Springer-Verlag.

Whitehead, A. N. 1969: *Process and Reality* (First published 1929). New York: Free Press.

Whitrow, G. J. 1959: *The Structure and Evolution of the Universe*. London: Hutchinson.

Whitrow, G. J. 1980: *The Natural Philosophy of Time*. Oxford: Clarendon Press.

Whitrow, G. J. 1988: *Time in History. The Evolution of our General Awareness of Time and Temporal Perspective*. Oxford: Oxford University Press.

Whorf, B. L. 1956: *Language, Thought and Reality*. Cambridge, Mass.: MIT Press.

Wilson, E. O. 1971: *The Insect Societies*. Cambridge, Mass.: The Belknap Press of Harvard University Press.

Yaker, H. 1972: Time in the biblical and Greek worlds. In H. Yaker, H. Osmond and F. Cheek (eds), *The Future of Time*. London: Hogarth Press, 15–36.

Yaker, H., Osmond, H. and Cheek F. (eds) 1972: *The Future of Time*. London: Hogarth Press.

Young, M. 1988: *The Metronomic Society*. London: Thames and Hudson.

Young, M. and Schuller, T. 1988: *The Rhythms of Society*. London and New York: Routledge.

Young, M. and Schuller, T. 1990: *Life after Work*. In press.

Zerubavel, E. 1979: *Patterns in Hospital Life*. Chicago: University of Chicago Press.

Zerubavel, E. 1981: *Hidden Rhythms. Schedules and Calendars in Social Life*. Chicago: Chicago University Press.

Zerubavel, E. 1985: *The Seven Day Cycle. The History and Meaning of the week*. New York: Free Press Macmillan.

Zohar, D. 1983: *Through the Time Barrier. A Study in Precognition and Modern Physics*. London: Paladin.

Index

DATE DUE

NOV 0 4 '95			
DEC 1 3 1995			
			Printed in USA